Another Economy is Pos

Another Economy is Possible

Culture and Economy in a Time of Crisis

Manuel Castells
Sarah Banet-Weiser
Sviatlana Hlebik
Giorgos Kallis
Sarah Pink
Kirsten Seale
Lisa J. Servon
Lana Swartz
Angelos Varvarousis

polity

First published in 2017 by Polity Press

Polity Press
65 Bridge Street
Cambridge CB2 1UR, UK

Polity Press
350 Main Street
Malden, MA 02148, USA

ISBN-13: 978-1-5095-1720-6
ISBN-13: 978-1-5095-1721-3(pb)

A catalogue record for this book is available from the British Library.

Library of Congress Cataloging-in-Publication Data

Names: Castells, Manuel, 1942- editor.
Title: Another economy is possible : culture and economy in a time of crisis
 / [edited by] Manuel Castells.
Description: Malden, MA : Polity, 2017. | Includes bibliographical references
 and index.
Identifiers: LCCN 2016038452 (print) | LCCN 2016051494 (ebook) | ISBN
 9781509517206 (hardback) | ISBN 9781509517213 (pbk.) | ISBN 9781509517237
 (Mobi) | ISBN 9781509517244 (Epub)
Subjects: LCSH: Financial crises. | Economics.
Classification: LCC HB3722 .A55 2017 (print) | LCC HB3722 (ebook) | DDC
 338.5/42--dc23
LC record available at https://lccn.loc.gov/2016038452

Typeset in 10.5 on 12 pt Sabon by
Servis Filmsetting Ltd, Stockport, Cheshire
Printed and bound in the Great Britain by Clays Ltd, St Ives plc

For further information on Polity, visit our website:
politybooks.com

Contents

CONTENTS

Figures and Tables

About the Authors

Sarah Banet-Weiser is Professor and Director of the Annenberg School for Communication at the University of Southern California (USC), Los Angeles. She is also Professor in the School of Communication, and in the Department of American Studies and Ethnicity at USC. Her teaching and research interests include feminist theory, race and the media, youth culture, popular and consumer culture, and citizenship and national identity. She teaches courses in culture and communication, gender and media, youth culture, feminist theory and cultural studies, including economic cultures. She is the author of the award-winning book *Authentic*™ (2014).

Manuel Castells is University Professor and the Wallis Annenberg Chair in Communication Technology and Society at the University of Southern California (USC), Los Angeles. He is also Professor Emeritus, University of California, Berkeley, where he was Professor of City and Regional Planning and Professor of Sociology from 1979 to 2003 before joining USC. In addition, he is a Professor of Sociology at the Open University of Catalonia, and a Fellow of St. John's College, University of Cambridge. He holds the Chair on the Network Society at the Collège d'études mondiales, Fondation Maison des sciences de l'homme, Paris.

Sviatlana Hlebik holds a PhD in Economic Policy, MS in Finance and Risk Management, and MSc in Economic Cybernetics. She is the author of works on monetary policy, banking, and alternative economic practices during the financial crisis. She currently conducts research on bank regulation. She works in the Financial Management Directorate, Cariparma Crédit Agricole, Parma, Italy.

Giorgos Kallis is an environmental scientist working on ecological economics and political ecology. He is a Leverhulme visiting professor at SOAS and an ICREA professor at ICTA, Autonomous University of Barcelona. Before that he was a Marie Curie International Fellow at the Energy and Resources Group of the University of California at Berkeley. He holds a PhD in Environmental Policy and Planning from the University of the Aegean in Greece, a Masters in Economics from Universitat Pompeu Fabra, and a Masters in Environmental Engineering and a Bachelors in Chemistry from Imperial College, London.

Sarah Pink is RMIT Distinguished Professor in Design and Media Ethnography, and Director of the Digital Ethnography Research Centre at the Royal Melbourne Institute of Technology. She is also Visiting Professor at Halmstad University (Sweden) and Loughborough University (UK) and Guest Professor at Free University Berlin (Germany). Her recent collaborative books include *Digital Materialities* (2016), *Digital Ethnography* (2016), *Screen Ecologies* (2016), *Media, Anthropology and Public Engagement* (2015), and the iBook *Un/certainty* (2015). She is the sole author of *Doing Sensory Ethnography*, 2nd edition (2015).

Kirsten Seale is senior researcher at the University of Western Sydney. Her current research interest focuses on informal urban street markets. She has examined how informal urban street markets facilitate the informal and formal economy not merely in terms of the traditional concerns of labor and consumption, but also in regards to cultural and spatial contingencies. Seale examines what these markets reveal about urban life in a time of globalized, rapid urbanization and flows of people, knowledge, and goods.

Lisa J. Servon is Professor and former Dean at the Milano School of International Affairs, Management, and Urban Policy, New School University, New York. Professor Servon holds a BA in Political Science from Bryn Mawr College, an MA in History of Art from the University of Pennsylvania, and a PhD in Urban Planning from the University of California, Berkeley. She teaches in the Urban Policy Program at the Milano School and conducts research in the areas of urban poverty, community development, economic development, and issues of gender and race.

Lana Swartz is a post-doctoral researcher in the Social Media Collective of Microsoft Research in New England. In fall 2016, she will join the faculty of the University of Virginia as an assistant professor of Media Studies. She is working on a book on money as communication, both as a form of information transmission and as a vector of relations, memory, and culture.

Angelos Varvarousis is a researcher based in Barcelona, at the Universitat Autonoma de Barcelona. He is a member in the Research and Development group of Barcelona, with a focus primarily on alternative economic practices in Greece.

Acknowledgments

This volume presents the results of the study undertaken by a collaborative international research network on alternative economic practices and their cultural foundations that investigated and met between 2011 and 2015. The annual meetings of the network took place in 2011–12 in Barcelona, at the Open University of Catalonia, and in 2013–15 in Paris, at the Collège d'études mondiales, Fondation Maison des sciences de l'homme.

The project was funded by the Collège d'études mondiales. The authors want to express their gratitude to Professor Michel Wieviorka, President of the Fondation Maison des sciences de l'homme, and to Dr Olivier Bouin, Director of the Collège d'études mondiales, for their intellectual encouragement and material support provided to the project over three years.

We also want to thank Mr Gilles Desfeux, of the Fondation Maison des sciences de l'homme, for his care in organizing our annual meetings in Paris, and Mr Jean Louis Cury, director of the Maison Suger, Fondation de la Maison des sciences de l'homme, for his hospitality in hosting our meetings in the historic venue of the Maison Suger.

The meetings in Barcelona in 2011–12 were organized by Ms. Noelia Diaz Lopez, from the Internet Interdisciplinary Institute of the Open University of Catalonia.

The coordination of the project was assured by Ms. Pauline Martinez, and by Ms. Reanna Martinez, at the Annenberg School of Communication, University of Southern California, Los Angeles. We thank them for their support.

Introduction
Manuel Castells

This volume emerged from the challenge to rethink the meaning of economic practices in the wake of the financial crisis of 2008 and beyond. While governments and financial elites reacted to the near collapse of financial capitalism by attempting to restore the conditions of business as usual, the economic, social, and human damage inflicted by the crisis prompted a reconsideration of the inevitability of unfettered capitalism as a fact of life. A number of economic practices appeared throughout Europe and the United States that embodied alternative values: the value of life over the value of money; the effectiveness of cooperation over cutthroat competition; the social responsibility of corporations and responsible regulation by governments over the short-term financial strategies, led by greed rather than long-term profit-making, that took the overall economy to the brink of catastrophe. From Spain to Greece, from the US to Australia, and to many other countries beyond our direct observation, we saw the blossoming of multiple experiences of innovation in organizing work and life: cooperatives, barter networks, ethical banking, community currencies, time sharing banks, alternative means of payment, etc., that paved the way for a fast-developing sharing economy in all domains of activities oriented toward the satisfaction of human needs. Furthermore, while some of these new economic practices appear to be a reaction to the inability of the standard economic operations to provide goods, services, and credit during the crisis, other innovations became increasingly visible when taking a broader look at the way economic transactions co-evolve with culture, technology, and institutions in a fast-changing society. This is the case with cryptographic virtual currencies, epitomized by bitcoin, which blended a libertarian, entrepreneurial spirit with information technology to provide an

1

alternative to standard forms of currency. In a very different vein, this is also the case of forms of banking for those at the bottom of the pyramid, who are creating a financial underworld with its own rules and effects – an underworld that can only be understood through the methods of participant observation that inform some of the work presented in this volume.

Yet, this is not a collection of diverse case studies. Because throughout our collaborative research and in this volume, there is a common theme that provides the link to our polyhedric observation. There are as many economic practices as there are cultures. If standardized forms of capitalism appear to provide uniformity to economic practices it is only because of the cultural domination of capitalism, of the different forms of capitalism, enforced by institutions whose rules result from power struggles institutionalized in the law – always in flux. Thus, when standardized economic practices do not mesh with people's practices, either because they cannot practice them in situations of crisis, or because they challenge the values embodied in financial capitalism, alternative economic practices appear. These are not necessarily anti-capitalist (bitcoin is not), but different from current capitalism. At the source of this observation is our common statement. The economy is not simply related to culture: economy is culture. Looking at a whole range of economic practices, some directly observed, others studied more broadly from a cultural perspective (such as feminist economics or ecological economics), we can understand the logic of social change at the heart of the economic system. If economy is culture and if cultures are diverse and often contradictory, a whole range of economic practices are equally relevant and equally able to organize the way people produce, consume, exchange, innovate, invest, and live. This is the terrain we explored for three years in our research network, moving freely between observation, quantitative analysis, theory, and practice. This is our project: to unveil the cultural foundation of all economic practices by focusing on those that, because they are "alternative" (to contemporary financial capitalism), make more visible the cultural content of their economic logic. We have constructed an argument, not just collected a number of research papers and theoretical elaborations. Our argument is this: economic practices are human practices that, as such, are determined by humans who embody their ways of being and thinking, their interests, their values, their projects. There is no abstract, inevitable economic logic outside human practice, a metaphysical, a-historical logic to which humans should conform. If they do, it is because they are compelled or induced to resignation. When they are not, they redefine the goals and means of their economic practices, as in all dimensions of their practices. There is no such thing as a non-human economy. There is, yes, an inhuman economy because it sometimes benefits certain humans who try to appropriate humanity as a whole for their own advantage until other humans think differently, practice differently, and end up creating alternative forms of production, consumption, and exchange. This is our story, the story of this book, told in a plurality of voices, but in the harmony of a shared intellectual purpose.

Paris, Barcelona, New York, Athens, Parma, Boston, Melbourne, Los Angeles
January 2016

Chapter 1

Economy Is Culture

Sarah Banet-Weiser and Manuel Castells

What is value?

Like all human activities, what we call "the economy" is made up of human practices framed by institutions, both embedded in specific cultures, as argued by Douglass North, Elinor Ostrom, and Viviane Zelizer, among others (North 1981; Ostrom 2005; Castells et al. 2012; Zelizer 2013).

Economic practices refer to practices of production, consumption and exchange. But of what? In principle of "goods and services." But the implicit materiality of this formulation is misleading, unless we extend the meaning of goods and services to everything. Because production, consumption, and exchange of knowledge is central to any economic system, as it is the production and consumption of culture itself. Moreover, contemporary economies are based on the production and exchange of financial value, an immaterial but also essential product and factor of production. Therefore, it appears that the object of economic practices is the generation and appropriation of value, whatever the material support of value is in every specific practice. This leads to the fundamental question: What is value?

A classical distinction in economic philosophy differentiates use value from exchange value. Indeed the first pages of Marx's *Capital: Critique of Political Economy* open with this distinction and with a thorough elaboration on their relationship.[1] The use value of

---

[1] Because Marx's analyses are well known, the authors do not consider it necessary to refer to full quotes, since we are using his ideas to construct, using a different approach, our own argument rather than summarizing his theses.

anything is what is useful to satisfy human needs and desires, and it is realized by its use and its consumption. Exchange value, in Marx's formulation, appears as the quantitative measure according to which use values of different kinds are exchanged. This relationship of exchange is constantly modified depending on time and place. However, Marx's conceptualization refers specifically to the capitalist mode of production in which the wealth of society depends on "the immense accumulation of commodities." Both use value and exchange value exist as commodities, and because commodities are different in quality, in order to be exchanged they need an exchange value measure that transforms different use values into a common measure of value. Therefore, the difference and interaction between use value and exchange value is internal to the logic of the capitalist mode of production and not, as is often thought, as an opposition between what humans want and like, and the capitalist process of commodification measured ultimately by money as a quantitative representation of exchange value.

What humans want and like, in Marx's own words, has use value only if it is a "useful thing." If it is not useful, the labor embodied in the "thing" has been wasted, and accordingly does not create value. Who, then, determines that something is useful? From the capitalist point of view there is no doubt: to increase the exchange value of the product, as determined by the mechanism of exchange value quantification, it is the marketplace, organized around the interaction of supply and demand as a means of allocation of scarce resources to satisfy ever expanding needs and desires. Thus, ultimately exchange value determines the actual value of use value. Yet, this is a logic internal to the process of capital accumulation in a society in which the entire social organization, including culture and institutions, is organized around the logic of capital. However, this logic is not an immanent feature of human nature (as the implicit essentialism of neoliberal ideology would have it; Harvey 2005), but the result of a particular social structure: capitalism in its different forms and stages of historical existence.

Therefore, economic value is exchange value, and exchange value is measured monetarily by the market. And the dominance of exchange value as the overarching value of everything is in fact an institutional feature, derived from the dominance of the institutions of capitalism over other institutional-cultural formations that are subordinated to the power of capitalism (Sennett 2006). Thus, in broader social terms, value, in a given social/institutional context, is what the dominant institutions and norms decide is valuable. Since the current global economy is capitalist, capital accumulation is the supreme value, in economic terms, and should translate in the capacity to buy everything with money, the material expression of exchange value in a fully commodified society.

However, economic organization is not tantamount to social organization, not even under capitalism. We live in a global network society structured around networks that follow different logics (Castells 2000, 2004, 2009). Each one of these global/local networks has its own principle of valuation. Thus if we consider that the power of the state, supported by its technological and organizational military capacity, is the supreme value that organizes societies, then value is what accrues this power in its various manifestations, as was the case with the Soviet Union and is still the case, largely, in China. If we say that in the last resort power resides in human minds, as humans are able to reverse the logic of institutions by their conscious actions, then major ideational systems are the holders of symbolic power, as is the case with religious institutions or mass media systems, and value will be measured by the extent and depth of adherence to God's Law (in its diversity), or by the extent and depth of influence of media systems to construct representations of the human mind in specific contexts.

Then, the most important issue is the relative hierarchy of these global networks among themselves in each context (Castells 2009, 2011). Of course, all of these networks interact, each one with its principle of valuation, but is there a dominant network? A meta-network that organizes the functioning of the others as specific manifestations of the value-making principle of that network? Would this be the alpha network of capital accumulation that is referred to by all other networks? In a strict sense yes, but this would only be the case if we all lived in a capitalist society and not just a capitalist economy. Empirical observation shows that this is not the case. The principles of state power preempt economic considerations in the case of military conflict or potential threats: national security is priceless. The value in this case is security or victory. Economic benefits come second, although we know of many cases in which wars and conflicts are used as additional means of capital accumulation, though not for capital in general, but for the corporate allies of the state. It is what the media call crony capitalism and what these authors call the political pillage of resources using the power of the state, not the market logic. Moreover, the last century saw the formation of communist states and statist societies in much of the world. The fundamental value for these regimes was the accumulation of state power, not capital. Capital accumulation was a means to provide the resources for the enforcement of state power, domestically and internationally. This is not only the past (although it supports our analysis of value making beyond the logic of capital even if this was in the recent past) but also partially the present in the case of some societies, particularly China, the second-largest economy on the planet.

The Chinese state largely controls, owns, and ultimately dominates the Chinese economy. While economic growth and capital accumulation is a major goal, and thus a key value for Chinese society as a whole, what is valuable for the institutions that shape and control the life of Chinese is the power of the Communist Party. In China, unlike in the US, what is good for Huawei is not necessarily good for the country. Rather, what is good for the Communist State is good for Huawei (among other things because it is the property of the state). China operates simultaneously in different value systems: capital accumulation in the global economy; state power accumulation in the institutions and organizations of China (including economic organizations); and symbolic power, through cultural legitimation, in the controlled media system and consumerism as a guiding norm for the politically decisive urban middle class (Hsing 2014).

As for religion, it is the most significant source of violent conflict in today's world. Imposing one's religion, in multiple sectarian versions, is the most important value for the multiple theocracies and would-be theocracies around the world. God's glory and service to God are the most important overarching values for billions of humans on the planet. Capital accumulation is only a means to broaden and deepen the kingdom of God. State power must be in the service of God. Otherwise it is a heretic institution that pretends to be superior to the law of God. This is the case in Islamic theocracies, but has been historically the case in Western countries as well: the Spanish conquest of America aimed primarily to convert the lost souls of the natives. The fundamental goal of the Reformation Church of England with the King/Queen as the nominal head of the Church was a merger of powers ultimately decided in favor of the state. In societies dominated by religious values, both by coercion and persuasion, value is defined by the conformity of behavior to God's Law.

Thus, since value making depends on the hierarchy of power between the networks that organize human life, including strictly speaking economic activities, values and value making are largely an expression of power relationships.

Largely but not exclusively, that is. Since power, in every network or dimension of society, is contradicted by counterpower, the principles of value making projected by the counterpower networks will interact

7

with those imposed/proposed by the institutions, and may result in different values as guiding principles of human behavior, including economic activities (Castells 2015). If we consider the economy as a set of practices organized around processes of production, consumption and exchange to generate value according to certain criteria of what is valuable, then the market and other forms of economic institutions will not be the exclusive domain of capital accumulation but the expression of different goals and projects coming from humans operating as economic subjects on their own, even disregarding the values proposed by the institutions of society. These counter-projects could come either from collective expressions of alternative forms of values or from autonomous individuals organizing their lives, and therefore their economic practices, around their own values, thus creating their own value-making procedures. We will illustrate our argument by considering two processes of value making that do not adjust to the norms of capital and yet have immense impact in the informational network economy in which we live: the open source economy and the rise of feminist economics.

However, before engaging in the analysis of alternative projects of value making, we will show how capitalist values are embedded in the social practices of the most fundamental capitalist institution in our economy: financial markets. We contend that financial practices are also culturally constructed, as the structures of capitalism evolve and change over time. Capitalism in the twenty-first century is characterized by the domination of capitalism by global financial capitalism, enacted by financial elites whose role and cultural underpinnings have been transformed in the network society under the impulse of neoliberal ideologies and politics (Harvey 2005; Crouch 2011; Engelen et al. 2011; Mason, 2015).

The culture of financial capitalists and financial institutions

Values do not exist in a social vacuum. They are enacted by individuals and embedded in institutions. Global informational financial capitalism as a specific form of capitalism has been shaped by a specific culture (Hutton and Giddens 2000). This culture is supported by financial practices because it fits the interests of the actors, the financial elites. Indeed, contemporary financial culture may be damaging for the interest of "the system" as a whole, because it threatens its stability. Yet, contemporary financial elites could not care less about the broader picture, as their behavior is guided by personal gain with

8

a quarterly horizon for their lucrative bonuses (Nolan 2009; Engelen et al. 2011; Murray and Scott 2012). This is exactly the specific culture we refer to, and this is the culture whose content and formation we analyze in this section of the chapter.

The culture of the contemporary financial elites is formed by the articulation of different cultural layers that in their historical weaving induce a specific financial culture:

The first layer is, historically, the Protestant Ethic, following the classic analysis by Max Weber. It can be defined as the search for salvation through accumulation of wealth by reinvesting profits to increase profits: earned value is used to expand the production of value. In terms of the culture of the actors, it is characterized as a *deferred gratification pattern.* Their primary goal is not to consume the yield of their labor but to obtain their reward in the afterlife and in family reproduction of wealth, transforming profits into assets that will accrue their value faster than earnings because they start from a higher level of accumulation (Piketty 2013). For these elites, there is little hedonistic consumption; their lives tend to be relatively austere (at least in historical comparison with our time). Profit making is the supreme value, both for the economy as a whole and for personal salvation and reputation.

The second layer is the culture of liberty, based on the assumption that the market knows better, as supply and demand are constructed by the free decisions of investors and consumers, guided by their rational choice in terms of self-interest. Adam Smith's "invisible hand" is the ultimate driver of the market, thus of the capitalist economy. This is the cultural tenet of *liberalism and neoliberalism* (Harvey 2005). The culture of liberty emerged historically as a reaction against the arbitrariness of state power and theocracy (Crouch 2011). In such context, the free exchange of economic value levels the field and allocates resources depending on supply and demand, and, as a derivative, the expectations of profits. The most important market in capitalism is the financial market. Liberalism advocates acknowledge the need for regulation of the market, including the financial market, by government and legal institutions. Indeed, North showed in his classic analysis that institutions are absolutely necessary for the market to work properly (1981). However, regulatory bodies aim for allowing rational choices to be processed in the market. Yet, values and rationality are not the same. Rationality is framed within a value system that is institutionalized. What is rational from the perspective of one set of values may not be from another. For instance, the paramount need of energy supply at a lower price may be highly beneficial

9

for the economy even if it is accomplished by the new technologies of fracking. But if the preservation of the environment in the most fundamental sense is brought into consideration, what appears to be a rational choice is actually an irrational, damaging decision. Based on neoliberal assumptions, the financial elites believe government intervention distorts markets, and so regulation should be limited to assure fair play in the rules of the game without interpreting the value content of these rules, so that the submission to maximizing the profit rate of private investment is paramount.

The third cultural layer underlying contemporary financial cultures is individualism, defined as the culture in which the unit of reference for the benefit of an action is the individual herself (Santoro and Strauss 2013). The emphasis on individual identity predisposes the direct connection for the financial operators between their personal projects and the market by acting in the market for personal gain in priority of maximizing profits for the shareholders whose capital they represent. The priority given to personal gain is only checked by the regulatory framework and by competition with other financial operators. Yet, here is where policy and institutions matter. Because under the conditions of deregulation the priority for individual gain derived from the culture of individualism translates into financial practices such as (a) defining the success of an investment in a financial operation by quarterly financial results, which ultimately leads the market as a whole to evaluate the results of corporations also in quarterly terms, meaning short-term gains, regardless of long-term prospects for the soundness of the investment; and (b) compensation for financial operators that is largely linked to performance bonuses. These bonuses depend on: (i) short-term evaluation by the market of the traded financial products; and (ii) volume of transactions; since the amount of profit is more important than the rate of profit, it increases the market power of those investors who accumulate a larger share of assets.

The fourth layer in financial culture is the culture of risk (Admati and Hellwig 2013). In the traditional rationale for capitalism, the reward for companies and individuals alike is justified by risk taking. The assumption is that if they fail in their risky investments they lose and become responsible for their losses. If they win, their audacity is rewarded by the market. However, the current strategies of financial elites tend to minimize risk for the individuals of these elites, through several mechanisms: (a) at the individual level, financial operators set up contracts that limit their legal responsibility, which provide "golden parachutes" in case they lose their jobs, and insure their wealth in the long term through their knowledge and contacts; (b) at the institutional level, financial elites count on government bailouts in case of crisis – the so-called "too big to fail" argument – while still cashing their personal bonuses (insured by contract) even if the company goes bankrupt; (c) the high volume of transactions they perform, which is the most important counter-risk mechanism for the financial operators; in some cases the investment fails, in others it is profitable, but ultimately it is their clients who lose or win. The operators, as intermediaries protected by their contracts and conditions, win in (almost) all cases, because their compensation is based on the amount of their activity, in addition to their share of the profits they obtain. Thus, in the practice of contemporary finance, *the culture of risk has become an ideological myth*, self-serving individually motivated financial practices. This is in sharp contrast with innovation-driven industries, such as the technology industries in which the entrepreneurs risk their capital and their jobs, and depend on their performance (Saxenian 2006). Indeed, this confirms Schumpeter's old fears (Schumpeter 1942) about the end of the culture of risk, the engine of entrepreneurialism and innovation, under the conditions of oligopolistic corporatization, typical of the financial industry.

The fifth cultural layer that frames the practice of financial elites is patriarchalism, defined as the structural assumption of the systemic power of males over females and their children. This is because patriarchalism, as a fundamental structure of all historically known societies, is transversal to any other form of social organization, including the economy. The meaning of patriarchalism in this context refers to unequal chances of opportunity for men and women in the management structure of key financial institutions. But even more important is the prevalence of masculine values in the practice of all financial elite members, men and women alike. These masculine values include the rejection of any criterion to evaluate financial practices other than the best performance in terms of profit making and the personal maximization of the benefits of any financial transaction, including those that do not benefit the shareholders. Winning at all costs, as in war or in politics, is the fundamental attribute of masculinity throughout history, and this is reflected in the ruthless practices of finance, in the winner takes all principle, and in the praise for extreme risk taking, and the ability to be bold against all odds, even if this endangers the stability of the economy and the preservation of the assets entrusted to financial managers. Moreover, the framework of masculinity, or masculine values, that shape financial culture acts to eclipse any other values – emotional, affective, reproductive – that are

11

modified to function in ways that actually sustain masculine values. So there is a double movement at play here: masculine values dominate financial culture to the extent that no other values are seen as legitimate, but it is precisely these other values that allow masculine values their dominance. An overwhelming male presence in the circles of higher finance characterized the industry in earlier stages of capitalism. However, in neoliberal capitalism, masculinity as a specific set of values is more decisive than the gender symmetry in the heights of finance, as the speed and complexity of global financial transactions requires a one-dimensional determination to beat the competition, regardless of the broader, potentially damaging consequences. The macho culture of young, daring financial wizards has its roots in the history of violence associated with the cult of manhood. It manifests itself in the bravados of the new financial entrepreneurs, such as those twenty-something managers that imagined the credit default swaps (CDSs) during a weekend meeting in Atlantic City.

We hypothesize that the above described cultural layers form, in their interaction and articulation, the core of the financial culture that led to triumphant global financial capitalism and ultimately to its crisis in 2008.

There is continuity between traditional and contemporary financial elites in one fundamental attitude vis-à-vis the institutions of society. They abhor trade unions. This is not just a matter of class ideology. It comes from their deep conviction that any control or limitation to their freedom to make decisions in an ultra-competitive and complex industry may lead to their being outperformed by other companies and individuals. They would rather pay more to their workers than allow them to unionize. Indeed, the financial industry displays, in general, the lowest rates of unionization among industries in most countries.

The financial industry's attitude toward governments is more complex. They oppose government interference, but they acknowledge the necessity of some sort of regulation and they count on governments as their guarantor in the last resort. Thus, in practice, they tend to buy politicians and place their representatives at the highest level of government, making sure their interests are well served. This is the case in the United States where Wall Street executives have traditionally served in the White House cabinets for both parties. In the world at large, in the twenty-first century we have observed increasing influence of the financial elites in governments and political institutions, as was demonstrated in the management of the financial crisis of 2008 with a massive transfer of resources from taxpayers to the financial institutions to bail them out without demanding personal or corporate responsibilities (Castells et al. 2012). In cultural terms, the prevailing attitude of the financial elites is the deep feeling that they are indispensable and that governments, all governments, must work for them and through them in a global economy built around inter-dependent financial markets. Arrogance and self-assurance, together with a thinly veiled disdain for politicians, characterizes the new financial elites.

Are the financial elites citizens of the world? Yes and no. Yes, in the sense that they feel they belong to a special class of cosmopolitans. They operate under similar rules in an interdependent financial system, with similar technologies, managerial techniques, and strategies. Their industry is largely global, and so they are as well. They work and live in global networks of cooperation and competition. Furthermore, they are often culturally glued by attendance to similar educational institutions around the world: business schools, law schools, and engineering schools of the top private universities in the world (for themselves and their children alike). And they socialize in similar private clubs and venues, attending exclusive meetings where they hobnob with non-financial elites (political, media, academics) in forums such as the Davos World Economic Forum, the Netherlands-based Bilderberg Group, or California's Bohemian Grove. So, yes, there is a cosmopolitan culture of global financial elites that is crucial for their management of the global economy in their own interests.

On the other hand, the global financial elite is in fact plural, and lives in the diversity of their cultural/national origins (Anglo-Saxon, Japanese, Arab, Jewish, Chinese, Russian, French, German, Latin American, etc.), with specific norms and codes of conduct, specific references to their cultural traditions and religions, and specific references to their own institutions. Simplifying the matter, we can say *they are culturally diverse but their network has a shared global, cosmopolitan identity.*

Thus, there is a new kind of financial elite, whose culture and behavior have internalized the norms and structures of the network society and of the global networked economy (Kahneman and Tversky 1973; Aldridge 1997; Castells 2000; Zaloom 2006). Individual financial operators may have personal values of ethics, professionalism, and service. But the operators that the new financial system requires, in generic terms, are disembodied economic actors that increasingly insulate the global financial markets, and themselves as well, from the human condition in all its multidimensionality (Ferguson 2013). They become material supports of abstract capital markets operating with

13

simulation models enacted with the gut feelings emerging from their feverish minds.

The passion to create and the value of creativity

Every major techno-economic transformation in history has been associated with, if not induced by, a specific cultural foundation. This was the case for the protestant ethic as the spirit of capitalism, in Max Weber's formulation. The rise of the networked economy, related to the technological paradigm of informationalism rooted in the revolution in information technologies, should therefore be supported by a new cultural formation. What is it? Pekka Himanen suggested an illuminating hypothesis in his 2002 book *The Hacker Ethic and the Spirit of the Information Age*. We know hackers are not malicious geniuses, in spite of the media confusion of technological innovators and destructive minds. Hackers, in the original concept that emerged in MIT's Artificial Intelligence Lab, are simply those technically able individuals who "hack" (that is, work relentlessly), moved by the passion to create new, cool technologies that open up avenues of thinking and doing in the context of one of the most extraordinary technological revolutions in history. Based in the history of discovery in the digital culture, and in the biographies of some of its main actors, Himanen's concept refers to the supreme value embraced by these hackers: not money making, not power, not fame, but the feeling of creating technological excellence, the understanding and shaping of a new world in the making, the fire in the belly of creation, pursuing their own path and only recognizing their peers and the authority of their community of excellence. These individuals, each one of them and their communities of reference, did change the world, as without their passion to create and their willingness to immediately and openly distribute their discoveries without copyright, the traditional corporations who were appropriating/stalling the technological revolution would have wasted its potential yield. The Internet ICP/IP protocols that created the most potent horizontal communication network in history were designed by Vint Cerf and Robert Kahn in 1973–5 and were immediately posted on the Internet. Tim Berners-Lee created the World Wide Web in his spare time after work and posted the server program on the Internet in 1990 for everyone to use and improve. The email systems, the email lists, GNU, Unix, Linux, and Apache were among the many free and open software programs that provided the technical basis for the rapid spread of digital communication networks around the planet, reaching seven billion mobile communication users; at the time of this writing, over 50 percent of the planet's adult population uses smartphones. Most of the key discoveries of the digital age that created the information economy and spurred productivity, thus creating wealth, were advanced by the culture and practice of open source, particularly in the key technology, computer software, the DNA of the technological revolution. Open source is based on the principle of free disclosure of the kernel (or alpha code) of any new program with the purpose of improving it by the work of a cooperative network of peers.

As Steve Weber (2004) has documented in his seminal book on open source, the community is structured with a meritocratic hierarchy based on reciprocity and moved by the reward of enhanced reputation among peers. In fact, this is not too different from the truly academic research communities, which thrive in the pursuit of science and are often spoiled and ultimately destroyed when the search for monetary gains prevails in the process of discovery. Free culture, in the terms of Larry Lessig, asserting the value of technological excellence, and the drive to create are the cornerstones of the wave of innovation that has transformed the world in the last four decades (English-Lueck 2002).

This is not to deny that out of this revolution driven by the passion of discovery a whole new business world emerged, including some of the most valuable corporations in today's world. Indeed, capital accumulation on a gigantic scale resulted from the harvest of innovation. But this is precisely the point. The value of creation for the sake of creation, not profit searching, has been the engine of creation of capital value in the information economy. And in the process of creating a new economy, many of the actors became instant billionaires. Yet, the value drivers of this economy are mainly cultural and psychological, rather than profit searching, excepting a few significant cases, particularly Bill Gates's Microsoft.

The lessons of the technological revolution can be generalized to the broader concept of creativity as the key inducing factor in the current digital economy. Creativity, and its derivative, innovation, are the key factors of wealth creation in the digital economy, and of meaning creation in the digital culture. But creativity and innovation emerge from the culture of creativity, not from the anticipated value of capital accumulation. And they only yield extraordinary value added in all domains if their products are networked in an open source logic, in which the interaction in the network increases their synergy and ultimately their value in any way this value could be measured.

15

Let us lay down the argument in a systematic way.

For the sake of clarity let us start with a precise definition of creativity and innovation. We understand *creativity* as the capacity to create, which is to produce a new knowledge or new meaning. The newness must be considered not from the point of view of the subject (e.g. what is new for me?) but against the stock of scientific and cultural products existing in a given society. *Innovation* is the process by which, on the basis of creativity, new value is added to a product (good or service) or to the process of production or distribution of a product. Value can be exchange value (e.g. money) or use value (something useful for society, for some institutions, for some organization, for the individual, or for a collective of individuals).

Creativity and innovation both involve, of course, a mental process, therefore a process of activating the mind and brain. But this mental process, while being rooted in our biological wiring, develops in interaction with a social context, namely cultural context (values and beliefs), spatio-temporal context (material forms of space and time, including the natural environment, that organize and frame social interaction), and institutional context (political institutions, legal environment). Furthermore, any mental process becomes a social process by crossing the biological boundaries of the individual that hosts the originating brain. *This border crossing is what we call communication.* Therefore, communication is the cornerstone of social life, and therefore of human life, since human life is social, as consciousness, our distinctive feature, is founded in communication. *Communication constructs culture,* which is the set of values and beliefs informing behavior, as they are enshrined, always in a conflictive way, in the institutions of society. Communication processes depend on the characteristics of the sender, on the characteristics of the receiver, on the context of the process, and, not least, on the technology of communication, that is by the material process through which the signals are produced, transmitted, received, and interpreted. There are distinctive forms of culture depending on distinctive technologies of communication, although the precise forms of interaction between culture and communication technology must be established by research rather than asserted by speculative claims. But we do know that *we live in a global, digital culture* that is inextricably articulated with a global, digital economy.

Thus, the process of knowledge production and meaning in our time, that is *the process of creativity, and its derivative, innovation, are specified by their form of communication, that is microelectronics-based, digitally formatted and transmitted communication built*

16

around telecommunicated computer networks and databases. Internet and wireless communication are at the heart of this digital environment of knowledge and meaning production.

Cultural creation and communication have been deeply transformed by the digitization of products and processes (Neuman 2016). The development of Web 2.0 and Web 3.0 have transformed the Internet by increasing the role of users as producers of both content and applications. New business models are redefining intellectual property rights in accordance with technological evolution. Thus, the traditional division between popular culture, high culture, and commercial culture is increasingly blurred (though this blurring does not take place solely because of technological changes). It follows a broadening of the scope of creativity, and the potential for creative processes to migrate from the domains where they are born to other fields of application. For instance, creativity in social software may spur artistic creativity in design or music. Or else, imagining virtual forms of social organization may induce experiments in business innovation or in learning processes, including a transformation of the education system. Moreover, thousands of people around the world are already experimenting with hybridization between virtual and non-virtual processes, and with the cross-fertilization of these experiments between different domains of human activity. The key is the interaction between different realms of application of these creative practices, e.g. video games and learning, collaborative art online, new forms of mass self-communication [what Castells (2009) has called mass self-communication], new business models that allow for free production and consumption of content, and new forms of citizen intervention in the polity of societies. There are multiple forms of creative initiatives that take advantage of the possibilities offered by new social software and the networks of digital communication. The new frontier of creativity research seems to be exploring the rivers of creativity currently flowing on the Internet to reconstruct both our theories of human creation and our practices of organizational innovation.

While creativity has always been at the source of human economic practices and cultural practices, there are specific processes in the digital culture that transform the inducement and effects of creativity, including:

(a) the ability to communicate, mix, and blend any product of any kind on the basis of a common, digital language;
(b) the ability to communicate from the local to the global and from the global to the local in real time or chosen time;

(c) the multimodality of communication;
(d) the interconnection of all digitized databases, finally creating the hypertext and realizing the Xanadu of Nelson's dream;
(e) the capacity to reconfigure all configurations, producing new meaning out of purposive multi-layering;
(f) the gradual constitution of a collective mind by networking in an interactive mode of countless brains;
(g) the multi-layered generation of innovation in all domains, including economic activity, thus weaving the creative, innovative economy and the culture of creativity and innovation.

As a result, in the digital culture, *creativity is not an exceptional moment of an exceptional mental breakthrough, but a way of life.* This is not the future. This is current practice for millions of people. It ranges from survival strategies (using mobile phones' lost call to communicate without paying); to the copy, paste, and add of students around the world; to synthetic securities and constantly reinvented derivatives in the financial markets; to the remix culture in musical creation. Inventing nothing new since Andrade's Manifesto Antropofago in the 1920s, Brazil has already proposed the syncretic notion of cultural creativity brilliantly realized by Gilberto Gil during the 1960s re-invention of Brazilian music. But in a context of light speed reconfiguration enacted by millions of minds in a relentless flow of communication of all kinds of cultural products and economies from around the world, *the production of new knowledge and new meaning goes beyond the creators to shift to networks of creation.* Because innovation ultimately depends on the ability to channel creation into each specific realm of activity, the transformation of creativity in the digital culture ushers in new processes of wealth creation and destruction, as well as new forms of expressing and feeling the human experience. In this sense the digital economy is more than ever a culturally produced economy.

However, the promise of an economy driven by creativity and innovation is hampered by a fundamental roadblock: sexism. It is truly extraordinary to observe the rarity of women among the hacker tribes, the creators of information and communication technologies, or the most innovative engineers in Silicon Valley (Neff 2012). This is in spite of the fact that in terms of users, the majority in social networking sites are women. They are users but not producers of networking technologies. The gendered entry barriers to the realm of innovation in a decisive technological field greatly curtails the innovation potential of industries and countries. Women may be

18

half of the human population, but they occupy a very small corner of the advanced sectors of electronic R&D. In many ways, masculinity structures the culture of creativity in much the same way that it structures the culture of finance, with restricted barriers of entry, a de-valuing of reproductive labor, and a privileging of a kind of technology that has historically excluded women.

The study by Cecilia Castaño (2010), in Spain and in Europe, advanced several hypotheses to explain the masculinist structure of creative culture. Among them: the sexist bias of the engineering schools and the engineering profession at large, inherited from a tradition of technological elitism often perpetuated by the professional organizations, at least in the European context; the male-dominated hierarchy of technology firms, particularly in telecommunications, the matrix of the electronics industry in several European countries; sexism in secondary education, since women in the school have historically been discouraged from studying mathematics and were oriented toward humanities by their teachers, according to the gendered division of intellectual work in most societies. Furthermore, most hacker communities were formed by small coteries of young techies, often along the cultural patterns of young male bonding, a logic that not only deliberately excludes women but also devalues and diminishes them. Thus, although there are a number of examples of remarkable women in technological innovation and in the electronics industry, the barriers women have to face to enter the world of technolocal excellence appear to be greater than in most other fields (in contrast, for instance, with medical research) (Castaño 2015). The prevalence of masculine values in the electronics industries has serious consequences for the characteristics of processes and products designed in the industry; for instance, the overwhelming proportion of violent, masculinist games in the important video game industry; or the narrow range of applications developed, until very recently, in the educational field. In this sense, in the wake of the 2008 crisis, information technologies for education were a driver in the new wave of innovation in Silicon Valley. And an unprecedented number of women were recruited to work on these products: another example of the persistence of a gendered division of labor, exemplified by the fact that women tend to represent the large majority of teachers in primary and secondary education.

Furthermore, the transformation of creativity and innovation in the *digital culture and in the digital economy is constrained and contradicted by the institutions of cultural production, consumption, and exchange that resulted from the domestication and commercialization*

19

of creativity and innovation in the industrial age and in financial capitalism. Therefore, rather than seeing the triumph of our collective mind as creators, we are currently suffering the consequences of the iron cage in which we enclosed ourselves out of the vertigo of our freedom.

This is why the transformation of value, in economic practices as in social practices at large, requires more than the projection of a passion by autonomous individuals, usually young and male. It can only result from the rise of new values in the human condition, including the demasculinization of the human condition, and the re-valuation of women needs to be on par with that of men. Since the most fundamental transformation of this human condition comes from the feminist challenge to the millennial patriarchal structure, it is our contention that the seeds for a redefinition of value, including economic value, as if people matter, are being planted in feminist culture. Feminist economics could be the harbinger of a new economic culture, thus of a new economy.

Feminist economics

It is clear that both financial and creative culture have been shaped and framed by masculinist and patriarchal values. How can we re-read economics from a feminist perspective? We began this chapter with a discussion of value. As we pointed out, value is determined by dominant social relations, institutions, and norms, which determine what will be valuable and what will not. In a world structured by patriarchy, dominant social institutions and norms are powerful in determining what kind of value gender relations and practices will have.

As a way to address structural economic gender disparities, feminist economics not only examines gender roles within different economies, but also critiques gendered biases in the discipline of economics. More than anything else, feminist economics seek to render women more visible within economies, as well as to re-value women as key players in every economy, even if their labor is not recognized as such by traditional economics (including Marxist theory).

In other words, to think of feminism from an economic point of view, or economics from a feminist point of view, not only indicates an examination of gender roles in the economy, as conventional economists might study this. In fact, in a neoliberal capitalist context, to think about feminism in economic terms has often meant a more popular practice, that of how women can enter the capitalist workforce, rather than re-imagining cultures of the economy from a *feminist* perspective. The difference between these is crucial: in the first instance, there is no critique of capitalism, but rather just an insertion of women and gender roles into an already established material framework – one that continues the work of capitalism and the way it is designed to create and sustain inequalities (Piketty 2013). In the second instance, the project is to re-imagine and re-think what is possible in cultures of economy, possibilities that include re-valuing women and thinking in new ways how more equitable gender relations might be part of the culture of economy.

Let's first turn our attention to the first instance of feminism and the economy, what we call popular feminism.

Popular feminism

For popular feminism, becoming *popular* has meant, among other things, something that feels familiar: commodifying and branding a movement. As Banet-Weiser has written elsewhere (2012), while we primarily associate brands with their material visibility (and audibility), through symbols, logos, jingles, sound, and design, the definition of a brand exceeds its materiality. More than just the object itself, a brand is the perception, the series of images, themes, morals, values, feelings, and authenticity conjured by it, the essence of what will be experienced, a promise.

Thus it is not wholly surprising that political movements, as well as political identities, have been re-imagined within a general context of neoliberal capitalism and financial culture as brands. Wikileaks has been branded, as has Occupy Wall St. But in the twenty-first century, feminism has been one of the most successful political brands, for a range of reasons. This brand is expressed in a number of forms, from popular media circulation to celebrity endorsement to a heightened visibility of female leadership.

Because branding is not only an economic process but also a cultural dynamic, the brand of feminism takes on a variety of forms. For example, in March 2013, Sheryl Sandberg's now both famous and infamous book *Lean In: Women, Work, and the Will to Lead* hit the bookshelves and generated an immediate media frenzy. In this book, it seems that for women, aspiration to capitalist contribution and of course capitalist excellence is really the issue and also the handy explanation for most of the data on wage and role discrepancy.

Entrepreneurialism and capitalist accomplishment are here the only routes to feminist political identity. What we see here and over and over again in the feminist positionality that Sandberg and her fans construct is the conflation of feminist politics with the ethics of capitalist production and participation. It is, for her, the shining example of what a feminist subjectivity could mean; nothing else exists. There are no other routes to feminist expression for Sandberg; the options are either career or feminist inauthenticity. And we are reminded of this often throughout the memoir. Feminism, it seems, is nowhere if it isn't leaning into capitalist success.

There have also been more conventional efforts to rebrand feminism, using the media platform of advertising and marketing to circulate feminism as a brand in wider culture. The twenty-first century has witnessed many marketing efforts to use feminism as a vehicle to sell products. For example, as Banet-Weiser has written elsewhere, Dove soap (parent company Unilever) is one of the most successful brands in feminine beauty and hygiene products (Banet-Weiser 2012). In 2005, the brand launched the "Dove Campaign for Real Beauty," defined as "a global effort that is intended to serve as a starting point for societal change and act as a catalyst for widening the definition and discussion of beauty."[2] The campaign featured billboard ads, advertisements, and videos on social media that asked consumers to reconsider dominant notions of feminine beauty and the body. Harnessing the politicized rhetoric of commodity feminism, the Dove Campaign for Real Beauty makes a plea to consumers to act politically through consumer behavior – in this case, by establishing a type of brand loyalty with Dove products, and in effect, branding a version of feminism.

This visibility of branded feminism incites a breathless excitement in the air about feminism in the contemporary moment. It lives in hashtags, best-selling memoirs, and in the popular press; on Tumblr, and on popular blogs; emblazoned on tank tops and embodied by pop stars. Beyoncé owned the embattled label at the 2014 VMAs, but even before her we had a host of "empowerment" feminism corporate initiatives: Verizon, Always, Cover Girl and then other empowerment organizations that focus on girls in STEM fields (Science, Technology, Engineering, and Math), such as BlackGirlsCode or GirlsCode. Today, popular "feminist" explorations and affirmations circulate in and across multiple media platforms with ease and frequency, creating a frenetic landscape of feminist discourse, and also firmly situating this feminist discourse within the contours of brand culture. In

---

[2] "Dove Campaign for Real Beauty," http://www.dove.us/#/cfrb/

fact, *Time Magazine* in 2014 listed "Feminism" in industry parlance as a "buzzword," forgetting that feminism is a complex movement, not a buzzword.

Aside from these efforts to reboot feminism as a kind of brand that finds expression in retail and celebrity culture, we also have literal rebranding efforts. In 2013 the fashion magazine Elle UK hired three advertising agencies, Brave, Mother, and W&K, to rebrand feminism. According to Elle UK, they invited "three feminist groups to work with three award-winning advertising agencies to re-brand a term that many feel has become burdened with complications and negativity" (Swerling 2013). Elle UK attempts to do what most successful branders do, take out the "negativity" and complexities associated with feminism, smooth out those inconsistencies, and produce a seamless, coherent, and recognizable narrative that defines feminism for all. Indeed, trying to reign in popular feminism and create it as a coherent brand has been difficult, not simply because of information glut, but also because there are as many overlaps and convergences as there are contradictions. As Lucy Mangan from the *Guardian* points out, in her critique of the Elle UK rebranding effort, "Feminism doesn't need rebranding. It just needs to overcome the people-pleasing instincts of its majority members and focus on a few core issues, and then beat the shit out of everything and everyone in its way until those issues are satisfactorily resolved" (Mangan 2013). This notion of "people pleasing" is at the heart of branding feminism; like other commercial efforts, the trick to branding is to not alienate consumer constituencies.

Of course, the problem is that feminism *is* alienating to some constituencies, and for good reason. While there is no singular definition of feminism, there is typically a shared goal of critiquing and challenging patriarchal structures. Since so much of the world is built on, and depends on the maintenance of, these structures, feminism should be *de facto* alienating. Feminist branding, then, is *not* an alternative economic practice, but rather works squarely in the service of dominant financial culture, shoring up dominant economic practices and processes, reifying feminism as a product. To return to the question of value, the value of feminism as a brand is measured in economic terms. If economic value is exchange value, and thus measured by the market, then we need to consider the market for feminism. If the dominant understanding of the market is derived from the dominance of capitalist institutions, this means that other institutional-cultural formations are subordinated to the power of capitalism. As we have argued, this power is not totalizing; there are rips and seams within the fabric of capitalism, and the economic organization of capitalism as the dominant institution doesn't eclipse totally cultural and political organization.

So how to understand the differences and similarities between branded feminisms, or what Roxane Gay calls "the popular media feminist flavor of the week," and those that recognize intersections and contradictions and also insist upon a structural critique of patriarchy and gender discrimination? This is the context in which we forget, as Gay reminds us, the "difference between feminism and Professional Feminists" (Gay 2014).

We need to think more carefully about this difference, especially in the context of alternative economic practices. Some iterations and practices of feminism are alternative, but these compete with those practices of "professional feminism," which is what dominant institutions and norms decide is valued in the contemporary moment.

Rather than valuing the reification, or commodification, of feminism, what if we were to take our attention off of the product and re-route it to practice? What does an alternative feminist economic practice look like?

Valuing care

To engage in feminist alternative economic practices means to actively re-theorize capitalism, and to reclaim the economy as a site that can be vibrant and productive for alternative economic activism. The increasing mediation and circulation of "neoliberal feminism" is, again, not an alternative economic practice. While we need to contend with the ways in which a popular or branded feminism brings public attention to gender discrimination and gendered practices, and thus could potentially offer a space for rethinking feminist politics in the contemporary moment, it doesn't challenge the normative practices and concepts of a neoliberal capitalist economy.

That is, branded and/or popular feminism is produced and articulated within what J.K. Gibson-Graham calls "essentialist and abstracted thinking about economy" (Gibson-Graham 2006). In order to have a truly alternative feminist economics, we need to interrogate the conventions and assumptions about capitalism, and challenge these conventions and assumptions in ways that profoundly redefine and reshape how we organize the economy and position ourselves as economic beings. As Gibson-Graham points out, "Where once we believed that the economy was depoliticized largely through its representations, we have more recently come to understand that its repoliticization requires cultivating ourselves as subjects who can imagine and enact a new economic politics. Bolstered by the upwelling of various movements across the world, we see the need not only for a differently theorized economy, but for new ethical *practices of thinking* economy and becoming different kinds of economic beings" (Gibson-Graham 2006: 14). Since the economy has come to depend (especially in neoliberal times, but also in historical periods of capitalism) on "feminized" or what Maya Weisinger calls "housewifized" work, we need to think in new ways about unpaid labor, maternal or reproductive labor, and networks of care (Weisinger 2012).

One ethical practice of "thinking economy and becoming different kinds of economic beings" is to revalue care work as an alternative feminist economic practice. The invisible labor that women perform in every economy has been critiqued from a Marxist feminist perspective, with a significant feminist mobilization around this issue in the US and Europe in the 1960s and 1970s. In particular, feminists in the 1960s and 1970s sought to reveal the way power relations function in terms of the economy, where individual empowerment was bestowed upon those who were able to maintain a position in the formal economy. This position, however, could only be sustained by labor in the informal economy, namely the household. As Weisinger (2012) points out:

> In the case of housewives, an entire economy is build upon the idea of free labor and care: the informal economy. Housewives do not get reimbursed for taking care of children, shopping, cleaning, cooking, etc. These are elements of support that are deemed necessary in order for the Male counterpart of the family unit to be able to work and provide for the family financially and to be able to develop in the formal economy, which is the ultimate definition of success in our society.

Feminists relied on Marxist theory in part because the Marxist concept of a "social whole" allows us to see the mutual shaping of family formation, reproductive practice, sexual construction, economic determinism, and the ideology of the "feminine." Additionally, this concept allows us to see the way in which these institutions are rooted in particular economic conditions. Marxist feminists then called attention to the material order of existence, and explored the dynamics of power and domination within that order.

Of course, while Marxist thinking gives feminists powerful tools for thinking through the dynamic of history and oppression, there are numerous limitations in the ways these tools have been framed by the men who developed them. Marxist feminists then had to modify these tools, and ask questions such as: What is material for women? What is the relation of women's material order to ideology? What is the limitation of Marxism for appreciating gender as a problem of social construction?

It is clear that there needs to be an expansion of the material realm for Marxism to be an analytic that feminists can use to "become different kinds of economic beings." A feminist framework needs to open up a definition of economy to include household labor, reproductive work, sexuality, and emotional labor and care work. Thus, an alternative feminist analysis should seek to expand the "economy" as a realm of production and exchange to an economy with a much wider geographic and conceptual sense. To get back to our earlier discussion of value, a feminist alternative economic practice would not only widen and deepen a Marxist notion of the economy, but would strive to decenter it altogether.

One way Marxist feminists attempted to widen the Marxist notion of the economy in the late 1970s was to call for wages for housework. This was a compelling argument that organizing domestic life, from cleaning to cooking to childcare, was absolutely crucial to maintain a capitalist economic system (as it was the necessary reproductive labor that allowed for the continuation of the productivity of waged labor), but went uncompensated. This debate centered on how, and whether, housework actually produced surplus value for capital (that is, women's free labor services not only men, but also capital; it is not only free labor, but because it is unwaged, it is not counted as labor) (Hartmann 1979; Federici 2012). This analysis *widened* the Marxist notion of economy, but still remained quite close to Marxist terms.

As Italian feminist Silvia Federici has detailed in her work, the Wages for Housework feminist movement sought to unmask the process of naturalization housework has undergone because it is unwaged, to demonstrate the capitalist logic of "waged labor," and to "demonstrate that historically the question of 'productivity' has always been connected with the struggle for social power" (Federici 2012: 8). The movement was crucial in that it revealed some of the main ways capitalist economies maintain power: by devaluing "entire spheres of human activity, beginning with the activities catering to the reproduction of human life, and the ability to use the wage to extract also from a large population of workers who appear to be outside the wage relation: slaves, colonial subjects, prisoners, housewives, and students" (Federici 2012: 8).

There have also been feminist efforts to *deepen* the Marxist notion of the economy, which aimed to develop a material basis for women's oppression that challenged Marxist terms more overtly. For example, reproductive work needs to be valued differently, not as a natural phenomenon but as a social one, which is to say that it is organized, controlled, and situated in particular ways, but also that reproductive work produces certain consciousness and ideology and can't be reduced to economic relations.

Sex, sexuality, subjectivity, and affect are also feminist mechanisms to deepen a Marxist notion of the economy, where, as Catharine MacKinnon points out, feminism permits us to wed and transcend Marx and Freud, and to understand the construction of sexuality not as the construction of subjectivity but rather as a dimension of the material construction of people in a system of domination and oppression. MacKinnon argues that sexuality is the material domain of women's oppression, and the construction of it within masculine terms is what makes men dominant and women subordinate (MacKinnon 1982). It is precisely the naturalization of this relation that makes the subordination of women appear to have no material base. Is women's subordination really not so material as class subordination? This is the question that was at the center of feminist efforts to deepen a Marxist notion of economy.

However, there are crucial problems within the attempts to use Marxist theory to understand gender relations of power. Importantly, the circumscription of the economic entails the simultaneous circumscription of what is political. The Marxist primacy of the economic means that the relations of production are seen as shaping all else, and in the contemporary moment the dominant relations of production are those of capitalism, so that capitalist relations are seen as shaping all other relations. Marx simply did not recognize the centrality of reproductive labor, regardless of whether he was discussing capital accumulation or an ideal communist society. To get back to Gibson-Graham, we need to get out of this kind of essentialist and abstracted thinking, and think about what it means to be different kinds of economic subjects. In other words, while widening and deepening a Marxist notion of the economy are necessary first steps, we need to *decenter* this notion of the economy, and imagine a different set of dynamics and parameters.

One way to think through this is to re-value care. As Evelyn Nakano Glenn has pointed out, it is important to have a society that values care and care work differently – which is very different than a society that values the branding and commodification of popular feminism (Glenn 2012). In the contemporary Western world (especially the US), care is a privatized good, its articulation and operation the

27

responsibility of the individual. A feminist politics of care would suggest that we decenter this dynamic, and understand that care is a collective right for both caregivers and those who need care. This would require a redistribution of social wealth in the direction of those that need care (primarily the elderly and children), and a commitment to constructing a collective form of reproduction (Federici 2012). The labor involved in the organization of the domestic sphere, the maintenance of the family, nurturing and emotional work are typically relegated to women and people of color, and is certainly not a priority of the state. A feminist economic politics of care reprioritizes care, understanding it as a crucial form of social reproduction, and challenges the linked ideologies of individual independence and family responsibility, and thus position caring and care work as a public social responsibility.

Care networks

As Federici has argued, the care of the elderly has always existed in a state of crisis within capitalist societies, "both because of the devaluation of reproductive work in capitalism and because the elderly are seen as no longer productive, instead of being treasured as they were in many precapitalist societies as depositories of the collective memory and experience" (Federici 2012: 116). As governments dedicate less and less state money to the care of the elderly, and places the burden of care on private individuals, it becomes clear that from a conventional economic viewpoint, care of the elderly (as well as others) is devalued, seen as the responsibility of the individual, and not considered a crucial element of the social reproduction of a nation or community.

Arlie Hochschild has written in *The Outsourced Self* that in the current historical moment, we have monetized intimate relations, moving from what she sees as a "world of villagers to one of outsiders" (Hochschild 2013: 55). She continues, "Along the way, we've also created a market in emotional states. Ironically, one of the feelings the market can sell us is the feeling of being authentically out of the market" (Hochschild 2013: 55). This has implications for care work, as one of the markets for "emotional state" is the market for care – care of the elderly, care for children. As we have been arguing, markets not only create norms, they rely on norms for a context; they are a continuous normative process. In the context of the market for care, the social institution of care work must be built up and maintained, and in conventional economics, the responsibility of this maintenance has primarily been on poorly paid women and people of color. And many elderly and families cannot afford to hire care workers, so the burden is placed (usually) back on women in families to provide this kind of care.

There have been recent practices that have addressed the individualism of care work, especially maternal care work. As Julie Wilson and Emily Yochim have written, the blogosphere has become a rich space for mothers to establish networks of care and community, leading to what they call the "momosphere" (Wilson and Yochim 2015). "Mommy blogs" (an unfortunate name, as it diminishes the potential importance of these communities by labeling them as the domain of the "mommy," so I will use "maternal blogs") have flourished in recent years, and have provided a digital space for mothers to collectively share their maternal labor and the real stresses and burdens of nuclear family life within neoliberal capitalism. While maternal and reproductive labor have always been central for the operation of capitalism, within neoliberal capitalism the role of reproductive labor is even more crucial, as the welfare state continues to be dismantled and more and more labor hinges on individuals and families. As Wilson and Yochim point out, the precarity of labor figures centrally through mothers and their labor

> for it is their labors as the keepers of the domestic realm that underwrite and make possible ongoing privatization and government through insecurity. In this way, the staggering upward redistribution of wealth over the past decades has been achieved on the backs of mothers, who are constantly adjusting their lives, labors, affects, and sensibilities in order to stabilize their increasingly shaky family scenes as their lifeworlds are looted. (Wilson and Yochim 2015: 673)

Importantly, digital care networks such as maternal online communities do important work in terms of re-valuing the labor of women. Yet, at the same time, this re-values women's labor for the individual women involved, rather than always challenging the structural invisibility of this labor. Wilson and Yochim call this "individualized solidarities" where the "aim of collectivity is the stabilization and valorization of individual nuclear families." This tension between individuals and collectivities is indicative of much of social activism in the current environment, including feminist economics.

That is, feminist economics, like the culture of creativity, challenges the individualism of neoliberal capitalism not only by re-valuing particular kinds of labor, but also insisting on a notion of the "commons" as a way to think about alternative economies (see Varvarousis and

Kallis, this volume). In fact, the same economic processes and logic that authorize neoliberal capitalism and privilege the individual to become a norm ironically allow for alternative economic practices, such as a feminist understanding of the commons. As Federici comments, the way that neoliberal capitalism seeks to make all things into markets also ironically works to create alterative spaces that are newly threatened by privatization. These new spaces, such as digital spaces like maternal blogs, means "that not only commons have not vanished, but new forms of social cooperation are constantly being produced, also in areas of life where none previously existed, as for example the Internet" (Federici 2012: 139).

The key here is to actively challenge the co-optation of the commons by either the market or the state. A feminist commons, one that recognizes the essential role of the reproduction of human life as a collective, and not a private, practice, is truly an alternative economy.

Conclusion: Economic practices beyond economics

It should be obvious that economic practices are shaped by cultural values. In fact, this elementary observation runs against standard economic analysis, and economic calculations, because neoclassical economics stands on top of an essentialist assumption of human nature: *homo economicus*, as a rationally oriented individual. Rationality is measured in terms of the best allocation of scarce resources to maximize personal utility. For this naïve formulation to escape the contradiction of a value-free utility, the personal satisfaction has to be equated to maximizing monetary gain. Indeed, there is a second assumption: that if money does not necessarily lead to happiness, at least it can buy it. Thus, satisfaction is circumscribed to what the market may offer. The loop is closed: economic value is equated to monetary value determined by the market in terms of the relationship between supply and demand as a mean to satisfy most needs and desires. Of course, mainstream economists acknowledge that this is an oversimplification of the diversity of human behavior. Life cannot be reduced to economic transactions, societies cannot be reduced to markets. However, all other human behavior is dispatched to the world of irrationality, with the economy being the domain of rational choice and quantifiable outcomes. So be it. Therefore, we need an explanatory framework powerful enough to account for the cultural diversity that guides human behavior to understand why people do what they do, beyond the strictly defined rationality paradigm. And because practices of production, consumption, and exchange are fully embedded in the social fabric of people's lives (beyond the parameters of economic models), we need a multifaceted cultural analysis to understand human practices, including economic practices. This is what we have attempted to propose in this chapter, relating to the analytical effort of the contributors to this volume in their specific inquiries.

References

Admati, A. and Hellwig, M. (2013) *The Bankers' New Clothes*. Princeton University Press, Princeton, NJ.

Aldridge, A. (1997) Engaging with promotional culture: organized business and the personal services industry. *Sociology* 31, 3, 389–408.

Banet-Weiser, S. (2012) *Authentic™: The Politics of Ambivalence in a Brand Culture*. New York University Press, New York.

Castaño, C. (2010) *Genero y TIC: presencia, posicion y politicas*. UOC Press, Barcelona.

Castaño, C. (ed.) (2015) *Las mujeres en la gran recession*. Catedra, Valencia.

Castells, M. (2000) *The Rise of the Network Society*. Blackwell, Oxford.

Castells, M. (2004) Informationalism, networks and the network society. In: Castells, M. (ed.) *The Network Society: A Cross-Cultural Perspective*. Edward Elgar, London.

Castells, M. (2009) *Communication Power*. Oxford University Press, Oxford.

Castells, M. (2011) A network theory of power. *International Journal of Communication* 5, 773–87.

Castells, M. (2015) *Networks of Outrage and Hope*, 2nd edn. Polity, Cambridge.

Castells, M., Caraça, J. and Cardoso, G. (eds.) (2012) *Aftermath: The Cultures of the Economic Crisis*. Oxford University Press, Oxford.

Crouch, C. (2011) *The Strange Non-Death of Neoliberalism*. Polity, Cambridge.

Engelen, E., Ertürk, I., Froud, J., Johal, S., Leaver, A., Moran, M., Nilsson, A. and Williams, K. (2011) *After the Great Complacency: Financial Crisis and the Politics of Reform*. Oxford University Press, Oxford.

English-Lueck, J.A. (2002) *Cultures@Silicon Valley*. Stanford University Press, Stanford, CA.

Federici, S. (2012) *Revolution at Point Zero: Housework, Reproduction, and Feminist Struggle*. PM Press, New York.

Ferguson, N. (2013) *The Great Degeneration: How Institutions Decay and Economies Die*. Penguin Books, London.

Gay, R. (2014) *Bad Feminist: Essays*. Harper Perennial, New York.

Gibson-Graham, J.K. (2006) *The End of Capitalism (As We Knew It): A Feminist Critique of Political Economy*. University of Minnesota Press, Minneapolis, MN.

Glenn, E. (2012) *Forced to Care: Coercion and Caregiving in America*. Harvard University Press, Cambridge, MA.

Hartmann, H. (1979). The unhappy marriage of Marxism and Feminism: Toward a more progressive union. *Capital & Class* 3, 2, 1–33.

Harvey, D. (2005) *A Brief History of Neoliberalism*. Oxford University Press, Oxford.

Himanen, P. (2002) *The Hacker Ethic and the Spirit of the Information Age*. Random House, New York.

Hochschild, A. (2013) *The Outsourced Self: What Happens When We Pay Others to Live Our Lives for Us*. Picador, London.

Hsing, Y. (2014) Development as culture: Human development and information development in China. In: Castells, M. and Himanen, P. (eds.) *Reconceptualizing Development in the Global Information Age*. Oxford University Press, Oxford, pp. 116–39.

Hutton, W. and Giddens, A. (eds.) (2000) *On the Edge: Living in Global Capitalism*. Jonathan Cape, London.

Kahneman, D. and Tversky, A. (1973) On the psychology of prediction. *Psychology Review* 80, 237–51.

MacKinnon, C. (1982) Feminism, Marxism, method, and the State: An agenda for theory. *Signs* 7, 3, 515–44.

Mangan, L. (2013) Why feminism doesn't need rebranding. *The Guardian*, November 16.

Mason, P. (2015) *Postcapitalism: A Guide Tour to Our Future*. Allen Lane/ Penguin, London.

Murray, G. and Scott, J. (2012) *Financial Elites and Transnational Business: Who Rules the World*. Edward Elgar, London.

Neff, G. (2012) *Venture Labor: Work and the Burden of Risk in Innovative Industries*. MIT Press, Cambridge, MA.

Neuman, W. Russell (2016) *The Digital Difference*. Harvard University Press, Cambridge, MA.

Nolan, P. (2009) *Crossroads: The End of Wild Capitalism and the Future of Humanity*. Marshall Cavendish, London.

North, D. (1981) *Structure and Change in Economic History*. W.W. Norton, New York.

Ostrom, E. (2005) *Understanding Institutional Diversity*. Princeton University Press, Princeton, NJ.

Piketty, T. (2013) *Le capital au XXIème siècle*. Editions du Seuil, Paris.

Sandberg, S. (2013) *Lean In: Women, Work, and the Will to Lead*. Alfred A. Knopf, New York.

Santoro, M. and Strauss, R. (2013) *Wall Street Values: Business Ethics and the Global Financial Crisis*. Cambridge University Press, New York.

Saxenian, A. (2006) *Regional Advantage: The Cultures of Silicon Valley*. Harvard University Press, Cambridge, MA.

Schumpeter, J. (1942) *Capitalism, Socialism and Democracy*. Harper & Brothers, New York.

Sennett, R. (2006) *The Cultures of New Capitalism*. Yale University Press, New Haven, CT.

Swerling, H. (2013) ELLE rebrands Feminism: what does it means to you? *Elle*, 1 October. Available at: http://www.elleuk.com/fashion/celebrity-style/articles/a2322/elle-rebrands-feminism/

Weber, S. (2004) *The Success of Open Source*. Harvard University Press, Cambridge, MA.

Weisinger, M. (2012) Housewifization. *Tapestries: Interwoven Voices of Local and Global Identities* 2, 1.

Wilson, J. and Yochim, E. (2015) Mothering through precarity: becoming mamapreneurial. *Cultural Studies* 29, 5–6, 669–86.

Zaloom, C. (2006) *Out of the Pits: Traders and Technology from Chicago to London.* University of Chicago Press, Chicago, IL.

Zelizer, V. (2013) *Economic Lives: How Culture Shapes the Economy.* Princeton University Press, Princeton, NJ.

Chapter 2

Economics Without Growth
Giorgos Kallis

Introduction

The early twenty-first century poses a different set of challenges to economics than the late nineteenth and early twentieth centuries, when the premises of current orthodoxy were founded. Then the core question was how to achieve growth; now it is how to manage and prosper without growth (Victor 2008; Jackson 2011). Then the question was how to produce wealth (Smith 1887); now it is how to live with enough (Skidelsky and Skidelsky 2012).

Developed economies find themselves in a unique constellation of: stagnation, for the first time since the Second World War (Summers 2013; Piketty 2014); ecological thresholds, especially catastrophic climate change, all but unavoidable if the global economy continues to grow at its current pace (Jackson 2011); and rising inequalities, accentuated by stagnation and the "neoliberal" turn (Harvey 2011; Piketty 2014). Growth is unsustainable, but degrowth is socially unstable in capitalist economies (Jackson 2011). A new economics therefore has to inform the question of how to make degrowth stable while reducing inequalities.

Standard economic models are inadequate for engaging with these questions. Their pre-analytic simplifications are partly derived from normative concerns of the past. The standard Solow growth model, for example, was designed to explain the origins of growth. Growth was attributed to the accumulation of capital and to the technological progress that drives productivity. Economists after Solow broke the productivity part down to human and social capital, energy productivity, or the quality of institutions. To reverse this and claim that degrowth would require a reduction of the capital stock, technological regression or dismantling of institutions and education systems is obviously missing the point. The question of the determinants of "prosperity without growth" is qualitatively different. The question is not how to undo growth, but how to create an alternative prosperous path that does not pass through growth. A different economics is necessary for a different economy.

As noted by Rezai et al. (2013), in the neoclassical model of equilibrium, prices automatically adjust to keep the economy in the optimal path of employment, investment, and expansion (or inversely, but much less frequently admitted, an optimal path of contraction if this is where the fundamentals lead). In reality the economy is more often than not out of equilibrium. The "adjustment of prices" following a crisis is full of suffering and rife in distributional conflict. Contractions are far from stable. It is the dynamics, and distributive consequences of a contractionary "adjustment" that we need to understand from a degrowth perspective. In the standard model instead, distribution is treated as a separate question to that of wealth, and an afterthought to efficiency.

Many scientists, not all of them economists, are motivated by the quest to develop a "new economics." These efforts are diverse and range from integrated dynamic or neo-Keynesian models of low or no growth (Victor 2008; Rezai et al. 2013; Jackson and Victor 2016), to the various qualitative and quantitative analyses coming out from the post-growth and degrowth literature (Kallis et al. 2012). This diverse community includes not only ecological, institutional, or political economists, but also geographers, ecologists, and sociologists. The research agenda is transdisciplinary (Kallis et al. 2012). It does not share mainstream economics' obsession with axiomatic micro-foundations, mathematical representation, and statistical generalization. It formulates instead logical or dialectical hypotheses, expressed verbally or mathematically, and it mobilizes both qualitative (e.g. case studies) and quantitative (e.g. econometrics) methods to investigate them.

This new economics has not emerged in a coordinated fashion (for a history of the degrowth literature, see Kallis et al. 2014). What I attempt in this chapter is to reverse the order, and look ex-post, especially at the degrowth literature, and discern its core principles and the new understandings it engenders. Part 1 presents six key ideas about the economy that characterize the degrowth literature: the economy as an invention (1), that is political (2), material (3), and diverse (4), whose key function is the distribution and expenditure of surplus (5), and which changes through a co-evolutionary process (6). I leave out a seventh dimension of the economy as a culture because it is treated in detail in the chapter by Banet-Weiser and Castells. Part 2 provides an alternative explanation of the crisis building on these principles. Part 3 positions the rise of the alternative economy movement (Conill et al. 2012) as a movement embodying this new understanding of the economy. Part 4 focuses on policies for managing without growth.

Part 1: Six core principles

The economy is an invention (Latouche 2005)

The idea of "the economy" is not a universal, a-historical one that has always existed. It is one whose genealogy and origins can be traced; and whose meaning has evolved over time, signifying different things in different periods and societies. Martinez-Alier (1990) notes the distinction made by Aristotle between "oeconomics," the management of the household, and "chrematistics," the making of money out of money. Foucault (1991) traces the birth of political economy between the sixteenth and eighteenth centuries, noting an extension of the notion of a household's "economy," i.e. the proper disposition of a household's people and things, to the population as a whole. For Foucault political economy marks a shift from sovereignty-based rule to "governmentality," i.e. governing populations for their own improvement, making them accomplices to their own (self) disciplining. "Statistics," literally the science of the state, is a product of this pre-occupation with the registering, governing and improving of populations. Using a Foucauldian approach, Mitchell (2002) unveils the methods of measurement, circulation, and exchange that materialized the novel idea of a national "economy," using Egypt as a case study. New statistics and indicators such as gross domestic product (GDP) were part and parcel of this abstraction of the national economy (Dale 2012).

The fact that the economy is an invented abstraction does not make it any less real. As any abstraction, it represents things and changes that correspond to – partially at least – actual experiences. Abstractions have real effects, often violent ones (Loftus 2015). Witness the social consequences from capital flows or austerity policies that respond to debt to GDP ratios. Nevertheless, abstractions they are, by definition incomplete and partial. For example, the dominant representation of the "economy" in standard models is that of a national system

36

with an endless circulation of goods and services between "firms" and "households." Natural resources are nowhere to be seen. There are no limits, inflows, outflows, or external checks to this circulation (Daly 1997). There are no distributions, institutions, politics, or other forms of power that govern, sometimes violently, this circulation. A different economics requires a different representation, starting with the acknowledgement that there is no single, universal, and objective representation of a thing out there called "the economy."

The economy is political (Polanyi 1944; Castoriadis 1997)

In mainstream models, the economy is seen as a system with its own laws and dynamics, governed by supply and demand. The goal is then to understand how the "invisible hand" of the market works. Normatively, the project is one of approximating as much as possible this equilibrium, "free market" ideal where supply matches demand. The state is to be kept outside this perfect balance. Since markets are optimal, when states intervene they reduce the quantity of wealth that could otherwise be produced (an exception allowed is the provision of public goods, the correction of externalities, and the smoothing of economic cycles; usually this is restricted to very specific cases such as military defense and policing).

Polanyi (1944) first pointed to the ideological construction of the "free market." The free market does not exist; it is made, Polanyi argued. The self-regulating market is nowhere to be found but in the fantasy of economists. The creation of conditions of market exchange where they do not exist involves state intervention and force. Examples include processes of accumulation by dispossession (Harvey 2003), from the enclosures of pastures that catalyzed capitalism to more recent institutionalizations of private property in the genome or the intellectual commons (Prudham 2007). The establishment of private property and market exchange is far from straightforward and involves heavy state investment in law, regulation, monitoring, and enforcement (Bakker 2003). Polanyi argued that the institution of fictitious markets and the transformation into commodities of things that were not produced to be commodities – most notably land, labor, and money – was at the heart of the great crisis of the 1930s. Socialism and fascism were two expressions of a "counter-movement" against the self-destructive expansion of the market.

From Polanyi's formulation, it follows that the economy cannot be but *political*. The choice, for example, to render central banks independent, or to deregulate financial markets is *a choice*, one

37

with distributive consequences and one that expresses certain social interests over others. By insisting on the retreat of the state and the liberation of the free market, the neoliberal doctrine is dressing up a political choice as a natural outcome (hence the language of "equilibrium"). Cornelius Castoriadis (1997) noted how the idea of a self-regulated economy with its own laws and truths has replaced religion as a source of "heteronomy" for secular societies, this set of externally-given laws to which the will of populations supposedly has to succumb. Democracy for Castoriadis implied "autonomy," the possibility for collectives to consciously reflect upon and (re)make their own institutions (and history), rather than making them, while attributing their creation to external forces, such as "god" or "the market."

In the degrowth literature there are calls "to exit" or "take back" the economy (Gibson-Graham 2006; Fournier 2008). These are not as contradictory as they seem. "Exiting" means escaping from the dominant view of an external economy with its own rules and laws, i.e. a recognition of the autonomy to shape what is the economy. "Taking back" means an exercise of the collective power to govern the economy toward different ends. Exiting, literally and physically, the mainstream economy is a means for creating new, alternative economies, economies with different laws and truths.

The economy is material (Georgescu-Roegen 1971)

Economic activity – production, exchange, or consumption – does not take place in a vacuum. It extracts and transforms inputs – energy and raw materials – and it produces undesirable outputs, such as waste or air emissions. Each society, like each organism, has a "metabolism," a pattern of material and energy throughput (Fischer-Kowalski 1997; Giampietro 2003). There is nothing immaterial in information services, such as a social networking site like Facebook. These embed vast quantities of materials and energy [what Odum (2002) called "emergy," embodied energy]: raw materials used for computers; energy used to power servers; or food, materials, and energy used to raise, educate, and move around the Silicon Valley entrepreneurs. The "immaterial" economy embodies a very material economy.

The economic process increases entropy as it converts high order matter and energy into low order energy (Georgescu-Roegen 1971). For Georgescu-Roegen, the entropic death of life on the planet is the ultimate physical limit; a transition from exhaustive fossil fuels, which once used are turned into high-entropy energy irreversibly, to "renewable" solar power, which will slow down the pace toward this entropic end. However, the presence or not of ultimate entropic limits has been disputed; and even if there are such limits, they probably operate in time horizons of millions of years, making them irrelevant for current generations. Nonetheless, specific stocks, such as oil or phosphorus upon which modern industry or agriculture depend, may be exhausted. This is a matter of specific, not ultimate limits.

A preferable conceptualization of the relationship between society and resources is that of co-evolution. Resources such as fossil fuels, or ecosystems such as the atmosphere, condition what societies can or cannot do in any given moment. Societies refashion such "limits"; industrialized agriculture overcame the limits of land productivity and oil substituted coal. In the process new limits and conditions were produced, such as soil pollution, erosion, exhaustion of phosphorus for fertilizers, or climate change. The "responses" to such limits, such as the development of nuclear power, tar sands, or GMOs, may increase the wellbeing of some (typically a few) at the expense of many others. It is more apt to think of the economy and social activity not as ultimately limited in an absolute sense by a surrounding planetary ecosystem (Daly 1997), but in a constant co-evolutionary relationship, whereby societies transform ecosystems, for better or for worse, and then have to adapt to their own transformations (Benton 1992; Kallis and Norgaard 2010).

Georgescu-Roegen's insight remains important insofar as the economic process creates negentropic order in some places, by increasing entropy elsewhere. Climate change is the result of the entropic shift of carbon emissions to the atmosphere. Increasing carbon emissions and concentrations in the atmosphere destabilize the climate with disastrous consequences, which will strongly determine future co-evolution. If all currently available fossil fuels were to be extracted, temperature on the planet would increase by 15°C. To stay within what scientists claim as the safe operating zone of 2°C change, by 2050 the global economy would have to become 130 times more efficient in its use of carbon if it were to grow at the same pace; in comparison from 1980 to 2007, efficiency improved by a mere 23 percent (Jackson 2011). Rich countries should start cutting their emissions by 8–10 percent per year (Anderson and Bows-Larkin 2013), when the best they have achieved are 1 percent reductions, and this during recessions. A reduction of economic activity, in Georgescu-Roegen's terms a slowing down of the entropic economic process, seems unavoidable, either voluntarily by planned degrowth or involuntarily by a disastrous change of the climate.

39

Another important insight of the material, or metabolic view, is that the production of energy and resources uses energy and resources itself. To drill oil, one spends energy; to extract uranium and silicon, and build and operate nuclear or solar power plants, also. The period of high growth has been associated with high energy productivity (or high energy surpluses) from oil and coal. It is not clear how cleaner renewable energies, with lower energy return on energy investment, will sustain high growth rates or an economy of the present scale. While a short-term Keynesian perspective can suggest that public investment in green infrastructures and renewable energy can be expansionary, in the long term this is unlikely to be the case, since one in effect is substituting energy sources of high productivity for sources with low productivity. Labor can substitute energy, but this is the inverse of the growth process. In conclusion, it is unlikely to have a "green growth."

The economy is diverse (Gibson-Graham 2006)

The economy of mainstream models is the capitalist economy of private property, wage labor, and market exchange, with firms producing for profit and households offering their labor for wages that allow them in turn to consume. In reality, this is only the visible top of the economy iceberg (Gibson-Graham 2006). Below the surface, there is a diversity of alternative markets (e.g. fair trade) or non-market exchanges (e.g. barters), alternative forms of paid labor or unpaid labor (e.g. domestic or volunteer work), and alternative enterprises (e.g. ethical banks or cooperatives) or non-capitalist enterprises (e.g. NGOs, collectives and associations, mutual care networks). In the degrowth literature, a lot of attention is given to "gift economies" (Mauss 1954), where goods and services circulate through networks of bonds and obligations without a logic of profit; or the "commons," where people pool or share resources and self-organize the institutions of their governance (De Angelis and Harvie 2014; Varvarousis and Kallis, this volume).

Care labor or non-market exchanges within families are obvious forms of non-capitalist economic activity permeated by logics of gift or commons. Urban food gardens, consumer-producer food cooperatives or time banks are newer "post-capitalist" reincarnations of such non-capitalist relations (Conill et al. 2012). These are not remains of – or regressions to – pre-capitalistic formations "not yet capitalized," unless one buys into the ideology of the "free market" as the final destination.

As Gibson-Graham (2006) argues, the market economy is supported by an immense amount of work conducted outside of it. Measured in monetary terms, alternative, non-capitalist practices may account for a very small part of the economy. But this is precisely because they do not produce for profit, and they are not part of the accounting system of the markets. If one takes into account the human activity or work time devoted to domestic, voluntary, and not-for-profit work, or, more challengingly, if one accounts for the social (rather than exchange) value produced by such work, it might be that the alternative economy is comparable to, if not bigger than, the formal economy. Without it, and without its unaccounted for "subsidies," the formal economy would not be sustainable, as it would have to compensate a reproduction that it now receives for free.

The central economic question is surplus, not scarcity
(Bataille 1927)

Surplus is produced when workers receive for their work less than their contribution to the product. It is also produced when those who do the reproductive care work that sustains an economy (the cooking, cleaning, childrearing or mutual aid) do not receive their share from this work or when ecosystem services provided for free from nature are exploited without being replenished. Fossil fuels have offered vast amounts of free work without which industrialization would not have been possible (a useful metaphor is that of "energy slaves": think of the invisible workers necessary to power an elevator or pull a car around).

Bataille (1927) argues that the key question of any economic system is not scarcity, but what to do with its surplus, for there is always more product than what is necessary to satisfy the basic needs of the producers. What distinguishes, for example, capitalism from other systems is not the creation of surplus, but what it does with it. The innovation of capitalism is that it invests a great part of the surplus to further production and further surplus creation (D'Alisa et al. 2014). This unleashes a growth potential unseen by any other civilization. The destiny of surplus, be it into pyramids, idle monks, potlatches, carnivals, or investment, gives a civilization its essence, according to Bataille (1927). Bataille argued that surplus needs to be regularly expended and dissipated, if it is not to accumulate beyond a threshold that its dissipation becomes catastrophic (e.g. by a war).

The economic process is ridden with distributive conflict over the contribution to, and the destiny of, surplus, or, differently seen, the allocation of costs (and benefits). Economic distribution conflicts concern the distribution of surplus between workers and capital, whereas ecological distribution conflicts concern the distribution of environmental goods and bads (Martinez-Alier and O'Connor 2002). Reproductive conflict is often gendered given that women are disproportionately charged with reproductive and care work.

Economic change is a co-evolutionary process (Norgaard 1994)

How do transitions from one system configuration, say feudalism, to another, say capitalism, take place? Norgaard (1994) and more recently Harvey (2011) propose a co-evolutionary model of change, whereby different spheres of activity interact and change one another in a mutually constitutive fashion. Norgaard sketched five broad spheres: technology, nature, values, knowledge, and institutions; Harvey, seven: technological and organizational forms, social relations, institutional and administrative arrangements, production and labor processes, relations to nature, the reproduction of daily life and of the species, and "mental conceptions of the world," the latter including relations of trust and cultural and belief systems.

Evolution means that epoch changes become evident with the passing of time; they are not perceptible as they happen. At any given point in time the different spheres are interlocked and hard to change, giving the impression of an immutable "system," such as capitalism. This hides the variation and diversity that always exists within each sphere. Such diversity is constantly renewed through pure novelty (what in biology are called "mutations"), intentional or unintentional (Kallis and Norgaard 2010). Mutual selection means that those variants of one sphere that best fit the dominant ones of another are the ones more likely to "survive" and multiply. Minoritarian interlocked sub-systems often co-exist "within the shell of the old" occupying and developing in niches, and expanding when the surrounding conditions change. Spatial separation facilitates niche differentiation and evolution. As new life forms have evolved in distant islands, new social and cultural forms may emerge in distant geographies or by groups that manage to spatially isolate and autonomize their territory, while networking to transfer its innovations (think of the Zapatistas movement).

Capitalism long co-existed within feudalism before finally evolving out of it. Connections were forged first, between new technological and organizational forms (firms, corporations, trade contracts, banks, investments) with institutional and administrative arrangements (abolition of monarchies and feudal privileges, enclosure of the commons, liberal democracy, laws protecting private property). These connections were more intense in geographical niches, such as medieval Venice, or later the Netherlands or England. New administrative arrangements were made possible in a context of new social relations, values, and struggles over competing institutions (Harvey 2011). The success of the new mode of organization benefited from – and facilitated – the advent of a whole new system of technologies, which in turn was possible because of access to and development of the vast reserve of fossil fuels (Norgaard 1994).

While everything seems interlocked in the short term, in the long term everything changes, not least as a result of external perturbations that change the selection environment, akin to "comets" or other cataclysmic punctuations in biological evolution. Co-evolution is a slow process for most of the time, punctuated by transitions to new equilibria in periods of revolutionary change (such as the bourgeois revolutions of the nineteenth century or the socialist revolutions of the twentieth).

Part 2: An alternative account of the crisis

With the above conceptual repertoire at hand, let me sketch an alternative explanation of the crisis, developing thoughts expressed in Kallis et al. (2009). The basic idea is simple: limits to growth were superseded with an expansion of credit. Money growth detached from the fundamentals could last only up to a point, before it spectacularly crashed.

Since the late 1970s developed economies entered a prolonged period of what has recently been called "secular stagnation" (Summers 2013). The high growth rates of the post-war reconstruction period came to an end and low or zero growth rates became the norm. The economy of production was reaching a limit for four reasons: the natural stabilization that follows rebound after a catastrophe or fast growth during convergence and catching-up; the fact that the bigger an economy gets the more difficult it becomes to grow at the same pace; the exhaustion of the potential of the great technological innovations of the nineteenth and early twentieth centuries (Gordon 2012), especially the lack of new breakthroughs in energy productivity (Ayres and Warr 2010); and difficulties in creating new demand outlets to absorb ever-growing surpluses (Harvey 2011). Plausibly, limits in the throughput rates of oil and raw materials also played a role (Martinez-Alier 2009).

Stagnation was overcome by an expansion of credit and the economy of finance made possible by private and public indebtedness. Private indebtedness took the form of housing and consumer mortgages, facilitated by the privatization of money, new money in effect being created by banks via loans (Mellor 2010). Paper exchanging for paper is now 20 times bigger than paper exchanging for real commodities. In some unique cases, such as Greece, where the state continued to control a large part of the economy, indebtedness took the form of public debt. In others the majority of debt was private, at least up until governments shouldered the damage or the risks of insolvent banks. In any case, the influx of money and loans, private or public, facilitated by the invention of new financial products, managed to sustain fictitiously high growth rates.

This was sustained by a co-evolution between a belief system structured around the benefits of the so-called free market and a set of political interventions that served to deregulate important spheres of economic life, not least housing markets, financial products, and the cross-border movement of capital. The fetishization of GDP growth and stock exchange indices, propelled by the deregulated fictitious capital, served to disguise the problematic fundamentals of the economy. In turn, the political shift of power enacted by the institutional changes that took place in the name of "liberating" the economy led to a major redistribution from income to capital and from low to higher incomes (Piketty 2014). Most of the proceeds of growth accrued to the few, while the living standards of the majority stagnated. In a vicious cycle, further and further indebtedness avoided the stagnation of demand. And as the few controlled more and more of the surplus, they cornered the political system, and ensured that the neoliberalization changes were there to stay.

The bubble burst in 2008 and oil may have had something to do with it. Continued growth, accentuated by rising resource demand from Asia, coupled with an oversupply of money and financial capital, led to a sustained increase in oil and commodity prices, starting in 2002. By 2007, oil prices passed a threshold that pushed the US economy over the brink of recession (Hamilton 2009) and catalyzed mortgage foreclosures (Kaufmann et al. 2011). The inability of poor households in the suburbs, hit by high gasoline prices, to pay "toxic" mortgage loans revealed the unsustainable exposure of many banks, and precipitated the financial crisis. Low growth expectations stifled investment, and started a negative spiral, which exposed the unsustainable levels of household indebtedness and bank exposure.

The rest of the story, with the contagion of the crisis to the

Eurozone, and the shifting of costs from banks to the public sector, followed by austerity policies and regressive redistribution, is well known. Growth in the pre-crisis period was sustained not only by finance-driven expansion, but also by an intensive strategy of exploitation, increasing surpluses by suppressing wages, and cutting down on welfare services and environmental regulations, shifting in effect costs from private enterprise to workers, unpaid caretakers, and the environment. The fictitious circulation of money and the growth of GDP were sustained while un-monetized ecosystems or care services, "gift" relations such as hospitality or mutual care, and public commons such as healthcare or education, were monetized and traded or produced for profit ("commodification"). Following Polanyi, the degradation of the essence of such relations and services by treating them as commodities is linked to the social, moral, and environmental crises that preceded and accompanied the economic crisis.

Furthermore, the encroachment of the market economy to new realms possibly reduced the diversity of the economy and demised alternative, non-capitalist forms of provisioning that in other periods may have secured basic needs during the collapse of the formal economy. In other words, the hypothesis is that commodification and the concomitant reduction of economic diversity made societies more vulnerable to the effects of economic crisis; or in other words, societies with a strong presence of non-capitalist economies weathered better the effects of the crisis than societies without.

Part 3: The alternative economy as an embodiment of the new economics

The crisis has been accompanied also by a notable expansion of alternative economies that are the subject of this volume, such as producer and consumer cooperatives, alternative food networks, urban agriculture and food gardens, time banks and alternative currencies or exchange networks. These are "alternative" because in one way or another, to a lesser or greater extent, they defy basic tenets of capitalist production such as private property, wage labor, and production for exchange and profit.

The movement of alternative economic networks can be thought of as a counter-movement in a Polanyian sense, against commodification; an attempt to "take back" and decommodify labor, nature, or money, increasing the diversity of the economy and hence establishing new, resilient structures, alternatives to the crisis-prone money economy.

The exit from the mainstream economy signified by the alternative practices is both physical, in the sense of ceasing to produce, consume, and exchange for profit inside the market, as well as cognitive, based on a different understanding of what the economy is, and how it works.[1]

While the degree of conventional politicization of alternative economic networks varies, this "exiting" and "taking back" of the economy is an explicitly politicizing act. The economy is no longer understood as an autonomous system, but as a means to an end, a system of relations governed to achieve the social and political goals of a collective, and it is the collective that is autonomous.

The model promoted by such collectives is also explicitly ecological (Conill et al. 2012), aware of the concrete materiality of its production and consumption. Projects such as urban agriculture or alternative food networks are repairing the "metabolic rift" of capitalist production (McClintock 2010), slowing down, like peasants before them (Martinez-Alier 1990), the metabolic and entropic rate of the economy. Artisanal organic farming, or a food consumer cooperative are probably less intensive modes of organizing production and consumption than a large-scale industrial farm or a multinational supermarket conglomerate (though they also use less fertilizers, pesticides, and fossil fuels in production or transportation). More workers and more resources are necessary *per unit of product*, as specialization and economies of scale are reduced, and long hours are spent in constant deliberation and horizontal decision-making. It is precisely such "unproductiveness" that makes these alternatives more ecological; less productivity per unit of product means that they can only produce less, and damage the environment less. This should not be a problem insofar as they create jobs with social value. But it is an inversion of the capitalist logic, whereby ever-rising productivity leads to surplus accumulation, which in turn fuels further growth and resource use.

[1] The Cooperativa Integral Catalana (CIC) in Barcelona is an illustrative example. CIC is a legally registered cooperative in Catalonia with 600 members and 2,000 participants, an umbrella structure for independent producers and consumers of organic food and artisanal products, residents of eco-communes and occupied houses, cooperative enterprises and regional networks of exchange (*"Ecoxarxes"*) that issue their own currencies (Carlson 2012). CIC has its own conceptual model of the economy, consisting of five co-centric cycles, with reciprocity and gift exchange at the core, followed by barter, then exchange in community currency, followed by exchange in non-state currencies, and lastly, exchange in conventional money. This conceptual model is materialized into an alternative economy, as exchange within the auspices of the Cooperativa is mostly done through gifts, barter, or local currencies, while exchange with external actors is in digital cryptocurrencies, and only where unavoidable, in euros.

Food cooperatives, for example, are not designed to accumulate, but to satisfy the needs for healthy food of their members. Growth is neither their objective, nor their result. Limits are embodied in the very constitution and practice of such projects. Similarly, community currencies or local/regional non-monetary exchange networks reduce the level and speed of capital circulation, by keeping it local, and directing it to concrete needs, rather than profit. This signifies a different governance and destining of surplus than in capitalist economies.

Part 4: New economic policies

New economics start from the vantage point that further growth of the market economy is neither possible nor desirable. The objective then becomes how to manage, or rather prosper without growth (Victor 2008; Jackson 2011). Understanding the economy as a system of surplus, with conflict over its distribution and destination, then the normative question, which is in essence a political one, is how to redistribute a non-growing, or even declining surplus, in ways that secure, or even improve wellbeing and ecological sustainability.

One first policy in this spirit is work-sharing. This involves regulation to reduce the hours of paid work without losses in enumeration, and to facilitate dignified (secure and adequately remunerated) part-time work. Less working hours per person means more jobs for everyone to share, even though the rising cost of labor might reduce some of the gains (Kallis et al. 2013). Without growth, unemployment increases as rising productivity renders labor redundant. Work sharing does not let any labor become surplus (Gorz 1994). In effect this is a redistribution of the productivity surplus from accumulation to liberated time (Gorz 1994). And it facilitates a redistribution of time from the market economy to the alternative economy or to care, reproduction, or simply idleness. There might be a limit, however, to how much work may be reduced, without a concomitant reduction of needs. If fossil fuels are exhausted, and there are less "energy slaves" in the future, humans will have to do more work, or suffice with much less (Kallis 2013; Sorman and Giampietro 2013).

The second policy debated is basic income, an income guaranteed to all citizens of a nation for life, with no strings attached (Raventos 2007). Models for Spain suggest that a basic income of €400–600 per month is possible without a major overhaul of the tax system, in effect leaving the after-tax income of the middle class unchanged, redistributing from the very rich to the poor (Arcarons et al. 2013).

A basic income ensures that no citizen falls out of society's safety net. A basic income is not necessarily a disincentive against paid work; compared to an unemployment benefit, it provides more incentives to work, since one does not lose it by getting a job. It also increases the options for those who want to devote more time to the alternative or reproductive economy, as long as they are willing to settle for less material goods, but have their basic needs covered. Like work-sharing, it is an institution that facilitates redistribution not only in favor of workers, but also in favor of those who perform alternative or care work. A basic income is not supposed to substitute for other basic welfare services that should be secured by the state free of, or at low subsidized cost, such as basic care, health and education, or public transportation.

A third set of policies revolves around the overhaul of the taxation system. First, this requires a shift from taxing work, which is a "good," to taxing resource use and environmental damage, which are "bads" (Daly 1997). One way is by gradual substitution of income tax by a carbon tax. This would have to be orchestrated in a way that maintains the progressive redistributive function of the former, and also accommodates the potential loss of tax base in the latter (as people may start consuming less carbon-intensive goods). Importantly this shift is not meant to increase the total amount of taxes (what will be lost through a carbon tax will be gained by reduced income tax), but to shift consumption from high-carbon to low-carbon goods, giving advantages to low-carbon enterprises or cooperatives.

A carbon tax may be neutral concerning the distribution between capital and labor, but this also has to be addressed, since without growth, the proportion of surplus going to capital will increase (Piketty 2014). The second component of a tax reform goes along the lines of redistribution suggested by Piketty (2014), with taxes on capital and big wealth, such as inheritance or estate taxes. More ambitiously, ceiling "income caps" can be introduced, instituting a maximum allowable ratio of lower to higher income, in effect a cap on inequality (Daly 1997).

The state can shape the distribution of surplus not only through taxation, social security, and labor regulation but also through investment policy, aiming at the satisfaction of concrete social needs. A "new economic" investment program, for example, could bring an end to public investment and subsidies for private transport infrastructure (such as new roads and airport expansion), military technology, fossil fuels, or mining projects. The funds saved can be used instead for the improvement of public rural and urban space, such

as squares or traffic-free pedestrian streets, to subsidize public transport and cycle hire schemes, or for the development of small-scale
decentralized renewable energy projects. A reallocation of funds and
institutional support toward alternative economies is also possible.

A fifth transitional proposal is for the state to take back control of
the creation of new money from private banks, what Mary Mellor
(2010) calls "public money." As things stand, private banks create
in effect new money by issuing loans. Money enters the economy
as debt. This is why money and debt grew out of proportion to the
real economy. While private banks can only issue money as debt
through loans, the state could also issue money free of debt to meet
public needs. For example, states could issue money to finance a basic
income or to subsidize cooperatives, care services, environmental
conservation, or renewable energy. Public money would improve
public finances, as states would reclaim seigniorage (the difference
between the nominal value of money and the cost of producing it),
and as they would no longer borrow from private banks to finance
public expenditures. It would also give more leverage to the state to
stimulate desired forms of consumption, and suppress others, for
example exploitative or environmentally-damaging consumption. A
public money system may include a nested hierarchy of currencies,
including supra-national/national as well as regional and local currencies. More conservative credit institutions, such as cooperative or
ethical banks, whose lending is not driven by profit considerations,
and already tend to have tighter balances of deposits and loans,
would stand to benefit from such a shift.

Finally, beyond redistribution it is necessary to ensure that certain
environmental minima are respected, thresholds that, if overcome,
risk catastrophic co-evolutionary outcomes. Such minima might
include setting land or resources aside and keeping them out of
production; leaving oil underground is an imperative, as if all known
oil reserves were to be withdrawn, the change to the global climate
would in all certainty be disastrous. Note that a strategy of using
resources more efficiently will never suffice on its own, insofar
as more efficient use reduces the cost of resources, and increases
demand. Efficiency increases the scale of resource use. A cap on the
scale instead can ensure that gains in efficiency liberate resources that
are not then directed to further growth (as such growth is capped).

One key environmental institution is an absolute and diminishing
cap on the total emissions of CO_2, including emissions and materials embedded in imported products. The problem is that no single
country can take the lead and limit its emissions and its growth. This

is not only because it might lose in relative competiveness, but also because gains from a localized reduction of resource use will be offset by increased use elsewhere as the relative cost of the resource will fall. This is why a global climate agreement is indispensable. The Paris agreement was better than what could have been, but is nowhere near enforcing a binding and mandatory decrease of carbon emissions.

From a conventional economics perspective, these six proposals are not desirable. They are interventionist and meddle with the functioning of markets. Economists would be quick to argue that they raise the cost of production factors, curbing growth, and reducing jobs. From the new economics paradigm, this is not a problem. The economy is political and the state is a core actor, which can decide how to direct economic flows, in ways that redistribute costs and benefits, and achieve democratically decided goals. The above policies redistribute from rich to poor, from capital to labor, from banks to lenders, from paid to non-paid workers, and from humans to ecosystems. There are no "immutable" laws to be obeyed, and there is no "perfect market" that will convulse such interventions. And reduced growth is not bad, if global environmental change is considered. Reduced growth does not need to mean fewer jobs, if work is shared.

Of course, the "perfect market" may be a fantasy, but it is one that is real in a world of free capital flows. A valid question concerns the feasibility of the above institutional changes in a globalized world where capital flight can undermine even more moderate interventions or sovereign attempts to rein in deregulated accumulation. As Greece or Argentina have discovered, the room for policy innovation is very little within common currency zones or restrictive free trade zone agreements. Politically speaking, change, if it were to take place, would have to be initiated in core nations of the global economy, those with the power to change international institutions.

Where would the demand for such change come from? Redistributive conflict is rife as a result of the crisis and the possible end of growth. But can alternatives emerge? Political economic analysis here has to be informed by the co-evolutionary model. The changes in institutional and administrative arrangements discussed above *cannot* emerge alone and in a vacuum, without mutually constitutive changes in other spheres. The alternative economic practices signify the existence of new variants in the spheres of "production and labor processes," "relations to nature," "reproduction of daily life," and "cultural and belief systems." These are variants that can be mutually reinforcing with redistributive institutions. The policies liberate time and divert resources to the alternative economy. Vice versa, the practices will

50

need to build up a social movement that can demand such new "new deals," the indignant movement being possibly an example of such incipient linkages (Varvarousis and Kallis, this volume).

For the time being, however, alternative economies occupy only very small niches (with only incipient networking), while there is no visible political momentum for institutional changes like the ones proposed, with local exceptions of course. The open question concerns the conditions under which the evolution of an alternative economy can be punctuated, and the difficulties for divergent evolutions in a globalized world where distances have been annihilated, and where divergence is punished by isolation. In effect, the search for prosperity without growth may be thought of as a global collective action problem, whereby everyone would be better off if that path was followed, but those who first take the lead stand to lose, as the system is geared to expand or collapse.

Conclusion

The new economics of degrowth reconceptualizes and reinvents "the economy." This reinvention is a political act, in that it both expresses a different political vision, one according to which the economy should serve social needs, and in that it requires political force in order to be realized. The new model sees the economy as diverse, material, and defined by how surplus is distributed between capital, paid work, care and voluntary work, ecosystem "work," and idleness and joy.

The crisis marks a disjuncture between the economy of finance and the economies of production, reproduction, and ecosystems. As the growth of the economy met limits, and as capitalism cannot operate without growth, finance and credit took off, redistributing in favor of those who control them. The exploitation of workers, care workers and ecosystems intensified as the pie stopped growing. The financial crisis therefore came together with a social crisis, an environmental crisis, and a "crisis of cares."

The responses provisionally discussed here, such as work-sharing, a basic income, or green and wealth taxes, aim to reverse politically this redistribution and create conditions for a shared prosperity without growth. A co-evolutionary understanding of (economic) change suggests that such institutional change requires a mutual adaptation of technological, belief, and productive or consumptive systems. I argued that the seeds of such incipient change can be traced in the

51

niches of so-called "alternative economies," but that the scale of these networks is far from the necessary size for a systemic change. The presence of variation, however, is important in and of itself, as change historically takes place through punctuations in periods of conflict and crisis, where what previously seemed to be small and stagnating niches find opportunities to quickly expand.

Acknowledgments

The author acknowledges the support of the Spanish government through the project CSO2014-54513-R SINALECO.

References

Anderson, K. and Bows-Larkin, A. (2013) Avoiding dangerous climate change demands degrowth strategies from wealthier nations. Available at: kevinanderson.info

Arcarons, J., Raventós, D. and Torrens, L. (2013) Una propuesta de financiación de una renta básica universal en plena crisis económica. *Sin Permiso*. III. Monografico Renta Basica.

Ayres, R.U. and Warr, B. (2010) *The Economic Growth Engine: How Energy and Work Drive Material Prosperity*. Edward Elgar, Cheltenham.

Bakker, K.J. (2003) *An Uncooperative Commodity: Privatizing Water in England and Wales*. Oxford University Press, Oxford.

Bataille, G. (1927) The notion of expenditure. *Visions of Excess: Selected Writings, 1939*. University of Minnesota Press, Minneapolis, MN, pp. 116–29.

Benton, T. (1992) Ecology, socialism and the mastery of nature: a reply to Reiner Grundmann. *New Left Review* 194, 1, 55–74.

Carlson, S. (2012) Degrowth in Action, from Opposition to Alternatives Building: How the Cooperativa Integral Catalana enacts a Degrowth vision. Master's thesis, Lund University.

Castoriadis, C. (1997) *The Imaginary Institution of Society*. MIT Press, Cambridge, MA.

Conill, J., Cardenas, A., Castells, M. and Servon, L. (2012) *Otra vida es posible: prácticas alternativas durante la crisis*. UOC Press, Barcelona.

D'Alisa, G., Kallis, G. and Demaria, F. (2014) From austerity to dépense. In: D'Alisa, G., Demaria, F. and Kallis, G. (eds.) *Degrowth: A Vocabulary for a New Era*. Routledge, New York.

Dale, G. (2012) The growth paradigm: a critique. *International Socialism* 134.

Daly, H.E. (1997) *Beyond Growth: The Economics of Sustainable Development*. Beacon Press, Boston, MA.

De Angelis, M. and Harvie, D. (2014) The commons. In: Parker, M., Cheney, G., Fournier, V. and Land, C. (eds.) *The Routledge Companion to Alternative Organization*. Routledge, London.

Fischer-Kowalski, M. (1997) Society's metabolism: On the childhood and adolescence of a rising conceptual star. In: Redclift, M.R. and Woodgate, G. (eds) *The International Handbook of Environmental Sociology*. Edward Elgar, Cheltenham, pp. 119–37.

Foucault, M. (1991) Governmentality. In: Burchell, G., Gordon, C. and Miller, P. (eds.) *The Foucault Effect: Studies in Governmentality*. University of Chicago Press, Chicago, IL.

Fournier, V. (2008) Escaping from the economy: The politics of degrowth. *International Journal of Sociology and Social Policy* 28, 11/12, 528–45.

Georgescu-Roegen, N. (1971) *The Entropy Law and the Economic Process*. Harvard University Press, Cambridge, MA.

Giampietro, M. (2003) *Multi-scale Integrated Analysis of Agroecosystems*. CRC Press, Boca Raton, FL.

Gibson-Graham, J.K. (2006) *The End of Capitalism (as We Knew It): A Feminist Critique of Political Economy*. University of Minnesota Press, Minneapolis, MN.

Gordon, R.J. (2012) Is US economic growth over? Faltering innovation confronts the six headwinds. NBER Working Paper Series, 18315.

Gorz, A. (1994) *Capitalism, Socialism, Ecology*. Verso Books, London.

Hamilton, J.D. (2009) Causes and consequences of the oil shock of 2007–08. *Brookings Papers on Economic Activity* Spring, 215–83.

Harvey, D. (2003) *The New Imperialism*. Oxford University Press, Oxford.

Harvey, D. (2011) *The Enigma of Capital: And the Crises of Capitalism*. Verso Books, London.

Jackson, T. (2011) *Prosperity Without Growth: Economics for a Finite Planet*. Earthscan, London.

Jackson, T. and Victor, P.A. (2016) Does slow growth lead to rising inequality? Some theoretical reflections and numerical simulations. *Ecological Economics* 121, 206–19.

Kallis, G. (2013) Societal metabolism, working hours and degrowth: A comment on Sorman and Giampietro. *Journal of Cleaner Production*, 38, 94–8.

Kallis, G. and Norgaard, R.B. (2010) Coevolutionary ecological economics. *Ecological Economics* 69, 4, 690–9.

Kallis, G., Martinez-Alier, J. and Norgaard, R.B. (2009) Paper assets, real debts: An ecological-economic exploration of the global economic crisis. *Critical Perspectives on International Business* 5, 1/2, 14–25.

Kallis, G., Kerschner, C. and Martinez-Alier, J. (2012) The economics of degrowth. *Ecological Economics* 84, 172–80.

Kallis, G., Kalush, M., O'Flynn, H., Rossiter, J. and Ashford, N. (2013) "Friday off": Reducing working hours in Europe. *Sustainability* 5, 4, 1545–67.

Kallis, G., Demaria, F. and D'Alisa, G. (2014) Degrowth. In: D'Alisa, G., Demaria, F. and Kallis, G. (eds.) *Degrowth: A Vocabulary for a New Era*. Routledge, New York.

Kaufmann, R.K., Gonzalez, N., Nickerson, T.A. and Nesbit, T.S. (2011) Do household energy expenditures affect mortgage delinquency rates? *Energy Economics* 33, 2, 188–94.

Latouche, S. (2005) *L'invention de l'économie*. Albin Michel, Paris.

Loftus, A. (2015) Violent geographical abstractions. *Environment and Planning D: Society and Space* 33, 366–81.

Martinez-Alier, J.M. (1990) *Ecological Economics: Energy, Environment, and Society*. University of Wisconsin Press, Madison, WI.

Martinez-Alier, J.M. (2009) Socially sustainable economic de-growth. *Development and Change* 40, 6, 1099–119.

Martinez-Alier, J. and O'Connor, M. (2002) Distributional issues: An overview. In: van den Bergh, J.C.J.M. (ed.) *Handbook of Environmental and Resource Economics*. Edward Elgar, Cheltenham, pp. 380–92.

Mauss, M. (1954) *The Gift: Forms and Functions of Exchange in Archaic Societies*. Cohen & West, London.

McClintock, N. (2010) Why farm the city? Theorizing urban agriculture through a lens of metabolic rift. *Cambridge Journal of Regions, Economy and Society* 3, 2, 191–207.

Mellor, M. (2010) *The Future of Money: From Financial Crisis to Public Resource*. Pluto Press, London.

Mitchell, T. (2002) *Rule of Experts: Egypt, Techno-politics, Modernity*. University of California Press, Berkeley, CA.

Norgaard, R.B. (1994) *Development Betrayed: The End of Progress and a Co-evolutionary Revisioning of the Future*. Routledge, New York.

Odum, H.T. (2002) Emergy accounting. In: Bartelmus, P. (ed.) *Unveiling Wealth*. Springer, Amsterdam, pp. 135–46.

Piketty, T. (2014) *Capital in the 21st Century*. Harvard University Press, Cambridge, MA.

Polanyi, K. (1944) *The Great Transformation: The Political and Economic Origins of Our Time*. Beacon Press, Boston, MA.

Prudham, S. (2007) The fictions of autonomous invention: accumulation by dispossession, commodification and life patents in Canada. *Antipode* 39, 3, 406–29.

Raventós, D. (2007) *Basic Income: The Material Conditions of Freedom*. Pluto Press, London.

Rezai, A., Taylor, L. and Mechler, R. (2013) Ecological macroeconomics: An application to climate change. *Ecological Economics* 85, 69–76.

Skidelsky, R. and Skidelsky, E. (2012) *How Much is Enough?: The Love of Money, and the Case for the Good Life*. Penguin, Harmondsworth.

Smith, A. (1887) *An Inquiry Into the Nature and Causes of the Wealth of Nations*. T. Nelson and Sons, London.

Sorman, A.H. and Giampietro, M. (2013) The energetic metabolism of societies and the degrowth paradigm: Analyzing biophysical constraints and realities. *Journal of Cleaner Production* 38, 80–93.

Summers, L. (2013) Why stagnation might prove to be the new normal. *Financial Times*, December 15.

Victor, P.A. (2008) *Managing Without Growth: Slower by Design, not Disaster*. Edward Elgar, Cheltenham.

Chapter 3

Analysis of Worldwide Community Economies for Sustainable Local Development
Sviatlana Hlebik

Introduction

There exist some contemporary forms of social and solidarity-based economies, a growing area of practice that is highly relevant to sustainable consumption studies. This chapter presents an analysis of worldwide community economies for sustainable local development that, on the one hand can benefit businesses, and on the other, can promote local welfare services, influencing governance and society groups. An empirical analysis has been conducted to assess the possible relationship between community currency systems and the countries' levels of social and economic development, as well as monetary indicators and macroeconomic, environmental, and financial features.

The increasing number of communities that are developing and using alternative currencies as a form of monetary exchange with their own means of payment explains the growing research interest and policy attention. These will empower local communities by helping them to increase their economic self-sufficiency and enhance their financial autonomy. Blanc (2011) has established that a local currency focuses on territorial activities and actors, principally in order to strengthen and build local resilience in a specific territory. A community currency achieves this by developing its social exchanges and reciprocity in a particular community. According to Blanc (2011), complementary currency is therefore governed by market exchange principles and aims at developing economic activities.

First, this chapter introduces some existing scientific foundations explaining why the variety of business models and economic tools discussed in this work can make the economy more sustainable.

Considering the multiplicity of a community's economies, it is important to examine several classifications. There are two different approaches proposed in this chapter. The first one describes its historical evolution and development. The second focuses on the typology of currencies, their purposes, and their functions.

Since the instruments analyzed in the present chapter are different from our mental framework, some examples of complementary economic tools have been introduced for the purpose of better understanding their functionality.

There are multiple types of community currencies (CCs) and among them is the Commercial Credit Circuit (C3) model, a professionally run business-to-business (B2B) complementary currency based on the model of the WIR system. This currency has been successfully operational in Switzerland, involving a quarter of all the business units in that country. Formal econometric analysis and other research methods have proven that the WIR acts as a significant counter-cyclical stabilizing factor that explains the proverbial long-standing stability of the Swiss economy.

Current consideration of the aims and types of CCs discovered that these reach beyond common forms of barter exchange, rethinking the role of money and implementing instruments to promote social values and sustainable local development. As Derudder (2011) noted: "Common motivations and core objectives of such initiatives revolve around strengthening solidarity and sharing in communities, developing local employment and galvanizing the economy."

This work is organized as follows: Part 1 presents a conceptual framework on how the operation of business models and economic tools of diverse types enables the development of structural benefits, making the economy more sustainable. Part 2.1 introduces classifications of the typology of currencies and the historical evolution of the generations approach to community currencies. Some examples presented in Part 2.2 allow for a much better understanding of their functioning mechanisms. Part 2.3 aims to present some statistical evidence on world system distribution, in terms of type, purpose, and medium of exchange. Data was collected by the Complementary Currency Resource Center. Lastly, Part 3 is dedicated to the empirical analysis on how these worldwide economic tools are related to country-level economic, social, and environmental factors, and also to the different aspects of the financial sector and money.

Part 1: Conceptual framework

Kash et al. (2007) demonstrated how characteristics of agents in a system can be inferred from the equilibrium distribution of money. The authors provided analysis for optimizing scrip systems and tolls for "computing equilibria by showing that the model exhibits strategic complementarities, which implies that there exist equilibria in pure strategies that can be computed efficiently."

Goerner et al. (2009) provided a solid empirical/mathematical basis for a quantitative measure of sustainability for a complex flow system. According to some ecological economists (e.g. Herman Edward Daly, Robert E. Ulanowicz), a flow system's long-term sustainability depends on reasonable equilibrium, size and internal structure (development). In ecosystems as in economies, size is measured as the total volume of system throughput: e.g. gross domestic product (GDP) in economies. Consequently, the flow-network sustainability can be reasonably defined as the optimal balance of efficiency and resilience as determined by nature.

Efficiency can be defined as "the network's capacity to perform in a sufficiently organized and efficient manner as to maintain its integrity over time" (May 1972), while *resilience* is defined as a "reserve of flexible fall-back positions and diversity of actions that can be used to meet the exigencies of novel disturbances and the novelty needed for on-going development and evolution" (Holling 1986). Both concepts are related to the levels of diversity and connectivity found in the network, but in opposite directions. A multiplicity of connections and variety plays a positive role in resilience. Representing economies as flow systems links directly into money's primary function as a medium of exchange.

According to Lietaer et al. (2010) "in economies, as in living organisms, the health of the whole depends heavily on the structure by which the catalyzing medium, in this case, money, circulates among businesses and individuals. Money must continue to circulate in sufficiency to all corners of the whole because poor circulation will strangle either the supply side or the demand side of the economy, or both."

Applying the complex flow framework to financial and monetary systems, it is possible to "predict that excessive focus on efficiency would tend to create exactly the kind of bubble economy which we have been able to observe repeatedly in every boom and bust cycle in history" (May 1972).

Enforcing a monopoly of a single currency that is maintained and tightly regulated within each country improves the efficiency of price

57

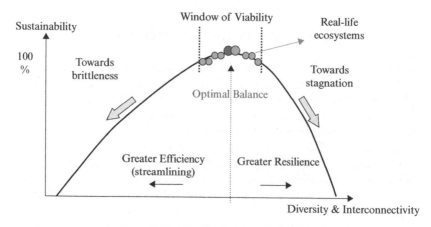

Figure 3.1: Window of viability

Source: Lietaer et al. (2010)

formation and exchanges in national markets. The mathematical foundation is that there exists only a single maximum for any given network system. It is curious to note that the optimal sustainability is situated slightly toward the resilience side, suggesting that resilience plays a greater role in optimal sustainability than does efficiency.

Figure 3.1 graphically illustrates Zorach and Ulanowicz's (2003) "Window of viability" in which all sustainable systems operate within a rather narrow range of health situated around peak sustainability that delimits long-term viability in the systems.

Many researchers such as De Long et al. (1990), De Bondt and Thaler (1987), Thaler (1999), etc., have observed market anomalies that are not explained by the arguments of the efficient market hypothesis. Nevertheless, the efficient market hypothesis is still the dominant paradigm for organizing and ruling the markets.

The global monetary system is becoming more fragile because a general belief prevails that all improvements need to go further in the same direction (thick downward arrow in figure 3.2) of increasing growth and efficiency. Based on efficiency of price formation and exchanges, the global monoculture of bank-debt money and floating exchanges were justified because they are "more efficient."

Figure 3.3 shows that since efficiency is the criterion considered most relevant, the overly efficient system can lead to system crashes and collapse. The main idea is that money circulates in our global economic network and is kept as a monopoly of a single type of currency – bank-debt money, created with interest.

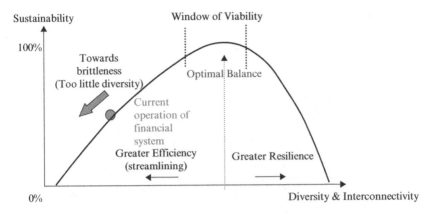

Figure 3.2: Monetary ecosystem

Source: Lietaer et al. (2010)

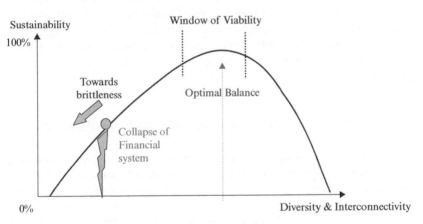

Figure 3.3: Systemic financial collapse

Source: Lietaer et al. (2010)

Different types of business models, instruments that can be used and accepted as a medium of exchange, facilitate the sale, purchase or trade of goods between parties. Many authors in modern economics literature use the "currencies" term in reference to "medium of exchange" because the implementation of these kinds of tools allows for a variety of "currencies" to circulate among private people and enterprises to facilitate their exchanges.

The thick upward arrow in figure 3.4 shows how the operation of

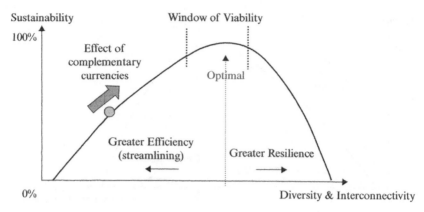

Figure 3.4: The effect of diverse complementary currencies

Source: Lietaer et al. (2010)

complementary currencies of diverse types enables reduced efficiency and increasing structural resilience, leading the economy back toward sustainability. This multiple form of "currencies" is frequently called "complementary" or complementary community currency (CCC) because they are operating as complements to conventional national moneys.

Part 2.1: An overview of typologies and classifications

There are wide-ranging socio-economic tools covering the economic, social, and environmental dimensions, and different classifications or typologies have only been introduced fairly recently (Schroeder et al. 2011).

Some of those classifications focus more on the technical and operational design features while others also integrate their different objectives, purposes, and visions (Martignoni 2012).

Here we briefly summarize two schemes:

- according to the historical evolution of the generations approach to community currencies by Jérôme Blanc;
- according to the typology of currencies after Kennedy and Lietaer (2004).

The scheme proposed in figure 3.5 distinguishes four generations. These generations are characterized by a "specific monetary

Denomination & Currency scheme type	Nature of projects & Space considered	Purpose & Guiding principle	Generation & Significant Case	Content overview
Community currency	Community & Social space (pre-existing or ad hoc community)	Defining, protecting and strengthening a community & reciprocity first, various distance to market	G1 & LETS, Trueque, CES	Inconvertible schemes; quite small openness to external economic activities
		Defining, protecting and strengthening a community & reciprocity first, various distance to local governments	G2 & Time Banks, Accorderie	Inconvertible schemes with time currencies, frequent partnerships, especially with local governments
Local currency	Territorial & Geopolitical space (territory politically defined)	Defining, protecting and strengthening a territory & redistribution or political control. Market first, generally distant from local governments	G3 & Ithaca Hours, Regio, Palmas, BerkShares	Convertible schemes; local businesses are included; interest of partnerships with local governments
Complementary currency	Economic & Economic space (production and exchange)	Protecting, stimulating or orientating the economy & market first, with links to governments and reciprocity	G4 & NU, SOL	Complex schemes oriented toward consumer responsibility or/and economic activities re-orientation and other purposes; partnerships are necessary
National currency	Territorial & Sovereign space	Sovereignty & redistribution or political control	–	–
For-profit currency	Economic & Clients of a for-profit organization	Profit & purchasing power capture	–	–

Figure 3.5: Historical evolution of the generations of community currencies

Source: Blanc (2011)

organization and specific relationships with the socio-economic world and with governments (local or central) as well" (Blanc 2011).

A first generation of CC schemes refers to the LETSystem (see figure 3.6 for a map of global LET systems). The LETS or LETS model is a local exchange trading system: "local employment and trading system or local energy transfer system is a locally initiated, democratically organized, not-for-profit community enterprise that provides a community information service and records transactions of members exchanging goods and services by using the currency of locally created LETS Credits" (Western Australia Government 1990).

The LETS program was founded by Michael Linton in the early 1980s on Vancouver Island in Canada and has been replicated in various countries and intensified, creating large networks, particularly since the second half of the 1990s. LETS networks used interest-free local credit that empowered members to issue their own line of credit at the point of purchase, creating a self-regulated mechanism.

The second generation appears with the time dollar schemes at the end of the 1980s in the US, since when they have been exported to various countries. The time dollar is the unit of exchange in a time bank. This kind of tool is a pattern of reciprocal service exchange based on trust and cooperation. Unlike traditional time banks, where the unit of exchange is the person-hour, time dollar schemes are earned for providing services and are spent receiving services. As the systems "providing help to people with social programmes they frequently develop partnerships with local governments and socially oriented foundations" (Blanc 2011).

Third generation schemes derive from the LETS model, generally implemented by non-profit organizations and sometimes with the participation of a community bank or local cooperative. This category with economic purpose increased significantly in the 2000s and is represented by German regio schemes, Brazilian community banks and US BerkShare. "They aim at dynamizing local economic activity by re-localizing a series of daily consumption expenses. The success of those schemes requires thus the inclusion of small local enterprises and shops, and sometimes bigger ones" (Blanc 2011).

The fourth generation is a new generation that is represented by multiplex projects in which local governments play a fundamental role. The implementation requires the combination of several objectives with particular focus on environmental issues. This type is aimed at encouraging sustainable behaviors, for example Rotterdam's NU (2002–3) local or organic product consumption, fair trade, and waste recycling; and the French SOL program, which combines a

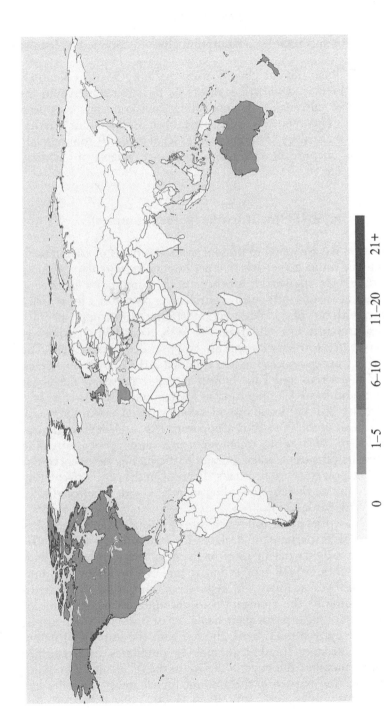

Figure 3.6: World map of LET systems

Source: Database of Complementary Currencies Worldwide: http://www.complementarycurrency.org

loyalty card for sustainable consumption close to commercial loyalty schemes.

Figure 3.7 illustrates the classification made by Margrit Kennedy and Bernard Lietaer (2004) that allows us to better understand the great variety of currencies, distinguishing their concepts, purposes, and functions. This typology aims to establish a scheme for classifying all forms of currency, differentiated as legal tender ("commercial" or for "social purposes"), medium of exchange, means of payment, cost recovery, etc.

Part 2.2: How it works (some examples)

In this section we are going to present some examples of complementary economic (monetary) tools that are designed to circulate within a specific zone, bringing wealth for those in the community, increasing liquidity, and consequently raising purchasing power in a local area.

We start with one of the oldest and most important complementary currencies presently in circulation: the WIR bank (*Wirtschaftsring-Genossenschaft*), formerly known as the Swiss Economic Circle. The WIR credit clearing association was founded in 1934 by businessmen Werner Zimmerman and Paul Enz in direct response to the Great Depression and has been operating in Switzerland for 80 years. It is now called the WIR Bank and provides conventional banking services. Its statutes enounce: "The WIR Cooperative is a self-help organization made up of trading, manufacturing, and service-providing companies. Its purpose is to encourage participating members to put their buying power at each other's disposal and keep it circulating within their ranks, thereby providing members with additional sales volume" (WIR Bank 1934).

The system works in the following way: a businessman who wishes to join as a WIR participant declares his intention to accept WIR booking orders as partial or total payment in any transaction with other participants. A WIR representative makes a preliminary examination of business acumen and reputation, subscribes to a credit bureau and submits the application to an admissions committee of three members: "Each participant has a set of booking order forms, similar to the conventional bank checks, with the imprint of name, address, and account number. In making purchases from another participating member, the buyer will give to the seller such a booking order after having written in the amount for whatever the seller has obligated himself to accept" (WIR Bank 1934).

Main Classification	Purpose		Medium	Function		Money creation process	Cost recovery
				Means of Payment	Medium of Exchange		
Specification	Legal tender		Commodity money, Coins, Paper, Electronic money, Hybrid forms.	Measure of Value	Store of Value	Real backing, Secured loans, Unsecured loans, Redeemable vouchers, Corporate vouchers, Customer loyalty currency. Mutual Credit Central issuance (flat) Hybrid forms.	No additional cost recovery. Fixed fees, Transaction fees, Interest charges, demurrage and other. Time-dependent charges, Hybrid forms
	Commercial	Social					
Finer Gradations	B2B, B2C, C2C, C2B	Elderly care, Pensioners, Unemployed, Education, Babysitting, Social contact, Cultural identity, Ecology, Other social objectives, Hybrid forms.	–	Payment in conventional currency, Payment in units of time, Payment with concrete objects.	Interest-bearing currencies, Interest-free currencies. Currencies with user fee. Currencies with a specific value in units of time. Currencies with expiry date, hybrids.	–	–

Figure 3.7: Typology of currencies after Kennedy and Lietaer (2004): *Regionalwährungen*, p. 268f., translated from German into English

Source: Martignoni (2012)

This mechanism stimulates rapid circulation of the money in order to generate increased sales among the members, stimulating spending account balances quickly. A main characteristic is no interest is paid on account balances, so the money is interest-free.

According to Thomas Greco (1994), WIR is an important case for monetary reformers and free exchange advocates to study: "While there may yet be some deficiencies in its operating policies, WIR has proven over a long period of time the effectiveness of direct clearing of credits between buyers and sellers as an alternative to conventional bank-created debt-money."

Let's take a look at another example of complementary economic (monetary) tools: liquidity networks as local trading systems using debt-free electronic currency schemes. Since a liquidity network seeks to fulfill one of the most important functions of many – that is it acts as a means of exchange – these kinds of tools address the liquidity constraint, that affect the ability of economic agents to exchange their assets and existing wealth for goods and services.

The Liquidity Network (http://theliquiditynetwork.org) was designed for Ireland but could be applied to any country during the downward spiral period, where there is increasing unemployment, high national debt, and the deterioration of loan quality induced by the recession and credit constraints:

> The aim of the Liquidity Network is to address the current liquidity problem – the slowdown in economic activity triggered by the credit crunch. Currently virtually all economic activity is powered by debt based credit – individuals and businesses borrow in order to finance their activities. Using the credit released by these loans they employ or do business with other individuals/businesses who in turn do business with their suppliers and so on. When the "seed" credit from banks dries up, as in the current crisis, the multiplier effect which normally helps to create liquidity efficiently acts in the reverse way and removes liquidity quickly. Liquidity Network aims to address this problem by creating an alternative "liquidity stream" which is not based on debt. (http://theliquiditynetwork.org)

The Liquidity Network uses a unit called the Quid. All trading is carried out electronically by mobile phone or over the Internet; it doesn't use notes and coins. The mechanism was devised by Richard Douthwaite and set up in Feasta, the Foundation for the Economics of Sustainability. It works as follows: businesses and every citizen with a National Insurance number can sign up for an account in which will be allocated Q1,000, which roughly equals €1,000. Every account holder can perform buy/sell operations exchanging Quid (Q);

however, accounts must be kept roughly in balance and the system does not allow them to go into deficit. Businesses that experience high turnover and balanced buy/sell exchanges would be allocated extra Q. In this way the system automatically provides liquidity.

Part 2.3: Statistical data overview

This section is aimed at presenting some statistical evidence collected by the Complementary Currency Resource Center ccDatabase. Graphical representation allows us to gain a much better understanding of annual growth of different types of systems and regional distributions of CCC across the world. Most complementary currencies have multiple purposes and/or are intended to address multiple issues.

Figure 3.8 represents the worldwide distribution of CC systems, showing that Europe, North America, and the Asia/Pacific zones are the regions with most experience of community currencies.

It is curious that in Europe, LETS is the most popular, followed by the Mutual Credit System, then the Commercial Exchange System (Database of Complementary Currencies Worldwide 2014), whereas in North America the Mutual Credit System and the Time Bank System prevail, and in the Asia/Pacific region, the Internet-based trading network Community Exchange System (CES) is more prevalent.

Relative distribution highlights the prevalence of LETS at 17 percent, followed by the Mutual Credit System at 10.7 percent, and the Community Exchange System at 14 percent. In terms of frequency, LETS in Europe and the Community Exchange System in Europe and North America are the most prevalent. As for South America, the "Sistema de Trueke" in Venezuela is very popular.

Most complementary currencies have multiple purposes, though nevertheless it is interesting to examine some types of patterns. North America and the Asia/Pacific region is frequently guided by "community development" aims, while Europe is more sensitive to the objectives of "contributing towards a sustainable society," "enhancing members' quality of life," "activating the local market," and also sharpening the importance of the "micro/small/medium enterprise development" mission. The data show the growth of complementary currency systems around the world. We can note that complementary currency systems have grown considerably, particularly since 2008 (see details in Appendix 1).

Alternative currencies encourage consumers to make purchases

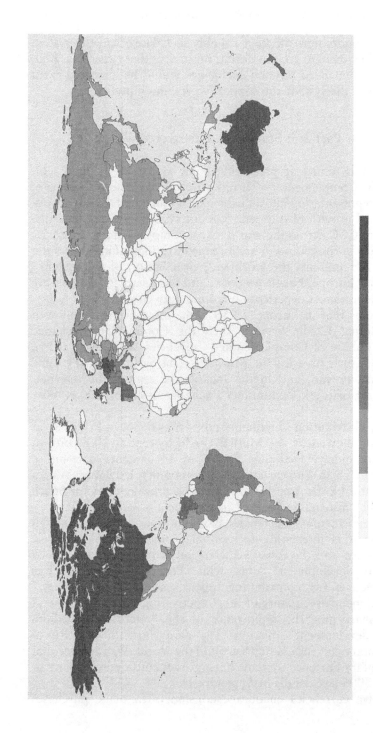

Figure 3.8: World map of complementary currency systems

Source: Database of Complementary Currencies Worldwide: http://www.complementarycurrency.org

within their communities rather than elsewhere in the country or abroad. "Buying local" circulates wealth in the region, reduces unnecessary imports, and helps avoid higher unemployment levels, supporters say.

Part 3: Relationship between the community currency systems and the country's level of social and economic development, different aspects of the financial sector and money

In order to examine this relationship, the Worldwide Database of Complementary Currency Systems has been used. This database, which contains all types of complementary currency systems in use in the world today, allows us to have information on the number of Community Currency Systems per single country and year; more precisely, it covers the period from 2006 to 2012 for 35 countries across the world. We also collected more than 200 variables from various sources. The information on the economic data series and the financial services were taken from the International Monetary Fund (IMF)/The World Economic Outlook (WEO) database, whereas the data relative to social, environmental, and education factors were selected from World Development Indicators.

As for the methodology, a generalized linear model (GLM) was used. (See Appendix 2 and Appendix 3 for details on the statistical model and description of the data.)[1]

Main empirical findings

Below we describe "highly significant" results obtained from empirical analysis. They have been grouped into different fields for clarity:

Macroeconomic features
- (−) **GDP growth (annual %) *T*−1.** The Complementary Community Currency (CCC) are negatively related with lagged GDP growth (annual %).
- (+) **Log general government gross debt.** The number of complementary practices is higher in countries and years with high government gross debt.

---

[1] The author is grateful to Fabrizi Enrico, Marco Riani, and Giovani Verga for their important statistical comments.

(+) **Risk premium on lending (lending rate minus treasury bill rate, %).** Community currency systems are positively related with risk premium on lending.

(+) **Government total expenditure as % of GDP.** The community tools are more used in countries and years with high government total expenditure as % of GDP.

These findings are crucial as they confirm widespread statements and convictions by founders and community members that CCCs are vitally useful and flourish during an economic recession.

Finance

(–) **Domestic credit to private sector (% of GDP).** This is an indicator of the movement of domestic credit to the private sector in contrast to CCC development. This result is fully consistent with the evidence discussed in this work. There are multiple types of CCs based on a mutual credit system that are activated especially during credit constraints. LETS networks used interest-free local credit where the participants issued their own line of credit, but there are also more evolved forms based on the successful model of the WIR system.

(–) **Bank nonperforming loans to total gross loans (%) T–1.** Complementary currencies have an inverse relationship with bank non-performing loans ratios. A bad quality loan has a higher probability of becoming a non-performing loan with no return. This result confirms the complementary function of community currencies because this means that a low level of this indicator, which shows the good quality of the banking portfolio, has a positive relationship with the development of CCCs.

Socio-demographic characteristics: population, education, gender

(+) **Log population (total).** A positive relation with CCC is discovered. In countries with a high population, it is more likely to find people, who for reasons of proactivity, ideological sensitivity, or economic needs, are inclined to experiment and implement complementary community tools.

(+) **Tertiary education, teachers (% female).** The positive relationship with the share of female academic staff in tertiary education evidences a positive influence for the diffusion of CCC.

(–) **Social contributions (% of revenue).** This indicator is negatively related to CCC. Social contributions include social security contributions by employees, employers, and self-employed individuals, and contributions to social insurance schemes operated by governments. Therefore this outcome is quite a logical explanation that these tools we are looking at are more stimulating where there are less social insurance benefits.

Monetary indicators

(+) **Money and quasi money (M2) as % of GDP.** Money and quasi money comprise the sum of currency outside banks, demand deposits other than those of the central government, and the time, savings, and foreign currency deposits of resident sectors other than the central government. This evidence is consistent with the claim that the CCC do not have a replace function and are not intended as an alternative to the national currency, but rather are complementary.

Internet and communication

(+) **Secure Internet servers.** Because electronic transactions are a dominant medium of exchange in CCC, it is obvious that there has to be a positive relationship with Internet technologies (see Appendix 1).

Entrepreneurship

(+) **New business density (new registrations per 1,000 people aged 15–64).** The indicators of new businesses registered positively with CCC experiences. It follows that in countries where there are people with an entrepreneurial mindset and the desire to work, but above all a climate more favorable for doing business (i.e. less bureaucracy, lower taxes, etc.), there is also an environment conducive to the development of CCC.

Climate and environment

(+) **CO_2 emissions (metric tons per capita).** Positive relations with carbon dioxide emissions are those stemming from the burning of fossil fuels and the manufacture of cement. As illustrated in Appendix 1, one of the purposes of the system is environmental conservation. Community currencies can play a role in better valuation of environmental resources (e.g. the Belgian e-Portemonnee that encourages businesses to adopt more environmentally sound practices). Increasing CO_2 emissions are blamed for global climate change. The positive and optimistic results of the analysis showed that there is higher sensitivity for incentivizing more sustainable behavior where the CO_2 emissions are elevated.

71

Conclusion

The global monetary system is becoming more fragile because of increasing growth and efficiency. Different types of business models, instruments that can be used and accepted as mediums of exchange, facilitate the sale, purchase, or trade of goods between parties.

Then, as a wide range of socio-economic instruments exist, covering the economic, social, and environmental dimension, we thought it useful to overview the classifications, following two approaches. The first helps us to understand the historical evolution, i.e. how they were developed. The second focuses on the typology of currencies, their purposes and functions.

Before proceeding with empirical analysis, with the aim of showing how different types of systems are distributed across different regions in the world, which type of exchange system and purpose of the system prevail the most, and which are less common, graphical statistical overview and data were entered (the main results of this description are shown in Appendix 1). Finally, using the Worldwide Database of Complementary Currency Systems, a statistical analysis was carried out to determine:

- whether the theoretical beliefs, sometimes the basis of the debate, are consistent with the quantitative approach; and
- because CCC is constantly growing, the existence of the possible relationship between Community Currency Systems and the country-level economic, social, and environmental factors, as well as the different aspects of the financial sector and money.

The outcome of this analysis is consistent with the existing affirmation that complementary currencies are particularly useful and a great help to people and businesses in times of crisis. In fact, many communities are implementing their own "complementary" currencies in the current economic crisis in an attempt to keep wealth in their area.

In the last few years, with the collapse of the global economy, there has been a revival of interest in the local economy and locally produced goods, with the United States and the United Kingdom showing particular enthusiasm, e.g. Berkshire Bank.[2] This is also true

---

[2] The secret behind Berkshire's success: "A trust-based system can be more efficient than a compliance-based system, but only if self-interested behavior among employees and executives is low" (Larcker and Tayan 2014).

for many European countries: alternative currencies are on the rise as the Eurozone crisis worsens. As the Eurozone crisis has worsened, the use of alternative tools has risen, for example in Greece where the deepening financial crisis has given rise to alternative trading mechanisms and developed a situation where several instruments could become more and more popular.

Economists have kept an eye on the WIR, the Swiss complementary currency, since it started in 1934. When there is an economic upturn, the turnover in WIR goes down. When business people are unable to sell their goods in Swiss Francs, they go into the WIR, and in the present economic climate, people are much keener on these types of solutions. Similar projects comparable to the WIR are ongoing in Germany, France, and other countries.

Regarding socio-demographic characteristics, empirical analysis shows that CCCs tend to prevail in countries with a high population and a poor social welfare system. In countries with a high population, they are more likely to be adopted by people for reasons of proactivity, ideological sensitivity, or economic needs inclined to experiment and implement complementary community tools. In addition, larger countries have more needs, which means more businesses, more consultation, more transactions, more people looking for credit, etc. As regards the outcome on the social welfare system, it is quite logical that these tools we are looking at are more stimulating where there are less social insurance benefits.

The indicators of new businesses registered positively with CCC experiences. It follows that the positive relationship of CCC experiences with indicators of new business density shows that encouraging environmental factors (i.e. less bureaucracy, lower taxes, etc.) promotes the development of CCC.

Community currencies can also play a role in better assessment of environmental resources (e.g. the Belgian e-Portemonnee that encourages businesses to adopt more environmentally friendly practices). Increasing CO_2 emissions are blamed for global climate change. The positive and optimistic results of the analysis showed that there is a higher incentive to create something that encourages sustainable behavior where there are CO_2 emissions.

It is shown in Appendix 1 that electronic transactions are a dominant medium of exchange in CCC, to which the expected result of a positive relationship with CCC Internet technologies was confirmed by the empirical analysis.

Interesting results were derived also in relation to monetary indicators and finance, i.e. the indicator of domestic credit to private sector move in contrast to CCC development. This result is fully consistent with the evidence discussed in this work. There are multiple types of CCCs based on a mutual credit system that are activated especially during credit constraints. An example of a business-to-business system is the Commercial Credit Circuit (C3) network. This is a technology that provides substantial liquidity at very low cost into the entire SME network. In this way the model provides transmission inside of networks from clients to suppliers and businesses increase their access to short-term credit as needed to improve their working capital and the use of their productive capacity. Since the liquidity, cash, and working capital are keys to the survival and growth of any company, it is essential that suppliers are paid immediately, injecting a considerable amount of liquidity at a very low cost in the SME network.

Finally, the evidence on money and quasi money indicators, consistent with the conceptual framework described in Part 1, confirm that these tools are "complementary" because they are operating as complements to conventional national currencies.

Financial globalization suggests that during non-crisis times, it is more convenient for market participants to use flat money rather than alternative means. Meanwhile, the community tools are an excellent remedy during economic recession. They support local business cycles and create social wealth.

Appendix 1

The initial design was as a local moneyless not-for-profit exchange which had similarity with the Local Exchange Trading System (LETS) that evolved into a more complex Internet-based trading global network, allowing its promoters to extend it to other regions/continents. In fact, the Community Exchange System is one of the main typologies present in South Africa, Australia, New Zealand, and Poland. Figure 3.9 shows the worldwide growth of complementary currency systems.

"Venezuela's barter systems are unique among contemporary CCC in that the initiative for their creation was taken at the highest political level by President Chávez himself" Dittmer (2011) noted. Chávez (2005) said: "[barter currencies] will be in the hands and soul of the people with its good judgment; they will be the system, the communities."

Observing the medium of exchange distribution, we can note that communities use the advantages of new information technologies,

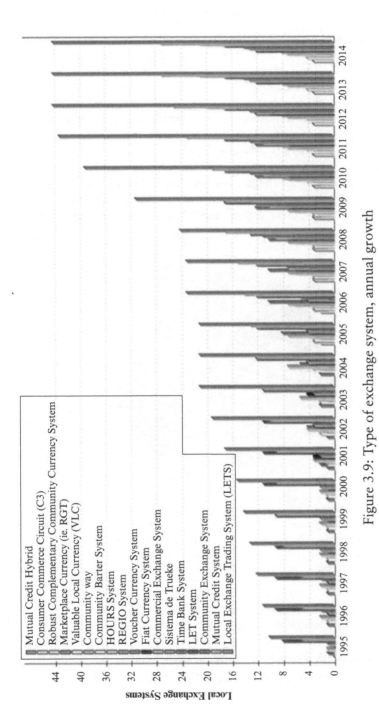

Figure 3.9: Type of exchange system, annual growth

Source: Database of Complementary Currencies Worldwide: http://www.complementarycurrency.org

giving preference to "electronic transaction" (see figure 3.10). It is more evident for the United States, Canada, Belgium, and Australia and conversely for Germany, where "Notes/Bills" are the most frequent medium of exchange.

Figure 3.11 shows that in relative terms "medium of exchange" has the following distribution: Electronic transaction, 19.5%; Notes/ Bills, 15.2%; Accounts, 10.5%, Electronic transaction using CES software, 7%; Accounts + Notes, 5.1%.

As for the variety of purposes and the relative world distribution of the most important of them – cooperation, poverty alleviation, environmental conservation, promoting a stable and sustainable economy, economic justice, create a new market, etc. – the multiple category

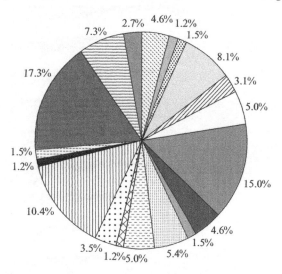

Figure 3.10: Type of exchange system (relative distribution)

Source: Database of Complementary Currencies Worldwide:
http://www.complementarycurrency.org

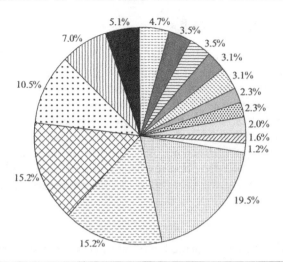

5.1% 4.7% 3.5% 3.5% 3.1% 3.1% 2.3% 2.3% 2.0% 1.6% 1.2%

7.0% 10.5% 15.2% 15.2% 19.5%

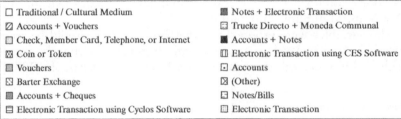

☐ Traditional / Cultural Medium	▨ Notes + Electronic Transaction
▨ Accounts + Vouchers	☷ Trueke Directo + Moneda Communal
☐ Check, Member Card, Telephone, or Internet	▓ Accounts + Notes
▨ Coin or Token	▥ Electronic Transaction using CES Software
▨ Vouchers	⊡ Accounts
▧ Barter Exchange	⊠ (Other)
▨ Accounts + Cheques	☲ Notes/Bills
☰ Electronic Transaction using Cyclos Software	▦ Electronic Transaction

Figure 3.11: Medium of exchange (relative distribution)

Source: Database of Complementary Currencies Worldwide: http://www.
complementarycurrency.org

"all reasons" makes up 49.4 percent, "contributing towards a sustainable society" 12 percent, "community development" 8 percent, and "activating the local market" 5.6 percent.

Appendix 2: Methodology

This model extends the linear modeling framework to variables that are not normally distributed. Poisson regression is often used for modeling count data. The GLM generalizes linear regression and allows the linear model to be related to the response variable via a link function. The log link function was applied for the Poisson regression. The model is:

$$\log(\mu) = \beta_0 + \beta_1 x_1 + \ldots + \beta_p x_p,$$

where μ is the count and log( ) defines the link function. This model also allows the magnitude of the variance of each measurement to be a function of its predicted value. Appendix 3 contains more detailed statistical information. There it is possible to consult: a list of goodness of fit statistics, Poisson regression coefficients for each of the variables along with standard errors, Wald χ^2 statistics and intervals, and p-values for the coefficients, etc. In addition, according to a test of the model form we provided to check if the Poisson model form fit our data, we demonstrate that the model fits reasonably well.

Description of the data

After an analysis was performed, we found very interesting significant variables. Tables 3.1 and 3.2 show summary statistics (Mean, Std Dev, Sum, Minimum, Maximum).

The variables were grouped together because they should be seen together. As debt levels rise, risk premia begin to rise sharply, faced with highly indebted governments. As Reinhart and Rogoff (2009)

Table 3.1   Summary statistics

Variable	N	Mean	Std Dev	Sum	Minimum	Maximum
w_25	270	104.60879	57.46501	28244	22.56075	241.17990
w_38	270	106.69313	59.40280	28807	11.66688	223.87316
w_141	158	40.54356	6.72466	6406	17.90211	68.68251
w_49	239	3.48537	4.03519	833.00406	0.16453	25.06939
lag1_w77	245	2.55172	3.70704	625.17234	−14.80000	14.20000
logx_41	264	3.89333	0.57420	1028	2.26975	5.46951
lag1_w11	218	5.15960	8.72002	1125	0.10000	61.80000
w_67	278	39.22036	19.91704	10903	10.00657	93.99816
logW_74	280	17.14665	1.30690	4801	15.23473	21.02389

Variable	Definition
w_25	Money and quasi money (M2) as % of GDP
w_38	Domestic credit to private sector (% of GDP)
w_141	Tertiary education, teachers (% female)
w_49	New business density (new registrations per 1,000 people ages 15–64)
lag1_w77	LOG GDP growth (annual %) $T-1$
logx_41	Log General government gross debt
lag1_w11	Bank nonperforming loans to total gross loans (%) $T-1$
w_67	Exports of goods and services (% of GDP)
logW_74	LOG Population (Total)

Table 3.2   Summary statistics

Variable	N	Mean	Std Dev	Sum	Minimum	Maximum
w_36	107	4.70378	8.22961	503.30499	−0.00231	36.62375
w_118	210	7.22287	4.20266	1517	0.41346	19.71596
w_131	227	26.89919	15.25939	6106	0.15336	58.92924
w_64	279	22189	65138	6190680	3.00000	487069
x_31	264	38.38237	10.42475	10133	18.02800	59.20300
x_33	264	−3.05801	3.64759	−807.31500	−16.60100	5.04200

Variable Definition
w_36   Risk premium on lending (lending rate minus treasury bill rate, %)
w_118 CO_2 emissions (metric tons per capita)
w_131   Social contributions (% of revenue)
w_64   Secure Internet servers
x_31   Government total expenditure% GDP
x_33   Government net lending/borrowing

highlight, countries that choose to rely excessively on short-term borrowing to fund growing debt levels are particularly vulnerable to crises.

Appendix 3: Statistical analysis

In this work, the generalized linear model has been applied. The Poisson distributions are a discrete family with a probability function indexed by the rate parameter $\mu > 0$: if it takes integer values $y = 0, 1, 2,\ldots y!$ The expectation and variance of a Poisson random variable are both equal to μ. The Poisson distribution is useful for modeling count data. As μ increases, the Poisson distribution grows more symmetric and is eventually well approximated by a normal distribution.

On the class statement we have two categorical variables: year and country (year key_code). We use the type3 option in the model statement as it is used to get the multi-degree-of-freedom test of the categorical variables listed (year key_code).

To help assess the fit of the model, we use the χ^2 goodness-of-fit test. This assumes the deviance follows a χ^2 distribution with degrees of freedom equal to the model residual. From the first line of our goodness of fit output, we can see these values are 54.9486 and 55:

p-value = 1 − probchi(χ^2, d.f.);   d.f. = 55; χ^2 = 54.9486;
p-value = 0.47659

This is a test of the model form: Does the Poisson model form fit our data?

We conclude that the model fits reasonably well because the goodness-of-fit χ^2 test is not statistically significant. If the test had been statistically significant, it would indicate that the data do not fit the model well. In that situation, we may try to determine if there are omitted predictor variables, if our linearity assumption holds, and/or if there is an issue of over-dispersion.

References

Blanc, J. (2011) Classifying CCs: Community, complementary and local currencies' types and generations. *International Journal of Community Currency Research* 15, Special Issue, D4–10.

Chávez, H. (2005) *Aló Presidente*. Televised broadcast, December.

Database of Complementary Currencies Worldwide (2014) Available at: http://www.complementarycurrency.org/ccDatabase/les_public.html

De Bondt, W. and Thaler, R. (1987) Further evidence on investor overreaction and stock market seasonality. *The Journal of Finance* 42, 3, 557–81.

De Long, B.J., Shleifer, A., Summers, L.H. and Waldman, R.J. (1990) Noise trader risk in financial markets. *Journal of Political Economy* 98, 4, 703–38.

Derudder, P. (2011) Cahier d'éspérance richesses et monnaies. *Monnaie en débat*.

Dittmer, K. (2011) Communal currencies in Venezuela. *International Journal of Community Currency Research* 15, Section A, 78–83.

Goerner, S., Lietaer, B. and Ulanowicz, R.E. (2009) Quantifying economic sustainability: Implications for free-enterprise theory, policy and practice. *Ecological Economics* 69, 1, 76–81.

Greco, T.H. (1994) *New Money for Healthy Communities*. Greco Pub., Tucson, AZ.

Holling, C.S. (1986) The resilience of terrestrial ecosystems: Local surprise and global change. In: Clark, W.C. and Munn, R.E. (eds.) *Sustainable Development of the Biosphere*. Cambridge University Press, London, pp. 292–317.

Kash, J.A., Friedman, E.J. and Halpern, J.Y. (2007) Optimizing scrip systems: efficiency, crashes, hoarders, and altruists. Eighth ACM Conference on Electronic Commerce.

Kennedy, M. and Lietaer, B. (2004) *Regionalwährungen: Neue Wege zu nachhaltigem Wohlstand*. Translated in French: *Monnaies Régionales: de nouvelles voies vers une prospérité durable*. Charles Léopold Mayer, Paris.

Larcker, D.F. and Tayan, B. (2014) Corporate governance according to Charles T. Munger. Stanford Closer Look Series. Available at: https://www.gsb.stanford.edu/sites/default/files/38_Munger_0.pdf

Lietaer, B., Ulanowicz, R.E., Goerner, S.J. and McLaren, N. (2010) Is our monetary structure a systemic cause for financial instability? Evidence and remedies from nature. *Journal of Futures Studies* 14, 89–108.

Martignoni, J. (2012) A new approach to a typology of complementary currencies. *International Journal of Community Currency Research* 16, Section A, 1–17.

May, R.M. (1972) Will a large complex system be stable? *Nature* 238, 413–14.

Reinhart, C. and Rogoff, K. (2009) *This Time Is Different. Eight Centuries of Financial Folly.* Princeton University Press, Princeton, NJ.

Schroeder, R.F.H., Miyazaki, Y. and Fare, M. (2011) Community currency research: An analysis of the literature. *International Journal of Community Currency Research* 15, Section A, 31–41.

Thaler, R. (1999) The end of behavioral finance. *Financial Analysts Journal 55*, 6, 12–17.

Western Australia Government (1990) LETSystems Training Pack. Community Development Branch, Department of State Development.

WIR Bank (1934) WIR Economic Circle Cooperative, Wirtschaftsring-Genossenschaft. Available at: http://www.wir.ch/

Zorach, A.C. and Ulanowicz, R.E. (2003) Quantifying the complexity of flow networks: How many roles are there? *Complexity* 8, 3, 68–76.

Chapter 4

Blockchain Dreams: Imagining Techno-Economic Alternatives After Bitcoin

Lana Swartz

Introduction

According to its advocates, the blockchain, the distributed ledger system underlying bitcoin,[1] is poised to radically transform society. Indeed, it truly is difficult to overstate the claims made by some blockchain enthusiasts. *Blockchain: Blueprint for a New Economy*, a 2015 introductory handbook for the technology published by O'Reilly begins, "We may be at the dawn of a new revolution" (Swan 2015). It goes on to assert that the "economic, political, humanitarian, and legal system benefits" make it clear that blockchain is an "extremely disruptive technology that would have the capacity for reconfiguring all aspects of society and its operations" (Swan 2015). Similar predictions are made in countless TED talks, pitch meetings, industry conference keynotes, blog posts, "white papers" that outline new technical methods, and "manifestos" that launch start-ups.[2]

The visions conjured by blockchain dreamers are ambitious and dazzling. Equipped with this technology, as one enthusiast put it, "Young entrepreneurs have realized that the possibilities are only hindered by their own imaginations" (Yuan 2015). But blockchain projects are, at present, a form of utopian science fiction: they may

---

[1] In general, I follow what has emerged as standard and do not capitalize the word bitcoin.

[2] Methodological note: this is the terrain of discourse that this research draws from. In addition to these documentary sources, I have been engaged in a multi-sited ethnography (Marcus 1995) of the networked field site (Burrell 2009) of bitcoin and blockchain systems and the communities that surround them since 2011, now close to five years. This includes interviews with participants and participant observation both as an observer and as a scholarly or critical expert at related events in San Francisco, New York, Los Angeles, Boston, Barcelona, London, Dublin, Amsterdam, and Sydney.

indeed map a coming reality, but for now, they are speculative visions. If blockchain dreamers are willing a future into being with their imaginations, what kind of future are they imagining?

This chapter investigates the alternative techno-economic future offered by these blockchain dreams. Even if these projects turn out to be vapor, the blockchain is meaningful as an inventory of desire. It is an engine of alterity: an opportunity to imagine a different world and imagine the mechanics of how that different world might be run. Embedded in those dreams is another question: How will this future be brought about? What is the link between today's vision and tomorrow's reality?

First, this chapter gives a short techno-social introduction to blockchain, including its emergence from bitcoin. It then maps the dissatisfactions and aspirations that are expressed in blockchain dreams, the alternative future world that just might be possible. Next, it compares these radical proposals to incorporative visions of blockchain within the finance industry. Finally, it draws from approaches in science and technology studies (STS) and alternative economic scholarship, to inquire after what the radical blockchain dream might learn from these less ambitious projects.

The bitcoin blockchain

Put most simply, a blockchain is a shared ledger. This concise definition captures the essence of the concept while allowing for the ample flexibility with which it is used. In even the loosest of applications of the concept, a blockchain is, first, a write-only ledger: a list of recorded entries that can only be added to, not erased or changed. Second, a blockchain is shared: it is maintained and accessed by a number of parties without one central host. Each "block" is a set of records-in the ledger. All parties can add blocks and can see when blocks are added, so the blockchain is a "chain" of "blocks."

The concept of a blockchain was, of course, developed not as a generic, multi-purpose ledger but for the purpose of assigning and transferring ownership of a new form of digital money, bitcoin. It was formally described by the pseudonymous Satoshi Nakamoto (2008) in "Bitcoin: A peer-to-peer electronic cash system," or, as it is most commonly termed, "the bitcoin white paper." The term "blockchain" does not appear in the white paper, but Nakamoto does describe bitcoin in terms of "blocks" and "chains." The blockchain envisioned in the white paper provides a decentralized ledger accounting for the ownership of every existing bitcoin. The bitcoin blockchain is the single record, shared and agreed upon by all nodes, of the ownership, past and present, of all bitcoins. In this way, Nakamoto describes "coins" as existing only as a "chain of digital signatures" (p. 2).

Ledgers are a common feature of most payment systems. In a highly simplified version of traditional payment systems, a centralized institution, like a bank, keeps account of who paid what to whom, crediting and debiting accounts accordingly. In contrast, with bitcoin, there is no bank keeping track of credits and debits. Instead, all node computers maintain the ledger of ownership of each bitcoin. To make a transaction, the owner broadcasts the transfer of a coin to all nodes. That transaction is collected into a "block," which is "chained" to all previously generated blocks to form the ledger hosted by all nodes. New bitcoins are generated for nodes as a reward for verifying blocks and adding them to the chain. The system protects against duplication or counterfeiting coins by verifying all blocks and ensuring that all nodes are in agreement. Each bitcoin is, in turn, really just an entry in the ledger. One trades in the rights to claim this bitcoin.

The bitcoin blockchain can be understood in terms of its social architecture as well as its technical features. The bitcoin blockchain is produced via a set of overlapping, sometimes inconsistent, ideological systems.

First, the bitcoin blockchain offers what Nakamoto calls a "new model of privacy" (p. 6). In the bitcoin blockchain, the owners and recipients of each bitcoin are pseudonymous, identified by cryptographic keys that function as addresses. Transactions, by virtue of being maintained on the blockchain ledger, are public, but the identities of the parties to the transaction are private, potentially even from each other. The publicity of bitcoin transactions stands in contrast to the traditional payment model, in which identities and transactions are kept private from the public by banks.

Previously, my collaborators and I have described the political values motivating the design of bitcoin as "digital metallism" (Maurer et al. 2013). There is no central authority, like a government, that issues bitcoins, instead, they are "mined" according to an algorithm that is thought to mimic a scarce natural commodity like gold. There is a limited number of bitcoins that become harder to mine at a steadily increasing rate. The value of bitcoin is "decentralized," allowing users to trade without reference to a central authority that underwrites the terms of the transaction. In metallism, these autonomous market transactions produce a broader, more total sociality of individual sovereignty and peership.

More recently, I have elaborated the theory of money and society implicit in bitcoin to include the concept of "infrastructural mutualism," which describes the way some enthusiasts value the ability to mutually build and support a collaborative platform upon which to transact, free from the prying eyes and inference of corporate intermediaries (Swartz forthcoming). Infrastructural mutualism is tied to the long history of peer production like free software, peer-to-peer production, and commonsing practices (see Benkler 2003; Bauwens 2005; Kelty 2008).

Both digital metallists and infrastructural mutualists share an investment in decentralization and autonomy. However, for digital metallists, the primary feature of bitcoin is the "coin," a value-bearing gold-like entity, which enables decentralized and autonomous value and therefore decentralized and autonomous market relations. For infrastructural mutualists, it is the blockchain, a decentralized, autonomous infrastructure with shared utility produced and maintained by all participants.

The blockchain after bitcoin

Beginning in late 2013, public attention seemed to shift from bitcoin as a currency to the underlying blockchain and other potential applications for it. By 2015, hype about the blockchain seemed to have fully subsumed that of bitcoin. The cover of Bloomberg Markets ran the headline "It's All About The Blockchain" (Robinson and Leising 2015). One observer wrote, "In the eyes of many the blockchain is seen as this disruptive piece of technology while Bitcoin is portrayed as a Napster-like experiment" (Ghalim 2015). Erik Voorhees, a well-known bitcoin entrepreneur, wrote on his blog, "2015 was the year the narrative changed. Bitcoin is out, blockchain is in" (2015).

Some of this interest was centered on so-called "Bitcoin 2.0" projects, that is, methods for extending the bitcoin blockchain. For example, there have been efforts to use the bitcoin blockchain to store information of all kinds – from marriage declarations to property records to sensitive information leaked by whistleblowers – in its immutable ledger. Other blockchain projects involved entirely new systems, functionally independent from bitcoin. Ethereum, perhaps the leading and most ambitious of the newer blockchain projects, is an ongoing effort to develop fully programmable, multi-use blockchain. As it is often explained, "Whereas Bitcoin could be described simplistically as a 'global spreadsheet,' Ethereum could be described

85

as a 'global spreadsheet with macros,'" referring to the mini bits of code that can be embedded to automate in programs like Microsoft Excel.[3]

Many blockchain projects are oriented toward revolutionary social, economic, and political change. I term these "radical" because they attempt to use the blockchain to bring about a new techno-economic order. Most of these initiatives are aligned with bitcoin's political themes: decentralization, autonomy, and privacy. Some are clever, simple repurposing of the blockchain. For example, there is Namecoin, which proposes to use a blockchain to operate a decentralized, domain name system for websites, outside of ICANN's governance (Isgur 2014). Other radical projects are more ambitious, aiming to produce holistic systems of decentralized, non-hierarchical, autonomous self-governance. For example, one start-up, Backfeed, proposes to produce a "distributed governance system for blockchain-based applications allowing for the collaborative creation and distribution of value in spontaneously emerging networks of peers" as well as "tools that enable large-scale, free and systematic cooperation between thousands of people without the coordination of any central authority."[4]

The spectrum of ideological commitments present in these projects resonates with values that have been present in bitcoin since its earliest days: digital metallism and infrastructural mutualism. In the digital metallist mode, blockchain produces the ultimate market mechanism, one that can trade in any form of value and exists beyond the domain of governments and the existing financial system. In the infrastructural mutualist mode, the goal is to produce peer-to-peer information systems that distribute resources and organize a new open networked commons.

In addition to these radical blockchain projects, there are also efforts to use blockchain technology to innovate within the existing financial system. One project is the Distributive Ledger Initiative launched in 2015 by innovation firm R3CEV, which has the support of large banks, including Bank of America, Barclays, Citi, Deutsche Bank, J.P. Morgan, Goldman Sachs, and HSBC (Stafford 2015). These initiatives pose challenges to the way that financial technology is currently implemented and propose to remake the backend infrastructure of banking. I term them "incorporative" because they do not necessarily seek

---

[3] See, for example, https://www.quora.com/What-is-Ethereum-in-laymans-term/answer/James-Z-2?srid=uEQu
[4] See http://backfeed.cc/explore-in-depth

to change the underlying financial system from a political or social perspective; instead, they seek to incorporate the blockchain into the existing system to make that system more efficient.

Incorporative blockchain applications benefit from the "revolutionary" aura of the radical projects, but for blockchain advocates who have more radical ambitions, these incorporative projects are seen as far afield of the original goals of bitcoin. When all the "peers" in a network are traditional financial institutions, can the network really be considered "peer to peer"? As Voorhees (2015) puts it, "Moving from a permissioned financial network between banks, to a permissioned financial network among banks, is no great step for mankind." But, perhaps ironically, no industry is more interested in or supportive of blockchain than banking, the one bitcoin was designed to circumvent.

Interest in the incorporative blockchain emerges from a milieu – the "fin tech" moment – where the financial and technology industries blur. Many of these projects exist as "start-ups," "accelerators," and "innovation labs" inside, or closely related to, large financial institutions. Behind some of this is what one engineer at a workshop described to me as "C-Suite FOMO" – the idea that high-level executives may suffer from "Fear Of Missing Out" on the next big thing. At a time when industry analysts suggest that Wall Street is losing the best and the brightest to Silicon Valley (see, for example, Duffy 2013; Egan 2014; Greenberg 2015), blockchain provides a fun, fascinating challenge to lure young talent back to Wall Street. The banks, eager to avoid being "disrupted," have summoned their ample resources toward blockchain innovation. In addition, there are plenty of bitcoin and radical blockchain aficionados who have professionalized their expertise and become evangelical fin tech consultants.

The distinction between radical and incorporative blockchain projects is not clearly defined and, in practice, there is a continuum between the two ideological modes. Because of its origin in bitcoin and continued relationship to cryptographic currencies, a blockchain is well suited to keeping track of a moving currency. It's not difficult to imagine how the leaders of libertarian radical blockchain projects may find themselves pursuing their (albeit short-term) rational self-interest by assisting a bank in the pursuit of more ordinary capitalism.

Similarly, while some radical blockchain initiatives are non-profit organizations or free and open source software projects, many are start-ups, and many of these start-ups receive support from many of the same funders and accelerator programs that support incorporative blockchain start-ups. Like the "sharing economy" before it, which began with visions of peer-to-peer commerce and quickly became platforms for on-demand task work, it's easy to see how start-ups with utopian visions might "pivot" (to use industry parlance) toward business models different from or even in opposition to their original goals.

Radical and incorporative blockchain projects represent different dreams about the future of value and society. Advocates of radical blockchain projects dream of a future in which institutions are disaggregated into millions of microsocial obligations backed by computerized contracts. They rarely articulate the intermediate steps through which such a future comes into being. While the dreams of incorporative blockchain advocates tend to lack the long-range vision of their radical peers, they focus instead on the short-term challenges of implementation. Concerned with the material constraints of the present, incorporative blockchain dreamers offer a vision of institutions transformed rather than destroyed.

Radical blockchain dreams

In one of the clearest descriptions of the radical blockchain dream, Noah Thorp, co-founder of blockchain start-up Citizen Code (2015), writes:

> People of the free internet, we now have the opportunity to create a world where we choose to work a 4 hour work week at our whim, collaborating globally with whom we like, freely choosing compensation in currency or equity, frolicking in our hyper-creative and artistic, fractally self-organized fluid work groups, protected from catastrophic risk by a basic income provided by our egalitarian peer to peer protocols. In this vision the tragedy of the commons is stamped out like polio by a collaborative network of trust and enforced by a consensus-based cryptographic protocol that ensures our aligned incentivization towards the expression of our personal and collective purposes.

This is a vision of an alternative society made possible by blockchain, a technological infrastructure. This infrastructure, like the society it is meant to power, is incipient, a powerful vision that feels to believers as though it already exists. It springs into being seamlessly, then persists seamlessly, providing a similar seamlessness to the relations it animates.

I characterize the radical blockchain dream by three components: futurity; decentralization and disintermediation; and autonomy and automation, which are elaborated in the following sub-sections.

Dreams of futurity

Blockchain dreamers are in a hurry to accomplish the future, which, as sociologist Anthony Giddens (1991) puts it, is always being "colonized" rapidly. If they don't dream the future now, someone else will. It is now "no longer optional," as one blockchain start-up founder put it, to passively await its coming (Swarm 2015). As soon as a proposal is offered – whether as a white paper, a slide deck, or a blog post – it is treated as though it already exists, ready to go. Indeed, blockchain projects exist in a particular temporality and have their own sense of the past and future, of change. It performatively leans into a future, always just around the corner, which might as well be here already.

Despite these heady visions, few post-blockchain projects currently exist, strictly speaking, in a fully functional form. Blockchain projects are regularly described as being fully ready to go, even though, so far, that is certainly not the case. In her introductory book, Swan (2015) describes an evolution from Blockchain 1.0 to 2.0 and 3.0, each of which relate to a more complex set of functions and a more comprehensive set of applications, but only Blockchain 1.0, the bitcoin blockchain, is currently implemented. The section entitled "Bitcoin 1.0 in Practical Use" numbers just three paragraphs. The rest of the book goes on to describe potential and theoretical applications, always in implied present tense.

This is technological fetishism with the implementation of that technology as almost an afterthought. As one journalist put it, "letting yourself get giddily far ahead of reality may be a requirement for participation in the blockchain revolution" (Rosenberg 2015). Perhaps this is the degree of audacious belief required to usher in a new techno-economic order. Their impatience mirrors the general future orientation of the Silicon Valley tech industry, amplified. Even in Silicon Valley, where technology is always one step behind its promises, blockchain advocates are unusually willing to operate as though a speculative future has already arrived in the present.

Dreams of decentralization and disintermediation

Many radical blockchain dreams envision new formations like decentralized autonomous corporations (DACs), decentralized autonomous organizations (DAOs), and decentralized autonomous societies (DASs). As Vitalk Buterin, founder of Ethereum and celebrated blockchain visionary, half-joked, "DAOism" is well on its way to becoming a quasi-cyber-religion" (2015). What kind of society is decentralized, autonomous? Or at least made up of decentralized autonomous organizations and corporations?

Nearly all blockchain believers agree that the key problem of our era is the role of "intermediaries" in all areas of society. According to this perspective, today's Internet is a tremendous disappointment. It is controlled by centralized platforms, marked by business models dependent on the collection of personal and social data, and complicit with state agencies like the NSA in the surveillance and flow of information. These systems are gently coercive, and there is no Internet outside of them. The individual is simply obliged to engage via these "trusted third parties" for all communication.

Blockchain, on the other hand, would do away with the need for this trust. It would be an infrastructure that is "decentralized and controlled by a multitude of people, in a vast peer-to-peer network" and thus can "altogether elude government regulations and controls" (Lujan 2016). As Ethereum's Stephan Tual describes it, "We just want to take the Internet to its logical conclusion: total decentralization" (Volpicelli 2015). Blockchain decentralization is seen as both an evolutionary next step and a return to an Internet free from intermediaries and therefore freer generally.

A key feature, then, of the blockchain dream is a network of peers. Instead of the increasingly centralized Internet, enthusiasts imagine a "huge number of decentralized devices that work together in a distributed mesh network, . . . decentralization on steroids" (Yuan 2015). Blockchain has been characterized as "radicalizing infrastructure": in its ideal form, gone would be the "monolithic resources with prohibitive barriers to entry, the quintessential server farmhoused in some distant industrial estate" in favor of "something immaterial and dispersed, or managed through flexible and transient forms of ownership" (O'Dwyer 2015).

In the blockchain dream, individuals will no longer "pay" to use intermediaries with data by passively working in what scholars call "the social factory" (see Gill and Pratt 2008). Instead, there will be no intermediaries because we will all be intermediaries, mutually producing a shared, trustless infrastructure and incentivized to do so with crypto-coins like bitcoin. If all individuals connect with each other directly via blockchain, the Googles, Facebooks, and Amazons will be made obsolete.

But the blockchain dream of decentralization is more expansive than just the disruption of the business models of intermediaries. It is also a dream of disintermediation, a dream of direct communication.

90

In the radical blockchain dream, decentralization and disintermediation are entangled and interdependent. Ethereum founder Vitalik Buterin (2014a) gives the example of book publishing:

> In the 1970s, if you wanted to write a book, there was a large number of opaque, centralized intermediaries that you would need to go through before your book would get to a consumer. First, you would need a publishing company, which would also handle editing and marketing for you and provide a quality control function to the consumer. Second, the book would need to be distributed, and then finally it would be sold at each individual bookstore. Each part of the chain would take a large cut; at the end, you would be lucky to get more than ten percent of the revenue from each copy as a royalty. Notice the use of the term "royalty," implying that you the author of the book are simply just another extraneous part of the chain that deserves a few percent as a cut rather than, well, the single most important person without whom the book would not even exist in the first place.

It's hard to see what isn't an intermediary to blockchain visionaries like Buterin. The work of publishing, of distribution, of bookseller each becomes just a chain of middlemen taking "cuts," adding friction.

Like publishing, almost all infrastructural components of existing information systems and economies are seen as, to use some of the terms that appear again and again, creaky, clunky, antiquated, byzantine, Kafkaesque. They are either predatory, incompetent, or both. Therefore, they are ripe for total disruption, destruction, and rebuilding from scratch with the blockchain. There is an almost moral disdain for mediation and the centralized infrastructures that enable it. And there is an almost moral obligation to decentralize and, presumably, disintermediate.

At the heart of the blockchain dream, then, there is a yearning for ever more direct communication. Ethereum takes its name from the classic element of aether, the quintessence that fills the universe. As communication scholar John Durham Peters (1999) points out, the cybernetic tradition of signal processing and the spiritualist tradition of telepathy meet in the ethereal dream of perfect communication. Ethereum promises peer-to-peer communication beyond the hassle of imperfect communication and, indeed, beyond the drudgery and domination of imperfect communication work.

But what is the infrastructural work of intermediaries, what service do they provide? Mediating, interfacing, making interoperability, smoothing interactions – this is all work itself. It is exactly the work that the blockchain dream is meant to obviate. And yet, the dream of directness is dependent on an ecosystem of hardware and software, all of which must be produced and maintained by someone.

In the one fully existing blockchain-based system, bitcoin, decentralization remains a challenge. Instead of developing capacities for lightweight protocols optimized for home computers or small-scale collectives to host the blockchain, metallist speculation in bitcoin the currency has lead to centralization of the infrastructure. Blockchain hosting has consolidated in the form of industrialized "mining" operations, with the top two pools operating 57 percent of the blockchain and five mining pools operating 80 percent.[5] There is the common suspicion that some of these pools might be owned by the same operator, which would mean further consolidation (Otar 2015).

Similarly, instead of transacting directly via the blockchain, most people use bitcoins via a new class of bitcoin-specific intermediaries: wallets, exchanges, debit cards, other payment portals. These do the work that financial intermediaries have always done: broker settlement and clearance, make equivalence between exchange rates, manage risk and fraud. What bitcoin entrepreneurs who have built these applications on top of the blockchain have discovered is that direct financial communication – like all communication – does not happen by magic. Bitcoin entrepreneurs have wound up rebuilding most of the payment system from the ground up.

By wishing away infrastructural work, the bitcoin ecosystem has become as centralized and mediated as existing systems. There is no reason to expect that newer blockchain projects will be any different.

Dreams of the autonomous and the automated

The word "autonomous" as it is used in the blockchain dream is polysemic and evocative of past dreams of alterity. It calls to mind the autonomia approach of anti-authoritarian left-wing theories and activists who sit at the intersection of socialism and libertarianism (see Lotringer and Marazzi 2007). It also evokes the liminal autonomy found in places, like Occupy encampments and Burning Man, which are seen by some participants as able to exist outside present society as a prefigurative site of alterity (Castells 2013; Turner 2009). It also references bitcoin, which was meant to function autonomous of states or banks. But in the new blockchain dream, autonomous means both something more and something else.

Although the term is slippery and controversial, blockchain

---

[5] See https://news.ycombinator.com/item?id=6894320 and https://blockchain.info/pools

enthusiasts have converged on the definition of a "decentralized autonomous organization" as something like a blockchain-based entity run without any external control, instead guided by a set of incorruptible rules and powered by smart contracts, markets in cryptocurrency, and AI (artificial intelligence) agents. Human stakeholders create smart contracts and use markets to express their preferences, and the AI enforces the execution of those contracts and market preferences. Autonomous, then, becomes not just about autonomy from authority, but automation. In the blockchain dream, the two are interconnected, the former dependent on the latter.

As Cameron and Tyler Winklevoss, eclipsed Facebook co-founders and bitcoin and blockchain entrepreneurs describe it (emphasis original):

> Crypto-currencies will also enable the first forms of *artificial life* ushering in a *"Second Machine Age."* While computers, machines and things (e.g., refrigerator) cannot open a bank account today, they will be able to plug into the Bitcoin protocol and behave like *rational economic actors* in the future. These computers known as *autonomous agents* (e.g., self-driving cars, drones) will own themselves, and if profitable, spawn children to create families or *autonomous corporations*. A *Trade Singularity* will occur, whereby trade between machines, computers and things, will exceed trade between humans. Uncreative tasks will become primarily automated causing goods and services to become much cheaper and living standards to rise.[6]

Fast Company describes blockchain entrepreneurs interested in DAOs as "the humans who dream of companies that won't need us" (Pangburn 2015).

Indeed, the problem, it seems, is people. As one enthusiast writes, "A smart contract automates the rules, checks the conditions and then acts on them, minimizing human involvement" (Frisby 2016). Again, inherent in this dream is the obviation of trust. The DAO makes it unnecessary to trust each other or a centralized third party because it automates all the processes that could be potential points of human maleficence or ineptitude. As Buterin puts it, "it's not even possible for the organization's 'mind' to cheat" (2015).

There is no need to try to cooperate, only engage in systems of consensus. Rather than "drafting, disputing or executing a traditional contract," even the most complicated business arrangements can be "coded and packaged as a smart contract" (Frisby 2016). Consensus is achieved through coordination via the automated capture,

[6] See https://winklevosscapital.com/money-is-broken-but-its-future-is-not/

quantification, and execution of social signals. Blockchain start-up founder Noah Thorp (2015) describes it:

> In my mind's eye the invisible streams of value soon to be represented by emerging protocols became visible. Beyond dollars and yen, the whole spectrum of reputation currencies, app coins, and machine economies streamed before my eyes in a rainbow of currency, equity, and distributed accounts.

These "machine economies," these "rainbow" of bitcoin-like cryptographic value tokens, become a perfect market to take care of everything, anything. This is a trust in markets as the primary drivers of automation. It is well beyond that of mainstream economists, most of whom at least implicitly recognize that market devices are designed by people to perform as much as measure the world (MacKenzie 2006). This is more aligned with what some are calling "fully automated luxury communism" or FALC.[7] As one major proponent of FALC put it, "There is a tendency in capitalism to automate labor, to turn things previously done by humans into automated functions. In recognition of that, then the only utopian demand can be for the full automation of everything and common ownership of that which is automated" (Merchant 2015).

When the blockchain dream is fulfilled, those tokens will circulate, and those who contribute in various ways will be incentivized by a market for those tokens, which become a form of equity in society in itself.[8] All of this will be automated, self-organizing, self-regulating, immune from human error or corruption, and therefore fair. In the meantime, however, these tokens can also be purchased. Joel Dietz (2015), founder of blockchain start-up Swarm says, "Unlike past revolutions, this is a revolution not to be joined, but to be owned." Early investors are purchasing stock in the very means of participation in the coming society.

In the blockchain dream, automation produces autonomy from hierarchies and institutions. This vision draws simultaneously from the far past and the far future, a kind of techno-primitivism. It is often described in terms of "swarms," "fractals," and other naturally-occurring complex patterns. As scholar and "chief alchemist" of Backfeed Primavera De Filippi said in her 2015 TED talk:

---

[7] See Fully Automated Luxury Communism. Tumblr: http://luxurycommunism-blog.tumblr.com/

[8] Ethereum began with a 42-day pre-sale for "ether," the coin-like "crypto fuel" that "powers" Ethereum (Buterin 2014b). In its first 12 hours, the pre-sale raised 3,700 bitcoins, which was, at the time, priced at US$2.3 million (Tanzarian 2014).

The animal kingdom contains numerous examples of individuals cooperating with one another to achieve impressive outcomes without the need for planning, control, or even direct communication between agents – examples are bees, ants, and schools of fish. Humans, however, have only been able to achieve goals cooperatively through the imposition of organizational hierarchies, centralized coordination, and rules. Blockchain technologies offer a new approach, allowing us to achieve large-scale and systematic cooperation in an entirely distributed and decentralized manner.

Julian Feder (2016) elaborates this idea on the Backfeed blog, explaining that blockchain allows "networks to arise spontaneously" that will "naturally" drive participants into coordination, "just like the simple response to pheromone exchange does for insect colonies." Blockchain is meant to provide humans with a kind of augmented hyper naturalness, a technological extension of an innate but alienated ability to self-organize. Achieving this future would mean a discovery of a more authentic human-ness. This is a perfected vision of humanity through both technology and markets.

But like the dream of decentralization, the dream of automation remains elusive. Without an existing functional blockchain to capture complicated ideas and negotiations, these groups must use communication technologies that do exist. Swarm, which described itself as poised to create "Civilization 2.0," used a Google Doc to publically brainstorm its plan for "fractastical distributed governance" (Swarm 2015). Despite big, present-tense promises, blockchain has not yet disintermediated Google, let alone the messy, frustrating processes of collective brainstorming.

The bitcoin project, again, the most fully realized blockchain implementation, is also struggling to use the blockchain for automated consensus. Beginning in 2015, there was strife in the bitcoin community over how to enable bitcoin to process more transactions more quickly. Several fixes were proposed, and consensus would be achieved by settling on the one that was run by the most miners and therefore "won." Crucially, this was not about "voting" because, as one forum leader wrote, "One of the great things about Bitcoin is its lack of democracy."[9] That is, no one could be "democratically coerced" into using one version of the protocol or another; instead, they would make the rational economic decision to run the version of the software the majority were running, or not. At present, the issue

[9] https://www.reddit.com/r/Bitcoin/comments/3rejl9/
coinbase_ceo_brian_armstrong_bip_101_is_the_best/cwoc8n5

has not yet been resolved. Bitcoin has not been scaled up sufficiently. For one leading core developer, Mike Hearn, who left in the wake of the debacle, this marked "the resolution of the Bitcoin experiment" in "failure" because it demonstrated that "the mechanisms that should have prevented this outcome have broken down" (Hearn 2016). Nevertheless, the dream of automated market consensus over the difficult work of cooperation remains.

The incorporative blockchain dream?

While it by no means has revolutionary aims, the vision of incorporative blockchain within the financial industry contains its own alterity. Precisely because its aims and context are so different, the incorporative orientation of blockchains as "fin tech" can perhaps provide a useful comparative. Indeed, as J.K. Gibson-Graham (2008) suggests, studying the economy as it is can surface and perform practices of an economy otherwise. The incorporative blockchain dream gives us some insight into what might be missing from the radical blockchain dream.

The incorporative blockchain dream isn't really a dream at all. It is boring. Despite the residual hype from the radical blockchain dream, incorporative blockchain projects do not seek to holistically remake society. Instead, they offer, as consulting firm Accenture Insights (2016) put it, a "platform to remedy existing pain points in the current banking landscape." The report describes potential applications, such as "Introduce unprecedented cohesion to the internal bookkeeping processes; Show a record of consensus with a cryptographic audit trail of transactions; Create near real-time settlement; Strengthen risk management through stronger auditability and counterparty ties" as well as "KYC/AML (Know Your Customer/ Anti-money Laundering data sharing), trade surveillance, regulatory reporting, collateral management, trading, settlement and clearing." This list is typical of the kind of applications being imagined for the incorporative blockchain. Nevertheless, it is a key convening for the financial services industry, a "once-in-a-generation opportunity to reimagine and modernize its infrastructure to address long-standing operational challenges" (DTCC 2016).

The incorporative blockchain offers a vision directly opposed to that of the radical blockchain in terms of futurity; decentralization and disintermediation; and autonomy and automation. Whereas the radical blockchain dream is marked by futurity, the incorporative blockchain dream is slow moving and risk averse. Whereas the radical blockchain dream values decentralization and disintermediation, the incorporative dream insists on governance and surfaces the work of intermediaries. Whereas the radical blockchain dream seeks autonomy built on automation, the incorporative blockchain dream imagines automation as a tool, not a replacement, for human work.

A slow blockchain?

Unlike the radical blockchain dreamers who bound enthusiastically toward the future, those interested in incorporative uses of the blockchain within financial institutions are slow moving and cautious. A 2015 report from the consulting firm McKinsey is representative: "The full potential of blockchain technology will only be realized through cooperation among market participants, regulators and technologists and this may take some time." A May 2016 report by the SWIFT institute notes that many in the industry were concerned that while blockchain technology may have potential, it is accompanied by an excess of "unrealistic expectations" with "relatively little short term pay off" (Mainelli and Milne 2016).

Again and again, at workshops and conferences on the blockchain, industry representatives ask whether or not implementing it will be "worth the cost of migration," question what the "added value" of doing so would be, and suggest that blockchain might just be a "solution in search of a problem." Beneath this corporate speak there is a critique of futurity and of technological fetishism. Beyond high-level enthusiasts and evangelical consultants who have crossed over from the radical blockchain, many people whose jobs it will be to implement blockchain are concerned with what it can actually do, and they are not in a particular rush to overhaul their entire system in the name of a technology that is very much in an early phase. As one industry consultant put it, "This is going to take a lot of work" (Peabody 2016).

This is precisely the lack of "agility" for which Silicon Valley regularly criticizes Wall Street, but it's a slowness and risk aversion rooted in an ethic of fiduciary care. Put another way: financial technology systems have to work. They can't be vaporware. The kind of wizardry like credit default swaps and high frequency trading might be valued on the trading side of big banks but it is not welcome in terms of the infrastructure that moves money around and keeps track of it. The following two sections describe the slowed temporality of

97

the incorporative blockchain dream in terms of the fiduciary labor it surfaces: the work of negotiating decentralization and automation.

But first, as a provocation, I want to consider for a moment the way in which the banking industry offers an alternative to the futurism of Silicon Valley and the radical blockchain. Perhaps ironically, because "the corporate banking revolution is a marathon, not a sprint," it may have more in common with the temporalities of many alternative economic practices and activism groups, who celebrate the virtues of slow (PYMNTS 2015). The incorporative blockchain, oddly enough, might share a mantra with the Spanish Indignados movement: "We are going slow because we are going far" (Roos 2011). Of course, the financial industry has the leisure of being the incumbent – indeed, perhaps the most powerful hegemonic system on the planet – yet the question is still posed: What would it mean to shift the temporality of change, to have a radical "slow blockchain" movement?

Centralization and intermediation

The vision for the incorporative blockchain is not, philosophically or practically, fully decentralized. Even leading incorporative blockchain evangelical Blythe Masters recognizes that total decentralization of infrastructure and authority would be "anathema to an industry in which client confidentiality is sacrosanct" (Robinson and Leising 2015). Instead, she advocates what have become known as "private" or "permissioned" blockchains (see Birch et al. 2016). In most proposals for this kind of blockchain, the nodes in the network are not voluntarist miners incentivized by mining cryptographic tokens, but servers maintained by member organizations. The result would be more like the Sabre Global Distribution System (GDS), a universal reservation database used by most major players in the travel industry, than anything imagined in the radical blockchain dream. This will not mean more decentralization; on the contrary, it will likely mean centralized ledgers produced by industry partners.

Incorporative blockchain would therefore be cooperatively produced platforms upon which to compete. Indeed, the payments industry has long been cooperative in many ways. The VISA network is one such site of "coopetition" – cooperation plus competition. It is an interface between merchants and customers who need not have accounts at the same bank (Stearns 2011). It is a functional method of negotiating the tensions between centralization and decentralization in practice. Blockchain technology itself still needs to be developed, but many in the industry note that "the harder work lies elsewhere,

98

in the domains of governance, rules development, regulatory change, back office optimization, and standards development" (Peabody 2016). This is not the work of disintermediation, it is the work of mediation.

The blockchain, then, becomes a site upon which to convene around problems and find solutions. Many interested in industry applications of the blockchain are agnostic about the technology itself. Instead, they are interested in easing "existing pain points" that make their work frustrating, and they are open to potential blockchain-based solutions. One financial technology columnist accounted for interest in blockchain in the following way:

1) It is dumb and bad for reasonably standard market transactions to take 20 days to settle because archaic procedures require market participants to fax each other documents and perform ancient incantations.
2) Market participants should get together and agree on a way to fix that.
3) That way should probably involve computers (Levine 2015).

The goal here is not to disintermediate the financial system but to determine how to be better intermediaries.

These conversations quickly zoom out, away from the specific affordances offered by the blockchain. Talk shifts from "blockchains" to "shared ledgers" to "shared databases" and onto a much larger range of technologies and practices. Soon, instead of talking about their "blockchain strategy," representatives of financial institutions are talking about pre-existing research on methods that accomplish what the blockchain promises. As one engineer told me, "We've been working on secure multi-party computation for a while, and calling it blockchain doesn't make it work any better, but it does make my boss more interested." The blockchain is more useful as rhetorical strategy than technological strategy.

The incorporative blockchain technology is creating an exciting context for the cooperative work of coming together to design a shared infrastructure, set standards, and decide on practice and protocol. As one employee of a major bank who works on a blockchain initiative told me, "Do I think it's going to change the world or even fin tech? I don't know. But it's a really exciting time to do what I do. No one has ever thought that rethinking these processes was interesting. Now it's all over the news."

The incorporative blockchain dream surfaces the infrastructural work of banking, and reorients the locus of excitement away from the trading floor and onto those who build information systems that have long been considered frictional and expected to be seamless and invisible. The embrace of centralization and intermediation offers a provocation to radical blockchain dreamers: *What if, instead of making decentralization and disintermediation goals unto themselves, we imagined what it would be to take seriously the hard work of infrastructural cooperation, of sharing?*

Not autonomy, not automated

Incorporative blockchain projects, by nature, are not autonomous from existing institutions. They are formed out of partnership within and between existing financial services companies. They engage existing regulators, both state and industry. While they sometimes envision using crypto "coins" in the operation of the system, they are not trying to move away from state currencies entirely, if at all. The incorporative blockchain dream doesn't offer social autonomy, nor does it offer personal autonomy predicated on automation. What the incorporative blockchain does offer, however, is a view of demystified automation.

Incorporative blockchain projects do not eschew automation entirely. Unlike radical projects, the goal is to create modernized information tools to confront the complexity of modern finance, not create systems that replace human inputs. There are no radical dreams of autonomy here, no independent "machine economies" or "companies that don't need us."

One representative example of an incorporative blockchain project is Nasdaq Private Market. In 2015, NASDAQ, in partnership with blockchain company Chain, announced this pilot project using blockchain technology to manage shares in private companies (Shin 2015). Historically, the process of managing shares in private companies has been time-consuming and labor intensive. Despite and because of this, documentation often lags behind reality, and as a result, records are often inaccurate. The blockchain method would streamline and automate much of this. Unlike proposals for DAOs, NASDAQ Private Market does imagine blockchain automation as a basis for enacting an entirely new paradigm, but as a more faithful recording device for an already existing complex environment.

Many incorporative blockchain projects focus on the development of "smart contracts," protocols that facilitate and enforce the negotiation of an agreement. Economist Susan Athey, who sits on the board of Ripple Labs, a shared ledger company, explains that the main utilities of smart contracts on a distributed ledger are, first,

100

that they "allow you to write a set of rules" and, second, that those rules would be executed on trusted information infrastructures (Shin 2014). The emphasis is on the work of figuring out how to write the rules, how to do the work of automation.

When automation is a professional rather than utopian practice, it's regarded as craft, as work: *techne*, not *episteme*. This is work for standards engineers, for those whose work involves the boring, bureaucratic labor of creating shared systems of operations and communications. As one consultant to the industry told me, "It's not magic beans, it's just software." At least for now, incorporative blockchain projects are focused not on doing away with work, but on the work of engineering new processes: automation as an interactive tool, managed by people.

Many in the industry are concerned that the blockchain, and automation in general, will empower engineers over MBAs and drive profits from banking to tech firms. This is likely to be true, and it may reflect a larger trend in society toward automation of the tasks performed by lower level employees that is far from unproblematic. But, these incorporative proposals do provoke questions for radical dreamers: What would it mean to imagine a blockchain that does not aim to replace people but is instead an extension of existing relations between people?

Conclusion

The biggest difference between the radical and the incorporative blockchain dreams is that the former has audacious goals to remake society for, as they see it, the better; whereas the latter has no such ambition. Beyond this obvious distinction, the incorporative vision prompts us to ask what a radical blockchain could do if it didn't insist on futurity, if it played a longer, slower game. What if it didn't have to altogether obviate trust between people; that is, if it were not fully decentralized and it didn't have to be autonomistic?

The incorporative blockchain surfaces the work of maintaining the blockchain. This isn't the work of big dreams, it's the work of sorting out the details. Lone geniuses, the Mark Zuckerbergs, Satoshi Nakamotos, and now the Vitalik Buterins, are celebrated for dreaming up new information infrastructures, but we are rarely invited to think about – much less celebrate – the everyday mundane work that maintains these infrastructures day after day.

Scholars of technology and society have called for greater attention

101

to this work of "maintenance" (see, for example, Jackson 2015; Downey 2015; Vinsel 2015). From system administration to regression testing to data cleaning, the information industries are made up of countless positions that are not only kept invisible but routinely dismissed and degraded as mere "friction," an inconvenient bug to be automated, outsourced or wished away. This isn't the veneration of "hard work" and productivity for its own sake. It's a rethinking of IT work as the part of labor that, when allowed to go unnoticed, perpetuates the techno-economic status quo.

I would like to suggest that the invisible work of the development and maintenance of technological systems, by virtue of its invisibility, can be seen as a form of infrastructural care work. As J.K. Gibson-Graham (2008) suggests, if we can learn to see the seamful work in seamless systems, we can glimpse the "diverse economy" in which we are enmeshed, one that includes the capitalist and non-capitalist.

In this way, the incorporative blockchain contains its own radical alterity. What would it mean if the radical blockchain dreamers found inspiration in the hidden cooperation that global capitalism is built on top of, instead of just imagining that market mechanisms work as if by magic? What would it mean for the radical blockchain moment if it were allowed to be boring?

References

Accenture Insights (2016) Are you exploring blockchain technology for your investment bank? Available at: https://www.accenture.com/us-en/insight-perspectives-capital-markets-blockchain

Bauwens, M. (2005) The political economy of peer production. *CTheory.* Available at: http://www.ctheory.net/articles.aspx?id=499

Benkler, Y. (2003) Freedom in the commons: Towards a political economy of information. *Duke Law Journal* 52, 6, 1245–76.

Birch, D.G.W., Brown, R.G. and Parulava, S. (2016) Towards ambient accountability in financial services: Shared ledgers, translucent transactions and the technological legacy of the great financial crisis. *Journal of Payments Strategy and Systems* 10, 2, 118–31.

Burrell, J. (2009) The field site as a network: A strategy for locating ethnographic research. *Field Methods* 21, 2, 181–99.

Buterin, V. (2014a) DAOs are not scary, part 2: Reducing barriers. *Ethereum.* Available at: https://blog.ethereum.org/2014/03/01/daos-are-not-scary-part-2-reducing-barriers/

Buterin, V. (2014b) Launching the ether sale. *Ethereum.* Available at: https://blog.ethereum.org/2014/07/22/launching-the-ether-sale/

Buterin, V. (2015) Superrationality and DAOs. *Ethereum.* Available at: https://blog.ethereum.org/2015/01/23/superrationality-daos/

Castells, M. (2013) *Networks of Outrage and Hope: Social Movements in the Internet Age*. Polity, Cambridge.

De Filippi, P. (2015) From competition to cooperation. *TEDxCambridge*. Available at: https://www.youtube.com/watch?v=aYOPcHRO3tc

Dietz, J. (2015) Swarm manifesto. Available at: https://gist.github.com/fractastical/b658c71573d92ebb9b19

Downey, G.J. (2015) Making media work: Time, space, identity, and labor in the analysis of information and communication infrastructures. In: Gillespie, T., Boczkowski, P.J. and Foot, K.A. (eds) *Media Technologies: Essays on Communication, Materiality, and Society*. MIT Press, Cambridge, MA.

DTCC (2016) *Embracing Disruption: Tapping the Potential of Distributed Ledgers to Improve the Post-Trade Landscape*. Depository Trust and Clearing Corporation, New York.

Duffy, T. (2013) Wall Street is losing the best and the brightest. *Wall Street Journal*, September 29. Available at: http://www.wsj.com/articles/SB10001424127887323623304579059592494840128

Egan, M. (2014) Talent wars: Silicon Valley vs Wall Street. *CNN Money*. Available at: http://money.cnn.com/2014/08/22/investing/wall-street-silicon-valley-talent/

Feder, J. (2016) From competition to cooperation. *Backfeed Magazine*. Available at: http://magazine.backfeed.cc/from-competition-to-cooperation/

Frisby, D. (2016) In proof we trust. *Aeon*. Available at: https://aeon.co/essays/how-blockchain-will-revolutionise-far-more-than-money

Ghalim, Y. (2015) Why we should drop the whole Bitcoin vs blockchain discussion. *Medium*. Available at: https://medium.com/@YacineGhalim/why-we-should-drop-the-whole-bitcoin-vs-blockchain-discussion-e3e38e9a5104#.bghtgxdzy

Gibson-Graham, J.K. (2008) Diverse economies: Performative practices for "other worlds." *Progress in Human Geography* 32, 5, 613–32.

Giddens, A. (1991) *Modernity and Self Identity: Self and Society in the Late Modern Age*. Cambridge University Press, Cambridge.

Gill, R. and Pratt, A. (2008) In the social factory? Immaterial labour, precariousness and cultural work. *Theory, Culture, and Society* 25, 7–8, 1–30.

Greenberg, J. (2015) Wall Street's scrambling to catch up with Silicon Valley. *Wired*. Available at: http://www.wired.com/2015/04/wall-street-silicon-valley-banks-play-catch-up-with-tech-startups/

Hearn, M. (2016) The resolution of the Bitcoin experiment. *Medium*. Available at: https://medium.com/@octskyward/the-resolution-of-the-bitcoin-experiment-dabb30201f7#.xrurew5mw

Isgur, B. (2014) A little altcoin sanity: Namecoin. *Coin Report*. Available at: https://coinreport.net/little-altcoin-sanity-namecoin/

Jackson, S.J. (2015) Rethinking repair. In: Gillespie, T., Boczkowski, P.J. and Foot, K.A. (eds) *Media Technologies: Essays on Communication, Materiality, and Society*. MIT Press, Cambridge, MA.

Kelty, C. (2008) *Two Bits: The Cultural Significance of Free Software*. MIT Press, Cambridge, MA.

Levine, M. (2015) Blockchain for banks probably can't hurt. BloombergView, September 1. Available at: https://www.bloomberg.com/view/articles/2015-09-01/blockchain-for-banks-probably-can-t-hurt

Lotringer, S. and Marazzi, C. (2007) *Autonomia: Post-Political Politics*. Semiotext(e), Cambridge, MA.

103

Lujan, S. (2016) Toward techno-anarchy: Blockchain tech will thwart government, transform society. *Bitcoin.com*. Available at: https://news.bitcoin.com/toward-techno-anarchy-blockchain-tech-will-thwart-government-transform-society/

MacKenzie, D. (2006) *An Engine, Not a Camera*. MIT Press, Cambridge, MA.

McKinsey and Company (2015) Beyond the hype: Blockchains in capital markets. Report. Available at: http://www.mckinsey.com/industries/financial-services/our-insights/beyond-the-hype-blockchains-in-capital-markets

Mainelli, M. and Milne, A. (2016) The impact and potential of blockchain on the securities transaction lifecycle. SWIFT Institute Working Paper No. 2015–007.

Marcus, G. (1995) Ethnography in/of the world system: The emergence of multisited ethnography. *Annual Review of Anthropology* 24, 95–117.

Maurer, B., Nelms, T. and Swartz, L. (2013) When perhaps the real problem is money itself! *Social Semiotics* 23, 2, 261–77.

Merchant, B. (2015) Fully automated luxury communism. *The Guardian*, March 18. Available at: http://www.theguardian.com/sustainable-business/2015/mar/18/fully-automated-luxury-communism-robots-employment

Nakamoto, S. (2008) Bitcoin: A peer-to-peer electronic cash system. Available at: https://bitcoin.org/bitcoin.pdf

O'Dwyer, R. (2015) The revolution will (not) be decentralised: Blockchains. *Common Transition*. Available at: http://commonstransition.org/the-revolution-will-not-be-decentralised-blockchains/

Otar, O. (2015) Mining consolidation: The bitcoin guillotine. *Bitcoin News Channel*, December 20. Available at: http://bitcoinnewschannel.com/2015/12/20/mining-consolidation-the-bitcoin-guillotine/

Pangburn, D. (2015) The humans who dream of companies that don't need us. Fast Company. Available at: http://www.fastcompany.com/3047462/the-humans-who-dream-of-companies-that-wont-need-them

Peabody, G. (2016) What blocks the blockchain? *Payments Views*. Available at: http://paymentsviews.com/2016/04/14/what-blocks-the-blockchain/

Peters, J.D. (1999) *Speaking Into the Air: A History of the Idea of Communication*. Chicago University Press, Chicago, IL.

PYMNTS (2015) Why the corporate banking revolution is a marathon, not a sprint. *PYMNTS*. Available at: http://www.pymnts.com/news/b2b-payments/2016/why-the-corporate-banking-revolution-is-a-marathon-not-a-sprint/

Robinson, E. and Leising, M. (2015) Blythe Masters tells banks the blockchain changes everything. *Bloomberg*. Available at: http://www.bloomberg.com/news/features/2015-09-01/blythe-masters-tells-banks-the-blockchain-changes-everything

Roos, J. (2011) We are going slow because we are going far. *ROAR Magazine*. Available at: https://roarmag.org/essays/marchabruselas-and-antibanks-in-paris-in-pictures/

Rosenberg, S. (2015) There's a blockchain for that! The code that secures Bitcoin could also power an alternate Internet. First, though, it has to work. *Backchannel*. Available at: https://medium.com/backchannel/how-bitcoins-blockchain-could-power-an-alternate-internet-bb501855af67#.mlndtx2pl

Shin, L. (2014) Susan Athey on how digital currency could transform our lives. *Forbes*. Available at: http://www.forbes.com/sites/laurashin/2014/11/24/susan-athey-on-how-digital-currency-could-transform-our-lives/#188df51a79e7

Shin, L. (2015) Nasdaq selects bitcoin startup Chain to run pilot in private market arm. *Forbes*. Available at: http://www.forbes.com/sites/laurashin/2015/06/24/nasdaq-selects-bitcoin-startup-chain-to-run-pilot-in-private-market-arm/#2f766ff252d7

Stafford, P. (2015) Blockchain initiative backed by 9 large investment banks. *Financial Times*. Available at: http://www.ft.com/intl/cms/s/0/f358ed6c-5ae0-11e5-9846-de406ccb37f2.html#axzz3y5HqclYN

Stearns, D. (2011) *Electronic Value Exchange: Origins of the VISA Electronic Payment System*. Springer, New York.

Swan, M. (2015) *Blockchain: Blueprint for a New Economy*. O'Reilly, Sebastopol, CA.

Swarm (2015) The Swarm skeletons. *Medium*. Available at: https://medium.com/@Swarm/meet-the-swarm-skeletons-83fb0627f438#.qkqea774y

Swartz, L. (forthcoming) *What Was Bitcoin?*

Tanzarian, A. (2014) Ethereum raises 3700 BTC in first 12 hours of ether presale. *Coin Telegraph*. Available at: http://cointelegraph.com/news/ethereum-raises-3700-btc-in-first-12-hours-of-ether-presale

Thorp, N. (2015) How society will be transformed by crypto-economics. *Medium*. Available at: https://medium.com/@noahthorp/how-society-will-be-transformed-by-crypto-economics-b02b6765ca8c#.46dy1nf8b

Turner, F. (2009) Burning Man at Google: A cultural infrastructure for new media production. *New Media & Society* 11, 1–2, 73–94.

Vinsel, L. (2015) The maintainers: A call for proposals. Available at: http://leevinsel.com/blog/2015/2/25/the-maintainers-a-call-for-proposals

Volpicelli, G. (2015) Smart contracts sound boring, but they're more disruptive than bitcoin. *Vice*. Available at: http://motherboard.vice.com/read/smart-contracts-sound-boring-but-theyre-more-disruptive-than-bitcoin

Voorhees, E. (2015) It's all about the blockchain. *Money and State*. Available at: http://moneyandstate.com/its-all-about-the-blockchain/

Yuan, L. (2015) Forget bitcoin, long live blockchain. *Medium*. Available at: https://medium.com/@L4yuan/forget-bitcoin-long-live-blockchain-5d4b55efce0b#.uo07vbozn

Chapter 5

Consumer Financial Services in the US: Why Banks May Not Be the Answer

Lisa J. Servon

The consumer financial services system in the US is broken. This system consists of mainstream banks and credit unions, "alternative" check cashers and payday lenders, and informal tools such as rotating savings and credit associations (ROSCAs) and loan sharks. In the last four decades, but particularly since the financial crash, consumer financial services has transformed into a system that no longer serves the needs of the lower and middle classes.

Policy makers and researchers are concerned about the growing numbers of Americans who have no bank account or who use "alternative" financial services (AFS) such as check cashers and payday lenders. In 2014, the FDIC reported that 17 million Americans are "unbanked" (they have no bank account) and another 43 million are "underbanked" (they have bank accounts but continue to rely on alternative financial services) (Burhouse and Osaki 2012). The numbers are more stark in low-income areas, and among racial and ethnic minorities (Cover et al. 2011). As many as 28.2 percent of low-income families (making less than $15,000) are unbanked and 21.6 percent are underbanked (Barr and Blank 2009). Black, Hispanic, and households of foreign-born non-citizens are also disproportionately underbanked. Only 48.7 percent of Hispanic households are fully banked; this figure falls to 45.8 percent in households of foreign-born non-citizens, and to 41.6 percent in Black households (Burhouse and Osaki 2012).

Policy makers and researchers have set up false dichotomies between the banked and the unbanked, and the financially "included" and "excluded." These frames are misleading. Labeling people as "banked," "underbanked," or "unbanked" presumes that relying exclusively on banks is the desired norm and that anything else is inferior. Similarly, the term "financial exclusion" assumes that people who do not have a bank account have no access to financial services. As this chapter demonstrates, these people are very much a part of the financial services system, sometimes by choice, sometimes because mainstream institutions fail to meet their needs, and sometimes because they are actively excluded.

These debates also ignore the interconnections between the different types of financial services providers and how they rely on each other to make their profits. Existing policy efforts tend to try to move the unbanked and underbanked to the banked category without a thorough understanding of the context in which they are making financial decisions and the viable options that are available to them (see, for example, the BankOn programs that began in San Francisco in 2006 and currently exist in 76 cities).

The purpose of this chapter is to tell the story of how the consumer financial services system became so dysfunctional and to show that key myths we hold about how low- and moderate-income people make financial decisions are incorrect. I discuss the three trends that have led to the current situation: (1) changes in bank practices and in policy relating to banks; (2) Americans' increasing financial instability; and (3) over-reliance on credit. Given this context, I will then show why it makes sense that so many people are turning to alternative financial services in greater numbers. Using data from participant observation and over 100 interviews, I will debunk four prevalent myths about the alternative financial services industry: (1) everyone needs a bank account; (2) people use alternative financial services because they lack financial literacy; (3) more regulation of alternative financial services will solve the problem; and (4) people who use alternative financial services don't save.

Methodology

This chapter relies on a deep literature and policy review that informed the sections on the trends underlying the dysfunctional financial services landscape. I also spent hundreds of hours embedded as a teller at RiteCheck, a check casher in the South Bronx, and as a teller and loan collector at Check Center in downtown Oakland, California. After working at each of these businesses, I interviewed 50 customers at each store. For one month, I volunteered as a staffer on a hotline for people having difficulty repaying their payday loans. I conducted a range of interviews with experts on banking and alternative financial services, policy makers at the Consumer Finance Protection Bureau and the FDIC, relevant researchers, the head of a subprime credit bureau, and consumer advocates. I attended local and national trade association meetings of check cashers and payday lenders, and conferences run by the Center for Financial Services Innovation.

My use of ethnographic and other qualitative methods allowed me to get as close to the issues I wanted to understand as I possibly could. By inhabiting a neighborhood-based financial institution that serves a largely banked/unbanked population, I was able to better understand the reasoning behind consumers' financial decisions. Spending a large amount of time in the neighborhood also enabled me to build trust and to get to know other ways in which people met their financial needs.

The three trends underlying the dysfunctional financial services landscape

Policy makers tend to decry the large numbers of unbanked and underbanked people, moving directly from the FDIC statistics to interventions that move people into bank accounts. This process misses the necessary step of analyzing a larger set of possible reasons that have led to the current situation. I found three trends that have taken place during the same period in which the alternative financial services component of the consumer financial services industry has grown: (1) changes in banking policy and practices; (2) greater reliance on credit; and (3) increasing financial insecurity.

Changes in banking policy and practices

Debates about the dangers of overly large banks have been going on since at least 1912, when then Democratic Party presidential candidate Woodrow Wilson wrote:

> The great monopoly of this country is the money monopoly. So long as that exists our old variety and freedom and individual energy of development are out of the question. A great industrial nation is controlled by its system of credit. Our system of credit is concentrated. The growth of the nation, therefore, and all our activities are in the hands of a few men, who, even if their action be honest and intended for the public interest, are necessarily concentrated upon the great undertakings in which their own money is involved and who necessarily, by very reason

of their own limitations, chill and check and destroy genuine economic freedom. (Wilson 1912)

The term "too big to fail" was actually coined in 1984 and was used to justify the government bailout of Continental Illinois, the nation's seventh largest bank, shortly after the branching bans began to be lifted and 24 years before the most recent financial crisis that made it a commonplace catchphrase (Haltom 2013). Congressman Stewart McKinney used the term in a Congressional hearing discussing the FDIC's decision to bail out Continental Illinois, the largest bank failure in US history. Between 1993 and 1997, 2,829 banks were obtained through merger or acquisition. Power became increasingly concentrated in a small number of banks.

Over and over, for more than a century, we've heard that banks are too big, and that they don't have our best interests at the center of their decision-making. The situation has only worsened since then. When Washington Mutual went under during the financial crisis in 2008, the bank was seven times larger than Continental Illinois had been. The four biggest banks collectively hold about half of total US bank assets, a total of $6.8 trillion (Schaefer 2014). The largest banks are enormous. Ellen Seidman, a Senior Fellow at the Urban Institute who has worked for decades in financial regulation told me, "I don't think you'll find a [bank] regulator . . . who thinks they are governable or regulable."

The unchecked growth of banks is hardly the only factor that created the situation we're in now. To understand what has happened, we need to go back to the beginning of the last century.

Early concern about harmful bank practices led policy makers to pass the Unfair or Deceptive Acts and Practices legislation in 1914 as a component of the Federal Trade Commission Act. These laws were reinforced by the passage of the Truth in Lending and Truth in Savings Acts in 1968 and 1991, respectively. These laws require that creditors disclose the costs and terms of credit and require that advertisements not be misleading or inaccurate, or misrepresent an institution's deposit contract (FDIC 2004). A second A, for Abusive, was added to the acronym in July 2010 when the Dodd–Frank Act was passed. Although it responded to real problems and was well-intentioned, UDAAP regulations differ from state to state, and are up to judges' interpretation of the terms "abusive" and "deceptive." The law has rarely been invoked since the passage of Dodd–Frank.

The Great Crash of 1929 intensified the focus on consumers. Policy makers responded to the crash by trying to ensure that what happened in 1929 couldn't happen again. The crash devastated so many families that it drove the next 40 years of bank legislation.

Between 1933 and the late 1960s, almost no new federal banking policy was made, and bankers and regulators acted cautiously within the newly growing economic landscape. Between 1941 and 1964, the number of bank failures nationwide was negligible – for context, only one Federal Reserve member bank in the Seventh District (serving Chicago and the Upper Midwest) failed during those years (Federal Reserve Bank of Chicago n.d.). In the mid-1960s the political climate again changed. The policy that's relevant to our story was made in the 1960s, when the intense activism we associate with that era caused Americans to reexamine a whole range of businesses, practices, and norms. A young Ralph Nader made a big splash with his 1965 book *Unsafe at Any Speed*, an exposé about the auto industry. The civil rights movement and the women's movement had gathered steam, and both movements converged on financial issues. In 1961, the US Commission on Civil Rights found that African-American borrowers were often required to make higher downpayments on homes and other major credit-based purchases, and pay off loans faster than whites (Westgate 2011: 382). Still, discrimination persisted. In urban neighborhoods, activists organized "bank-ins," to protest credit discrimination and bring attention to the problem, both to decision-makers at the bank and community members on the whole.

A spate of new federal banking legislation – the first that had been passed in over 30 years – was passed. The Truth in Lending Act (TILA), passed in 1968, the 1970 Fair Credit Reporting Act, and the Equal Credit Opportunity Act (ECOA) of 1974 all aimed to level the playing field for people seeking all kinds of loans. TILA required that banks disclose key information – annual percentage rate (APR), complete loan terms, cost – before extending credit. The Fair Credit Reporting Act regulated collection of credit information and access to credit reports in order to ensure fairness, accuracy, and privacy of the personal information kept by credit reporting agencies. And ECOA focused on discrimination, making it illegal to deny credit on the basis of "race, color, religion, national origin, sex or marital status, or age ... or because all or part of the applicant's income derives from any public assistance program" (15 USC § 1691). Together, these three pieces of legislation demonstrated a new commitment to consumer protection by mandating greater transparency on the part of banks. Some states also took the initiative to mitigate discriminatory lending practices. In 1964, California passed legislation requiring

110

state-chartered savings and loans to submit certain lending data to the Commissioner.

Since before the Great Depression, federal and state banking regulation aimed to limit branch banking. The passage of the McFadden Act of 1927 prohibited interstate branch banking in the United States. Some states passed laws further regulating intrastate savings and loan (S&L) branch banking. For a century, all branch banking was prohibited in Illinois, beginning with the passage of the State Constitution of 1870, which specifically prohibited branch banking, until a 1983 state law repealed branching restrictions.

Similarly, until 1982, Pennsylvania banks were allowed to branch only in the county where their head offices were located and in contiguous counties (Jayaratne and Strahan 1999). A number of other states also severely restricted intrastate branching before 1985, but relaxed or eliminated these regulations by 1991, including Kansas, Montana, Nebraska, Oklahoma, Texas, and Wyoming. Only Colorado, Minnesota, and North Dakota made no changes to the restrictiveness of their state branching regulations during those years. Other states restricted branching based on town population: New York and Oregon prohibited branching when the town population was less than 50,000 people. New Hampshire prohibited branching in towns with populations of less than 2,500 people, but only if there was another bank within the town. Hawaii restricted branching within Honolulu (Calem 1994).

States enacted restrictive bank legislation in order to limit the power of banks, due to concern that if banks became too big they would gain too much political and economic power. Many customers feared that deposits made in small towns would be siphoned to make loans in the state's larger financial centers, leaving small businesses and local communities without adequate available capital. Branching restrictions were also intended to protect banks from excessive competition from bigger banks (Rice and Davis 2007).

In 1977, the passage of the Community Reinvestment Act (CRA) facilitated the growth of bank branching. The CRA sought redress to the severe shortage of available credit in lower-income neighborhoods and, in states without severe restrictions on branching, S&Ls were incentivized to locate in underserved areas. The effects of this legislation happened in tandem with the easing of regulations restricting branching on the state level. Fifteen states passed legislation allowing branching between 1970 and 1985, as did another dozen by 1989. Although the idea behind the CRA was to make financial services more accessible in low-income communities and communities of

111

color, the branches that resulted did not have the same knowledge of the local communities as independent banks did. Community connected banks and relationship banking was no longer the norm in most states by 1990.

The Riegle–Neal Interstate Banking and Branching Efficiency Act of 1994 permitted interstate bank branching, and represented a turning point in banking regulation. By allowing interstate branching, it allowed larger banks to easily grow bigger, often by buying single branch and small banks in large metropolitan areas, particularly those that spanned state lines, such as the Washington DC metropolitan area.

Following deregulation in the 1980s, the number of S&Ls fell sharply as larger banks bought out smaller banks, and a number of smaller thrifts closed, unable to keep pace with growing competition. Between 1986 and 1995, the Federal Savings and Loan Insurance Corporation (FSLIC) and the Resolution Trust Corporation (RTC) closed 1,043 thrift institutions, approximately half of the total number in the US.

In December 2010, *The New York Times* Dealbook reported that there were 734 thrift institutions operational in the US (Protess 2010). This dramatic drop in the number of thrifts over the last few decades means that individual consumers have many fewer choices in where they can bank, which creates less incentive for banks to compete to best service customers. By 1999, virtually all of the protections that had been created following the Great Crash had been eliminated. Congress passed the Financial Services Modernization Act, known as Gramm–Leach–Bliley, that year, allowing banks to engage in both commercial and investment activities. Once again, depositors were left unprotected from the consequences of banks' high-risk investment strategies.

We all know what happened next. In September 2008, Lehman Brothers collapsed, sending panic through the stock market and threatening to bring down the world's financial system, and creating a "credit crunch" as taxpayer-financed bailouts held up the limping finance industry (The Economist 2013). The crisis was brought on by irresponsible mortgage lending to subprime borrowers – primarily people with poor credit history who struggled to repay their loans. The risky mortgages were bundled in supposedly low-risk securities by financial engineers at big banks, while in fact these weak mortgages retained their risk. Banks used finance instruments in unsafe ways, betting against themselves and creating a vulnerable financial environment. But regulators like the Fed also were to blame; by failing to exercise sufficient oversight, they allowed the Lehman Brothers collapse to happen, leading to the downward spiral that caused the largest economic downturn since the Great Depression.

Commercial banks still see service to consumers as a poor stepchild, secondary to their core business. With the expansion allowed by deregulation, they have branched out (literally) to the depository and loan services previously provided by community-based thrifts, but because the profit returns from these services are much smaller, retail banking is not treated as a priority by the nation's largest banks.

There is a connection between the lack of quality, affordable financial products and the "too big to fail" mentality. There are currently 6,900 banking institutions in the US and ten of them hold 80 percent of total deposits (Hryndza 2014). As banks have grown larger and their numbers have dwindled, they have become less and less responsive to the needs of consumers. Big banks have focused on profit at the expense of their customers. Perhaps not surprisingly, the alternative financial services industry has grown significantly during the same period that banks have consolidated and become more expensive to use.

Greater reliance on credit

Over the past several decades, Americans have relied increasingly on credit. Low interest rates and easy access to credit made credit cards a simple option for people experiencing financial stress. In 1983, only 43 percent of US households had a MasterCard, Visa, or some other general purpose credit card. By 1995, that number had risen to 66 percent. As of 2010, 68 percent of families had one or more credit cards. That means roughly 152 million consumers (two-thirds of adults above age 18) were holding 520 million credit cards in 2010 (Canner and Elliehausen 2013).

Credit card companies also sought new markets with aggressive marketing, eventually targeting riskier customer segments. In 2005, credit card companies sent nearly six million pre-screened solicitations to consumers, or 20 solicitations for every man, woman, and child in the US. As companies' tactics changed, so did the mix of cardholders. In 1995, cardholders were more likely to be single, to rent instead of own their homes, and to have less seniority at work than they were in 1989. These new borrowers were riskier than previous cardholders. They had a substantially higher debt-to-income ratio, which meant that even small drops in income could lead to financial distress. New borrowers were also more likely to work in unskilled jobs with wages dependent on the business cycle.

One means of evaluating the composition of credit card borrowers is to look at those who were targeted with credit card solicitations. According to an analysis by the Federal Reserve, about 63 percent of individuals received credit card solicitations in 2007. This rate dropped to 27 percent by 2009. Individuals with credit scores in the lowest quartile (who pose a higher risk of default) received about 11 percent of credit card mailings in 2007. By 2009, that number had dropped to only 2 percent (Canner and Elliehausen 2013).

Credit card companies raised credit limits in the period leading to the Great Recession also. The median available credit per card increased about $900, or about one-third, and the median outstanding balance rose from $1,100 in 1989 to about $1,700 in 1995. In 2010, most families that held credit card debt owed relatively stable amounts. The median owed by families carrying debt was $2,600. However, the average amount owed by US households in general is significantly higher at $7,100 (Canner and Elliehausen 2013). When considering only those families who are in debt, average household debt is $15,224 (Federal Reserve Board 2014).

The cost of using credit cards has also risen, and policy has abetted rising costs. Consumer debt has grown along with the deregulation of the credit card industry beginning with the 1978 Supreme Court ruling of *Marquette v. First Omaha Savings Corp.*, which virtually eliminated interest rates on credit cards. In 1996, the *Smiley v. Citibank* decision did the same for credit card fees, allowing them to be determined by the lender's home state. Prior to this decision, credit card late fees averaged $16; in 2007 the average late fee was $34 (Garcia 2007).

One of the most significant impacts of the Great Recession was a change in the way consumers managed payments. As more consumers faced financial constraints and made difficult choices, many chose to prioritize their credit card payments over their mortgages; they needed the liquidity to make ends meet (Vornovytskyy et al. 2011; TransUnion 2014). The credit card industry abetted this trend; low interest rates and easy access to credit fueled an increase in credit card debt that peaked in January 2009, six months into the financial crisis (Garcia 2007; Canner and Elliehausen 2013).

In the aftermath of the financial crisis, the use of credit cards has declined as banks tightened lending standards; less credit was available to consumers as they lost their jobs (and income). Between 2000 and 2011, households became less likely to hold credit card debt. In

2000, 51 percent of households held credit card debt. In 2011, the percentage had decreased to 38 percent (Vornovytskyy et al. 2011). Twenty-nine percent of Americans don't own any credit cards, the highest proportion since 2001, and those holding credit cards have 3.7 cards, down from 4 in April 2001.

These changes have occurred because of a combination of changes in policy and practice by lenders, not solely because of changes in consumers' behavior. In some cases, frugal borrowers paid off their outstanding balances. In other cases, as consumers struggled to make payments, credit card companies experienced a rise in delinquencies and charge-offs. Card issuers responded to these conditions by changing the terms offered on credit cards, the amount of credit offered to borrowers and the strategies used to market their products (Garcia 2007; Canner and Elliehausen 2013; Athreya et al. 2014).

These changing dynamics of the credit card industry are one reason that an increasing number of consumers turn to payday loans. These loans are perhaps the most hotly debated topic in the area of consumer financial services. It used to be that you could walk into a bank and get a $500 loan with just a signature. If you were white, at least. Greg Fairchild, professor of management at UVA, told me his father called those loans "white man's loans." Now, no matter what your race or gender, those days are gone. Payday lending is a $90 billion industry; there are more payday lending stores than there are McDonald's and Starbucks combined (Graves and Peterson 2008).

The contraction of credit has also caused people to juggle their available credit and to use payday loans in ways that seem counterintuitive without complete knowledge of individuals' situations. Some of the people getting payday loans also had credit cards on which there was still available credit. It would seem that they should use the credit cards before getting a payday loan, right? Not necessarily. Tim Ranney relays a conversation he had with the head of risk for a major credit card company who asked him, "Why are people taking out loans instead of using their cards?" Ranney told me, "This guy was implying that these people weren't smart enough to make the 'right' decision. I laughed in his face. 'They're protecting the card!' I told him. People don't want to use their last available credit line." In these cases, the credit card is the safety net. Whereas failure to repay a payday loan won't affect a consumer's credit score, failure to repay a credit card will.

In order to truly understand the problem of reliance on credit, it is necessary to analyze what consumers are using credit for. When we do this, we see an increase in the number of people using credit cards to pay for basic needs. In 2006, one out of three families reported using credit cards to pay for basic necessities such as rent or mortgage, groceries, utilities, or insurance (Garcia and Draut 2009). Across the board, people are substituting credit for income, a strategy that is unsustainable. And, as credit has become more difficult to obtain, consumers have turned increasingly to expensive forms of small dollar credit, such as payday loans.

Widespread financial uncertainty

The changes in banks and credit cards discussed above have led to changes in the context in which we make financial decisions. During the same period that banks became more expensive to use and the use of credit expanded, conditions for American workers declined. Despite decades of increased productivity, the typical American family has experienced a steady decline in inflation-adjusted income since 1972 (Garcia and Draut 2009). Between 2000 and 2004, people at all income levels experienced a decline. The hardest hit were those in the lowest 20th percentile, whose wages effectively decreased 1.5 percent (Garcia 2007). Minimum wage workers are older and more educated than they used to be (Cooper and Hall 2013).

Declining wages have combined with a rising cost of living to make Americans' financial situations even more precarious. Between 1984 and 2004, the cost of living has increased 90 percent due to the rising costs of healthcare, housing, and transportation (Dēmos 2007; Garcia 2007). Income volatility doubled between 1973 and 2004 (Hacker and Jacobs 2008). The average cost of higher education – a key indicator of future financial mobility – increased by 165 percent (in 2005 dollars) between 1970 and 2005. In the ten-year period between the 2003–4 and 2013–14 school years, prices for undergraduate tuition, room and board increased 34 percent at public universities and 25 percent at private schools (US Department of Education 2016). In addition, childcare is now a significant expense for families, whereas it was virtually non-existent as an expense as recently as a generation ago (Garcia 2007).

As a result of this squeeze between decreasing income and increasing cost of living, many people have begun to substitute credit for income, an unsustainable strategy (TransUnion 2014). Starting around 2000, many households began to use credit cards to cover basic expenses after first liquidating their savings and draining equity from their homes (Garcia 2007). Andrew Ross coined the term "creditocracy" to describe the current situation, one that emerges when the cost of goods, regardless of how staple, has to be debt financed and when indebtedness becomes the precondition for meeting basic needs.

Fifteen percent of Americans had poor credit scores (300–599) prior to the recession. By 2010, more than 25 percent were in this category (Whitehouse 2010). This change, combined with the contraction of credit discussed above, means that Americans are increasingly turning to expensive sources of credit such as payday loans and auto title loans. Although the research about whether these sources of small dollar credit are helpful or harmful to consumers, it is clear from the surge in usage of these loans and the reasons consumers cite for using them that financial insecurity has reached a crisis point.

Findings

The combination of these three trends correlates highly with the increase in the use of alternative financial services (AFS). Policy makers continue to push consumers to use banks instead of alternative financial services, but they rely on false assumptions about the differences between mainstream and alternative financial services businesses and the people who use them. Policy also fails to incorporate an understanding of the changing environment as laid out above.

The research for this section of the paper focuses on the time I spent embedded as a teller, loan collector, and hotline staffer, and on the interviews my research assistant and I conducted with over 100 customers of the businesses where I worked. This research enabled me to challenge four myths about what policy makers and researchers call "financial inclusion." The first myth is that everyone needs a bank account. The second is that financial literacy would lead most people to make different (read *better*) decisions. The third myth is that the problem lies with the providers of alternative financial services, as opposed to the mainstream banks or broader systemic factors. And the fourth is that people who use alternative financial services lack mechanisms for saving. These myths and the stories we tell about the people who use AFS are detached from actual people's lives, and lead us to believe that the problem is confined to a small, marginal group, when in reality it is an enormous problem that affects us all.

Myth #1: Everyone needs a bank account

The agenda of the FDIC is to move the unbanked and the underbanked to bank accounts. The underlying assumption is that these

117

Americans are underserved and that banks are the appropriate route to the "financial mainstream." However, the FDIC's arguments lack recognition of the complexity of the situation. The agency's economicinclusion.gov website, for example, highlights only the downside of check cashers and payday lenders, and only the benefits of banking. A growing number of people do not have enough money to enjoy these benefits.

When I interviewed RiteCheck and Check Center customers about why they chose to frequent these businesses, they cited three reasons: cost, transparency, and service.

Policy makers, consumer advocates, and the media criticize check cashers for their high fees (Fox and Woodhall 2006; Choi 2011). However, when I asked customers why they used a check casher instead of a bank, they often told me that they found banks to be too expensive. Zeke, a RiteCheck customer I interviewed, told me that he had had a bank account in the past but that he had closed it after losing his job. "I'd like to go back, but I can't afford the monthly charges," he said. Zeke has been a RiteCheck customer for two years. Maria left her bank for the same reason. "The fees were just ridiculous!" she said.

Indeed, banks have become more expensive, and the increases in charges relate directly to the changes in policy discussed above. Policy, starting with Glass–Steagall, has attempted to keep banks from engaging in the kind of risky behavior that led to the Great Crash of 1929 and the 2008 financial crisis. Legislators have also required banks to serve the entire public without discriminating. Invariably, restrictions on banks in one area have led them to increase fees and rates in another.

The Community Reinvestment Act (CRA), discussed above, provides just one example of this dynamic. CRA was intended to combat redlining by requiring banks to provide banking and credit services to all communities. The law essentially grafted consumer services onto a system that had pulled away from consumers. CRA prohibited banks from engaging in other, more profitable services, such as mergers and acquisitions, unless regulators determined that the bank was in compliance with the law. Unfortunately, the law has never had very sharp teeth. It did incentivize banks to open branches in low- and moderate-income areas, but these branches were not always profitable; the customers in these neighborhoods have less money to save and invest than their wealthier counterparts, and checking accounts – a staple product for most consumers – do not make enough money for banks.

Banks therefore began to charge more for their services. They instituted a range of new fees and raised existing charges on everything from ATM withdrawals, which more than doubled between 1998 and 2011, to wire payments, debit card replacements and paper statements. The availability of free, non-interest bearing checking accounts decreased from 76 percent in 2009 to only 39 percent in 2011, and the average monthly service fee on checking accounts increased 25 percent in one year alone, from 2010 to 2011 (Bankrate, Inc. 2012).

Trust and relationships are another key reason people choose to use check cashers. Banking has grown increasingly depersonalized. Technology has abetted changes in the way we bank, and these changes have lowered costs for banks. While banking has become less relationship oriented, check cashers have maintained this focus on the customer. I experienced this when I worked behind the teller window, and the customers I interviewed also told me stories about the service they had received.

Nina, who has lived most of her life in the Mott Haven section of the South Bronx, where the store I worked in is located, told me that her mother had been very ill and that the RiteCheck staff had called to ask about her. "So we can be family," Nina said. "We know all of them."

Being a regular at a check casher also brings more tangible benefits. Marta, another regular, came to my window one afternoon with a government-issued disability check to cash. When I input her information into my computer, a message popped up indicating that Marta, a middle-aged Puerto Rican woman, owed RiteCheck $20 on every check she cashed. It turned out that Marta had recently cashed a bad check. Rather than charging her an overdraft fee or closing her account, as a bank might, RiteCheck had worked out a plan for her to pay back what she owed in $20 installments. On that particular day, Marta told me, she could not afford to pay the $20; she needed her entire check to cover an unexpected expense. We allowed her to cash her check and keep the entire amount (minus the regular fee).

Many customers also told me that a lack of transparency at banks contributed to the costs they incurred; they found it difficult to predict when and what they would be charged. Banks are required to provide customers with disclosure agreements when they open a checking account. These agreements, on average, are 111 pages long, and the language is difficult to penetrate. The date on which monthly fees can be withdrawn is subject to change. Customers who are living close to the financial edge, a category that is increasing, need transparency. Check cashers also have very clear and easy to read signage, as opposed to banks, which have virtually no signage. Consumers who are not familiar with banks have difficulty understanding what they can do in banks and what it will cost. Walking into a check casher feels more like walking into a fast food restaurant. Every service available is posted in large font on signs that span the top of the teller windows, along with its price.

Myth #2: People use AFS because they lack financial literacy

Policy makers believe that people would make different choices about how they manage their finances if they had better information. What became more apparent to me as I worked in these businesses was that people lack good options more than they lack financial literacy. Many of the people I interviewed paid a high price to get their money or to borrow money because they had no alternative.

Many of the payday borrowers I interviewed knew that they would be unable to pay their loans back on time, but they saw no other way out of the situations they found themselves in. Azlinah, one of my fellow tellers in Oakland, took out five loans ranging from $55 to $255 each when her car broke down and she needed it both to get to work and to take her young daughter to daycare. The loans cost $15 for every $100 borrowed; all were due on the date of her next paycheck. Azlinah, a 22-year-old single mother, took the bus for a few weeks, but found it impossible to get to work and daycare on time. When the due date came, Azlinah could not repay the loans; she needed every dollar of her paycheck to pay the rent and utilities, and to buy food. So she paid the loans back and immediately took out others, paying a whole new set of fees and effectively extending the length of the loans. When the lenders tried to withdraw what she owed from her checking account, her account didn't have enough money to pay out, and she was hit with overdraft fees that quickly mounted to $300. Suddenly, her debt had skyrocketed.

As a teller, Azlinah understood that these loans can be problematic. Day after day she deals with customers who pay off their loans and immediately take out another. "I know it's bad," she told me. "I knew what a payday loan was."

Working as a teller and a counselor, I learned that the customers I served often paid high prices for their money because they needed every penny they could get as soon as it became available to them. Banks routinely hold checks for several days until they clear, while check cashers enable customers to get their money (minus a fee) immediately. Joe Coleman, president of RiteCheck, told me that

120

his customers would rather pay a flat fee that they understand than get hit with unexpected charges and overdraft fees at a bank. He explained that people trust his tellers and continue to return because they find RiteCheck to be less expensive than the local bank, and because they value the transparency, the convenience, and the service they receive: "Let's say a customer gets paid on Friday. If he brings his check to us, he gets his money immediately. He can pay his bills right away, go food shopping over the weekend. If he goes to the bank, his check won't clear until sometime the next week. He'll be late on his bills. And if he writes a check and it hits his account before the check he deposited clears, he'll be hit with an overdraft fee for more than $30 – much more than the fee he would have paid us."

Michelle, a young RiteCheck regular, came to my window one morning to withdraw money from her Electronic Benefits Transfer (EBT) card. The New York State Office of Temporary and Disability Assistance (OTDA) delivers cash and Supplemental Nutrition Assistance Program (SNAP) benefits on these cards. The state deposits benefits into an electronic account that recipients can access by swiping a card at an ATM or a terminal like the one I used at RiteCheck. RiteCheck charges a $2 flat fee for any withdrawal regardless of the amount. Michelle asked me to withdraw $10 from her account; she would get $8 back and pay what amounted to a 20 percent fee. Even though EBT recipients are allowed two free withdrawals each month from certain ATM machines, these machines only dispense money in certain amounts. Most machines have a minimum withdrawal of $20.

The majority of EBT customers I worked with and talked to needed every dollar they could access as soon as it became available to them. This behavior is logical; it is also expensive. Michelle needed that $8 right then; she could not wait to accumulate enough money in her EBT account to be able to pay a lower price per dollar. This is the same dynamic that results in people paying high prices in local delis rather than shopping at discount stores that require buying in bulk. A well-paid job, a steady car, and space to store bulk goods means that spending $200 at once can save money over the long term. The benefits of bulk shopping, like the benefits of banking, are not equally available to everyone.

Working people increasingly need this kind of liquidity also. Carlos came into RiteCheck often to cash checks of several hundred to a few thousand dollars for his small contracting business. One Thursday afternoon he came through the door dressed in work clothes and passed a $5,000 check through my window. I scanned the check, counted out his money, and slid the $4,902.50 through the window. The $97.50 fee – 1.95 percent of the face value of the check – is regulated by state law. New York, which is one of the most highly regulated states, has one of the lowest fees in the country.

There are at least two different reasons why Carlos would pay nearly $100 to get his cash quickly. If he is like many contractors operating in New York City, he relies at least in part on undocumented workers, who are unlikely to have bank accounts. If Carlos had deposited his check into a bank, it would have taken too long to clear for him to have paid his workers on time. Another possibility is that Carlos was hired to do a job that needed to be started quickly. In that case, he would need the cash in order to purchase materials. Michelle's and Carlos's stories illustrate that they did not make irrational decisions and that more financial literacy likely would not have changed what they did. This does not mean that alternative financial services work perfectly for the people who use them; for many people, though, they make more sense than banks.

Myth #3: Alternative financial services providers are to blame for the problems of the "unbanked" and "underbanked"

Consumer advocates and policy makers believe that the alternative financial services industry is driving the problem of financial exclusion. Researchers, financial regulators, and the media use words like sleazy, predatory, and abusive to describe check cashers and payday lenders (Noah 2010; Montezemolo 2013; Johnson 2014). As a result, solutions to the problem of "financial exclusion" have focused on further regulating these businesses or making them completely illegal. Although additional regulation is likely warranted, regulation will not eliminate demand. Policy recommendations need to focus on the nature of demand – on the conditions that lead people to seek these products and services. The increasing demand stems from the trends outlined earlier in this paper.

During the time I worked as a credit counselor, I talked to Jeannine, a woman in her thirties who moved to Virginia from Pennsylvania after losing her job. Jeannine quickly found a new job but she had to wait a month before receiving her first paycheck, and she needed money to secure an apartment and cover her moving expenses. She turned to payday loans to get her through the transition. Another hotline caller, Mae, took out a loan to move her mother from a "horrific" nursing home to a better one. "I knew I couldn't handle the debt," she told me, "but I couldn't leave my mother in that place. I would do anything to help my mother. Wouldn't you?" Both Jeannine and Mae soon found themselves with debt they could not handle, but it is hard to argue that they made poor decisions given their circumstances.

Myth #4: People who use AFS don't have good ways to save

The fourth myth about check cashers and payday lenders is that they inhibit savings. Savings is clearly a problem in the US. The US has one of the lowest savings rates among all developed countries. In the first quarter of 2013, the personal savings rate was 2.6 percent, down from 5.5 percent in 2009 and 3.9 percent in 2012. In comparison, in 2012, the savings rate in France was 12.3 percent, Germany was at 10.5 percent, and Sweden was at 10 percent (Kramer 2013).

It is true that check cashers and payday lenders do not take deposits; given the way they are regulated, they cannot. A few, like RiteCheck, have figured out a way around this problem. RiteCheck partners with a local credit union, Bethex FCU, to offer customers a seamless way to save. RiteCheck customers can open a Bethex account and deposit money into that account at any RiteCheck store. Many of my interviewees also told me they did not trust banks with their money. Some participate in rotating savings and credit associations – ROSCAs – informal groups that are often rooted in immigrant communities. Others save at home. Mike, a regular RiteCheck customer, told me he had a bank account but closed it because he does not like banks. He does save, however, and described his savings process like this: "You gotta put pressure. You say this is what I'm going to spend for the month, and this is what I'm going to put away, even if it's a hundred dollars. You make sure you don't touch those hundred dollars. That's the key." When I asked Mike where he saved, he said "I put it in a drawer. Put it in the closet and I don't touch it, and it doesn't bother me because I budget everything else. Once I budget everything else, then it all adds up."

Many of the people we met who use ROSCAs earmark this money for building assets. Carmen is using the money she saves in a tanda to build a home for her mother in Honduras; it will be completed this year. Maribel uses the tanda to pay her tuition at a local community college. Even though she has had to provide for her two younger siblings since their mother was deported to Mexico several years ago, Maribel has been able to avoid student loans. She studies early childhood education and plans to get her BA next and then her master's degree at Columbia. She works part-time at a daycare center on

Manhattan's Upper East Side and goes to school in the evening. She beams when she tells us her younger brother is in college, and that her sister will be starting this fall.

Conclusion

The dysfunction that characterizes the consumer financial services industry is the product of decades of policy and practice and it will not be changed overnight. Creating an atmosphere that once again delivers on the social contract Americans can count on to reward their work and give them the confidence and resources to invest in themselves and their families will require significant changes in the public and private sectors. It also calls for collective, grassroots action. It requires a movement.

Policy makers must reframe the conversation based on a better, more complete understanding of what consumers actually do and why they do it. The policy conversation about "financial inclusion" needs to extend beyond banks, payday lenders and check cashers to informal practices and new products that don't fit neatly into the old categories. Further, any regulation of consumer financial services must be accompanied by policy that reverses the decline in real wages and addresses increasingly entrenched income inequality.

Fix the regulation. The alphabet soup of current bank regulation is opaque, confusing, and may be inhibiting innovation. Change has been incremental, and the result is a patchwork quilt of policy that is difficult to understand.

When banks are evaluated to determine whether they're serving consumers well, the process generally consists of regulators doing a lot of box-checking. The problem is that checklists often fail when we really want to know the answer to questions like, "Is this practice fair?" and "Would I sell this product to my mother?"

Make it easier for consumers to get quality information. Financial decision-making is wrapped in a veil of mystery, and the topic of personal finances triggers a range of emotions in us, the majority of them unpleasant. Suze Orman has built her career by recognizing how deeply past experience and perceptions of self-esteem shape the way we deal with our money. Typing the term "Money Shame" into Google yields 164 million results.

The consumer financial services industry is much more complex than it used to be. This is good news and bad news. The good news is that I should be able to find a credit card that meets my needs and a

124

budgeting tool to help me keep track of my spending. The bad news is that it's incredibly difficult to wade through the information available in order to make decisions, and to figure out which information is reliable. Montel Williams is the celebrity spokesperson for Money Mutual, a payday lender. He also has close to 78,000 Twitter followers. Nerd Wallet has 11,000 followers. If I'm a Montel Williams fan and I've never heard of Nerd Wallet, whom do I trust?

Make work pay. This recommendation has nothing to do with consumer financial services, at least on the surface. But the market, in the form of alternative financial services, is responding to the condition consumers find themselves in. Declining wages, escalating costs of education, healthcare, and childcare, and extreme income volatility have combined to create a triple whammy that lies at the root of the crisis in consumer financial services. When we focus solely on rules and regulations, we are treating only the symptoms of the problem rather than working to find a cure.

Broaden capital ownership. One way to ensure people can deal with the inevitable ups and downs life brings is to enable everyone to build a nest egg from an early age. The American Saving for Personal Investment, Retirement and Education (ASPIRE) Act of 2013 proposes to establish a savings account for every American at birth. Each account would be endowed with a one time, $500 contribution ($1,000 for children in households earning below the national median income) from the federal government. The accounts would incentivize savings, and account holders would not be able to withdraw funds until they reached the age of 18. The UK has had a system of children's savings accounts in place for many years.

This chapter demonstrates that the "banked/unbanked" frame currently applied to consumer financial services is inaccurate. Instead of categorizing people according to whether and how much they use a bank, we need to understand whether they have access to safe, affordable financial services. Too many people are lacking this asset, which is critical for fully functioning in the economy and in civil society.

References

Athreya, Kartik, Sánchez, Juan M., Tam, Xuan S. and Young, Eric R. (2014) Labor market upheaval, default regulations, and consumer debt. Working Paper No. 2014-002A, Federal Reserve Bank of St. Louis. Available at: http://research.stlouisfed.org/wp/more/2014-002.

Bankrate, Inc. (2012) Free checking gets rarer as ATM fees and other checking account fees continue to rise. Press release, September 24. Available at: http://phx.corporate-ir.net/phoenix.zhtml?c=61502&p=irol-newsArticle&ID=1737572&highlight

Barr, M.S. and Blank, R. (2009) Savings, assets, credit, and banking among low-income households: Introduction and overview. In: Blank, R. and Barr, M.S. (eds) *Insufficient Funds: Savings, Assets, Credit and Banking Among Low-income Households*. Russell Sage Foundation, New York.

Burhouse, S. and Osaki, Y. (2012) 2011 FDIC national survey of unbanked and underbanked households. Federal Deposit Insurance Corporation, Washington, DC.

Calem, P. (1994) The impact of geographic deregulation on small banks. *Business Review*, November/December, 17–30.

Canner, G. and Elliehausen, G. (2013) Consumer experiences with credit cards. *Federal Reserve Bulletin* 99, 5, 1–36.

Choi, C. (2011) Reporter spends month living without a bank, finds sky-high fees. *Huffington Post*, May 25.

Cooper, D. and Hall, D. (2013) Raising the federal minimum wage to $10.10 would give working families, and the overall economy, a much needed boost. Economic Policy Institute. Available at: http://www.epi.org/publication/bp357-federal-minimum-wage-increase/

Cover, J., Fuhrman Spring, A. and Garshick Kleit, R. (2011) Minorities on the margins? The spatial organization of fringe banking services. *Journal of Urban Affairs* 33, 3, 317–44.

Dēmos (2007) Higher and higher education: trends in access, affordability, and debt. Young Adult Economics Series. Available at: http://www.demos.org/sites/default/files/publications/yaes_web_execsumm.pdf

The Economist (2013) Crash course. *The Economist*, September 7. Available at: http://www.economist.com/news/schoolsbrief/21584534-effects-financial-crisis-are-still-being-felt-five-years-article

FDIC (Federal Deposit Insurance Corporation) (2004) Unfair or deceptive acts or practices by state-chartered banks. Financial Institution Letters, March 11. Available at: https://www.fdic.gov/news/news/financial/2004/fil2604a.html

Federal Reserve Bank of Chicago (n.d.) *Chicago Fed History: 1940–1964*. Available at: https://www.chicagofed.org/utilities/about-us/history/chicago-fed-history-1940-1964

Federal Reserve Board (2014) Aggregate revolving credit survey. Available at: http://www.federalreserve.gov/releases/g19/hist/cc_hist_sa_levels.html

Fox, J.A. and Woodhall, P. (2006) Cashed out: Consumers pay steep premium to "bank" at check cashing outlets. Consumer Federation of America. Available at: http://consumerfed.org/pdfs/CFA_2006_Check_Cashing_Study111506.pdf

Garcia, J. (2007) Borrowing to make ends meet: the rapid growth of credit card debt in America. *Demos*. Available at: http://www.demos.org/publication/borrowing-make-ends-meet-rapid-growth-credit-card-debt-america

Garcia, J. and Draut, T. (2009) The plastic safety net: how households are coping in a fragile economy. *Demos*. Available at: http://www.demos.org/publication/plastic-safety-net-2009-how-households-are-coping-fragile-economy

Graves, S. and Peterson, C. (2008) Usury law and the Christian right: Faith-based political power and the geography of American payday loan regulation. *Catholic University Law Review* 57, 3, 637.

Hacker, J. and Jacobs, E. (2008) Income volatility: Another source of growing economic insecurity. Economic Policy Institute. Available at: http://www.epi. org/publication/webfeatures_snapshots_20080528/

Haltom, R. (2013) Failure of Continental Illinois. *Federal Reserve History.* Available at: http://www.federalreservehistory.org/Events/DetailView/47

Hryndza, M. (2014) *An Introduction to Clever: An Initiative of the Campaign for Better Banking Fiscally.* The Center for Urban Research and Learning at Loyola University, Chicago, IL.

Jayaratne, J. and Strahan, P.E. (1999) The benefits of branching deregulation. *Regulation* 22, 1, 8–16.

Johnson, A. (2014) Bank of America will use database to screen for payday lenders. *The Wall Street Journal,* June 16.

Kramer, L. (2013) America's savings crisis: your spending habits may be to blame. ICI 2013 General Membership Meeting. *CNBC.com.* Available at: http://www.cnbc.com/id/100700580

Montezemolo, S. (2013) Payday lending abuses and predatory practices. Center for Responsible Lending. Available at: http://www.responsiblelending.org/ state-of-lending/reports/10-Payday-Loans.pdf

Noah, T. (2010) Legal usury: The skeevy business of payday loans. *Slate,* October 5.

Protess, B. (2010) Thrift banks long decline. *NYT Dealbook,* December 8. Available at: http://dealbook.nytimes.com/2010/12/08/thrifts-last-stand/

Rice, T. and Davis, E. (2007) The branch banking boom in Illinois: A byproduct of restrictive branching laws. *Chicago Fed Letter,* May

Schaefer, S. (2014) Five biggest U.S. banks control nearly half industry's $15 trillion in assets. *Forbes,* December 3. Available at: http://www.forbes.com/sites/ steveschaefer/2014/12/03/five-biggest-banks-trillion-jpmorgan-citi-bankamerica/

TransUnion (2014) 2014 payment hierarchy study. Available at: http://media.mar ketwire.com/attachments/201403/233081_PaymentHierarchyInfographic2014 FINAL.jpg

US Department of Education, National Center for Education Statistics (2016) Digest of Education Statistics, 2014 (NCES 2016-006), Chapter 3. Available at: http://nces.ed.gov/fastfacts/display.asp?id=76

Vornovytskyy, M., Gottschalck, A. and Smith, A. (2011) Household debt in the US 2000 to 2011. US Census Bureau. Available at: http://www.census.gov/ people/wealth/files/Debt%20Highlights%202011.pdf

Westgate, M. (2011) *Gale Force.* Education and Resources Group, The Woodlands, TX.

Whitehouse, M. (2010) Number of the week: Default repercussions. *The Wall Street Journal,* July 31.

Wilson, W. (1912) The Democratic Party's appeal. In: The Political Parties: Their Appeal to the Nation by the Presidential Candidates William H. Taft, Woodrow Wilson, Theodore Roosevelt, Eugene V. Debs, Eugene W. Chafin, Arthur E. Reimer, special issue. *The Independent,* October 24.

Chapter 6

Commoning Against the Crisis
Angelos Varvarousis and Giorgos Kallis

Introduction

There is a documented growth of alternative economies in contexts of crisis, from time banks and community currencies, to social centers, clinics or agro-ecovillages, in diverse places from Argentina (Abramovich and Vázquez 2007), to Spain (Conill et al. 2012), or Greece (Vathakou 2015). Why do such alternative economies emerge and grow in some places (say Greece or Spain), but not others (say Italy or Portugal)? What explains the often punctuated take-off and exponential growth of such practices in a condensed period of time? And finally how do new alternative projects negotiate internal differences and conflicts, how do they stabilize themselves (or not), and how do they relate to the state and the markets? These are some of the questions addressed in this chapter.

In a context of secular stagnation and limits to growth (Jackson 2009; Kallis, this volume), there is a growing interest in alternative economic practices that produce new forms of "common-wealth," wealth that no longer relies on more and more money. While in places like Greece or Argentina, alternative economies are a new phenomenon, in other places there is a long lineage of experimentation with alternatives, traced back to the 1960s student and counter-cultural movements or even the Paris Commune previously (Ross 2002, 2015). The questions concerning the sustainability, effects, and legacy of such alternative attempts within a hegemonic capitalist system remain pertinent. But here we are interested in something different: first, the dynamics of emergence of such alternatives, and the factors that catalyze them in an early phase of growth; and second, the – perhaps – novel ways that contemporary movements try to deal with the dilemmas faced by their predecessors, especially those of openness versus closure, and of their relationship to the state and the capitalist economy (Harvey 2000). Each generation – from the Paris Commune, to Paris '68, to the Indignados and the Occupy movement – might reinvent the wheel, yet each does so in its own distinct way and with different afterlives and effects.

We address these questions with an emblematic empirical case: Greece. The economic depression in Greece is the greatest ever faced by a developed country.[1] While unemployment and poverty sky-rocketed, alternative commoning projects flourished. Before 2008, there were only a handful of such projects; today there are more than 600. How and why this happened is the subject of this chapter. This is the first in-depth examination of the whole spectrum of alternative economic practices in Greece, and the first attempt to link them to pertinent theoretical debates.

Our contribution to the analysis of alternative economies is theoretical and conceptual. First, we propose to think of alternative economies as new forms of commons (De Angelis 2013b). Second, we argue that an early stage of liminality is catalytic for the take-off of new commons. And third, we observe that the evolution of a patchwork of new commons follows a rhizomatic pattern. Our core thesis is that *the commoning movement in Greece benefited from a liminal state of unfixed identity, dominant in the period of the occupied indignant squares, and then blossomed as a rhizome. It now faces challenges of maturity in terms of its internal and external relations.*

Part 1 explains the key concepts and theoretical terms used in this chapter: commons and commoning; liminality; and rhizomatic movements. Part 2 provides contextual information on the Greek crisis and outlines the fieldwork methods. Part 3 traces the origins of the new commons in the occupied squares and Greece's indignant movement, and Part 4 details its rhizomatic expansion in health and food provision, education and cooperative production. Part 5 discusses how the movement handles internal conflicts and democracy, how it attempts to organize at higher scales, and how it relates to the state and the market.

---

[1] Greece's peak-to-trough decline of GDP by 33 percent (and still falling) is worse than the USA's 27 percent decline during the most acute phase of the Great Depression.

Part 1: Conceptual framework: commons, liminality, and rhizomes

Elinor Ostrom's 2009 Nobel Prize in economics marked a rising interest in the study of the commons. Ostrom (1990) researched the conditions under which collective forms of governing resources can work. Ostrom documented that more often than not communities self-organize and manage to control access and use of shared resources. The "tragedy of the commons" (Hardin 1968), where open access destroys a common resource, is the empirical exception, Ostrom showed.

Ostrom treated the commons as a "thing" to be governed, mostly a material entity such as a forest, an aquifer, or a public infrastructure. The main drive behind commoning in Ostrom's work is "benefit" and this is always bounded to an economic reasoning directly related to a community's survival. Ostrom, however, forgets that the very concept of benefit itself is determined culturally and historically. As Harvey (2012)[2] argues, the commons is not "a particular kind of thing" but "an unstable and malleable social relation between a particular self-defined social group and those aspects of its actually existing or yet-to-be-created social and/or physical environment deemed crucial to its life and livelihood." De Angelis (2010) gives a tri-partite definition of the commons which includes the *common-pool resources*, i.e. the natural, human, or intellectual resources shared, the *community* that creates and/or governs these resources, and the process of *commoning*, that is the overtime institutionalized process of coming together to pool and govern resources (see also D'Alisa 2013).

The first generation of literature that followed Ostrom's work studied the governance of still existing, pre-enclosure resource commons. Recent studies instead investigate the making of new physical or digital commons like urban gardens, social centers, Wikipedia, Linux, time banks, or producer-to-consumer cooperatives (Bollier 2014). This is what in this volume we call *alternative economic practices*, or what others call *"alternative spaces"* (see Gibson-Graham 2008; Gritzas and Kavoulakos 2015), or *"solidarity economies"* (Vathakou 2015; Kioupkiolis and Karyotis 2013). We approach, instead, alternative economies and practices as *"commoning projects,"* emphasizing processes of cooperation and sharing that not only produce new forms of economy but rather also new forms of living in common, while

---

[2] Quoted also in Stavrides (2015).

distinguishing them from governmental, private, or church solidarity initiatives that are top-down or charity-based.

A claim we advance and which is new in the literature is that many of these new commons are, or have passed, or have been generated through, what we define as *liminal conditions*, before evolving into more stable structures. The inspiration comes from anthropological studies of the "rites of passage" (Van Gennep 1960 [1908]), the ambiguous and ambivalent processes that a subject enters when it loses its established identity and before obtaining a new one.[3] As Victor Turner (1977) puts it "liminal entities are neither here nor there; they are betwixt and between the positions assigned and arrayed by law, custom, convention, and ceremonial." This condition of "in-betweeness" characterizes both the individuals who participate in commoning projects foregoing at least temporarily their fixed identities, and the institutions that govern the projects.

What does the concept of liminality add to the understanding of the commons? In Ostrom's theory, the commons are governed by *fixed* communities (Wade 1988; Ostrom 1990; Steins and Edwards 1999). "Define clear group boundaries" is the first principle that Ostrom proposes for a successful management of the commons. Recent literature though questions this fixity and communities are not conceived necessarily as homogeneous (Agrawal and Gibson 1999; De Angelis 2010; Stavrides 2015). In liminal commons, instead, the community of the commoners *shines through its absence*. Some kind of community of course is temporarily emerging for the production of the common. But this is always precarious and often dissolves. The borders of a liminal community are not only blurred. They actually do not exist as such. Liminal commons, in other words, are not defined by exclusion. Because of this they are more likely to *happen* in spaces where exclusion is not likely or desirable, such as a public square.

In a liminal commons, the glue that brings the actors together is the practical production of the common. A collective identity is neither a precondition nor the purpose of the process and is discouraged when it puts obstacles in the way of common production. Sharing,

---

[3] This is not the first use of "*liminality*" outside anthropology. Several scholars have connected liminality with sociological, geographical, and philosophical studies (Szakolczai 2009; Thomassen 2009; Stavrides 2013b). The potential of the concept is not fully realized yet (Szakolczai 2009; Thomassen 2009). Anthropologists themselves have linked liminal periods and liminal subjects to horizontality and equality and to the – partial or complete – collapse of the dominant social structures, situations akin to that of the current crisis, insisting that liminality can illuminate the formative aspects of transitory social periods and revolutions (Turner 1977; Olaveson 2001; Szakolczai 2009; Thomassen 2009, 2014).

solidarity, or horizontality are not introduced as indisputable *a priori* identity values. They emerge as their worth is experienced in practice, in solving practical problems or in organizing collective action. As the subjects enter a liminal condition where dominant social taxonomies and identities are contested, "collective inventiveness" (Stavrides 2015) flourishes. Liminal subjects are more open and more vulnerable to imitate social behaviors and practices that offer a possible way out from the uncertainty that the liminal phase is associated with.

The institutions that are performed in this kind of commoning and that define what is to be shared and how are also characterized by liminality. Liminal institutions are not fixed but precarious and fluid and they emerge and perish within decentralization–recentralization dynamics. They unify, not exclude the diverse potential commoners and they promote the non-antagonistic co-existence of different perceptions. Whereas in Ostrom's approach, the commons are regarded as "nested" institutions between the private and public typically requiring support from institutions at higher levels in order to operate (Ostrom 1990; Steins and Edwards 1999), liminal commons emerge within uncertainty and a reversion of social taxonomies and ordering, operating as deliberative processes without linkage to "higher" institutions.

Our theory of liminal commons is radically different from theories of collective action that celebrate difference and claim that the contemporary collective action unfolds around the cultural capital of a "politics of selves" (Lichterman 1996; McDonald 2002). These theories too criticize the idea of collective identity, arguing that in contemporary movements this has been replaced by a personalized "public expression of the self" (Lichterman 1996). Whereas this may have some value in describing some contemporary movements, especially those dominated by a "middle-class culture," the liminal commons presented here are not the outcome of an individualism that propels a self-actualization process. They are the result of the loss of an established identity, which allows space for a precarious and fluid "we" to emerge. People do not only express publicly themselves; they propose, even incompletely and contradictorily, an alternative social organization.

Finally, we argue that the new (liminal) commons unfold and expand as a "rhizomatic movement" (Castells 2012). A rhizomatic movement is one that has no center or periphery, does not begin from or end at a specific point. Its nodes are either not connected or connected mostly through unforeseen encounters, following a decentralization–recentralization process (Zibechi 2010). The nodes of the rhizome are not stable but appear and disappear within a highly accelerating spiral; multiple nodes can be added to the movement without previous control of whether or not they are compatible with the network.

Not all networked movements are rhizomatic. The transition town movement,[4] for example, is a networked movement, without center or periphery, but in which, differently from a rhizome, there is a bigger stability of nodes. The connection of the nodes is not the outcome of unforeseen but of planned encounters, whose aim is to deepen an organic collaboration and not a temporal exchange of experiences as in rhizomes. Moreover, in a network there are usually checking mechanisms which ensure that new nodes are compatible with the existing structure and a minimum agreement is usually regarded essential for an expansion to occur.

Before proceeding to explain the rhizomatic origins and evolution of Greece's new commons, let us explain the political-economic context.

Part 2: Greece's great depression

As of 2013, 1.4 million Greeks were unemployed, 27.5 percent of the total workforce, up from 7.2 percent in 2007 (Matsaganis 2013). For the 18 to 25-year-olds, unemployment increased from an already record high of 36.6 percent in 2009 to 65.0 percent in 2013 (EL.STAT 2009, 2013). Around 450,000 families have no working members (Insurgenta Iskra 2014). For those that do work, things are not much better: the median monthly gross wage fell from €1,997 in 2009 to €1,048 in 2015 (EL.STAT 2015). Minimum salaries declined from €751.5 in 2009, to €586.1 in 2013 (Vaiou 2014). VAT increased from 9 percent and 13 percent to 23 percent, while taxes on property, including small property, increased 514 percent between 2010 and 2014 (EL.STAT 2014). Consequently, the purchasing power of wage earners plummeted by 37.2 percent (Vaiou 2014).

Numbers do not capture the grim everyday reality, but indicatively, suicides increased 62.3 percent between 2007 and 2011 (EL.STAT

---

[4] The transition network movement is a grassroots movement that is primarily based on community projects seeking increased resilience in response to peak oil, climate destruction and economic instability (Hopkins 2008). It aims at creating local community bonds that uphold values that are primarily defined by a theoretical and practical framework that contains specific rules such as "12 ingredients." The movement has also developed various ways to register and monitor new and already registered projects.

2012); almost half of those committing suicide in 2012 were economically inactive (Insurgenta Iskra 2014). Cases of major clinical depression increased 248 percent between 2009 and 2011 (Economou et al. 2013). Some 145,000 children face food insecurity and hunger (PROLEPSIS 2013; Insurgenta Iskra 2014).

Rather than a direct effect of GDP decline, Greece's great depression is the outcome of austerity policies implemented to deal with public debt. Public debt had increased from €141 billion in 2000 to €263 billion in 2008, yet international institutions were praising Greece as late as 2008 for its economic performance. This was a debt-fueled growth (Lapavitsas 2012). From 2008, a period of repetitive recessions commenced, increasing the cost of borrowing, and rendering Greece's debt unsustainable. Unable to borrow from the private bond market, Greek governments reached a series of agreements ("memorandums") with the "Troika" of institutions (EU, IMF, and European Central Bank) which led to austerity and cuts in public services (e.g. 36 percent cuts for education). Pensions were on average reduced by 30 percent and salaries in the public sector 20–35 percent (Hadjimichalis 2013). Public expenditures decreased, but because of the decline in economic activity caused by austerity, debt kept growing and new debt was simply used to service old debt and interest.

A social crisis had preceded the debt crisis. The benefits from the early 2000s growth were not evenly distributed (Kaplanis 2011; Dalakoglou 2013). The term the "700 Euros generation" was coined prior to 2008 for young university graduates without access to well-paid jobs (Dalakoglou 2013). The number of immigrants without papers soared and became a new source of inequality (Dalakoglou 2013; Hadjimichalis 2013). The supposed economic miracle of the 2000s was based on credit expansion, cheap migrant labor, the construction of public works, and a real estate bubble (Kaplanis 2011), linked to the Olympic games of 2004 (Stathakis and Hadjimichalis 2004; Hadjimichalis 2013). Socio-spatial inequalities emerged for the first time with such intensity in the urban centers of Athens and Thessaloniki (Dalakoglou 2013). In December 2008, the social crisis came to a boiling point in the student-anarchist neighborhood of Exarchia in Athens (Vradis and Dalakoglou 2011), when a policeman killed a high-school student. A revolt erupted in Athens and in over 60 other cities in Greece, and days of clashes with the police ensued (Hadjimichalis 2013). The increasingly unequal urban space became the site and stake of the conflict (Stavrides 2013a).

The December 2008 revolt evolved into a confrontational

anti-austerity movement. The conservative government responded with new and more brutal crackdowns by the police and an intensification of surveillance (Fillipidis 2011; Dalakoglou 2013). It is within this context of crisis and fear cultivated by media and politicians (Douzinas 2013), versus resistance and revolt, that a new commoning movement was born. December 2008 was a moment of rupture. Urban space was reclaimed, including the conversion into a people's park of the garage lot where the high-school student was killed, urban gardens and parks in other parts of the city, resistance against the enclosure of Ymittos Mountain, and clashes against the opening of a new metropolitan landfill in the periphery of the city (Dalakoglou and Vradis 2011; Dalakoglou 2013; Hadjimichalis 2013). The next section traces precisely the rhizomatic evolution of these battles into a new movement of commoning; the role of the indignant movement that occupied the central squares in Athens and other big cities in 2011 was catalytic.

Analysis of the indignant squares (Part 3) is based on published material, participant observation by the first author, and conversations with participants in commoning projects asked to reflect on this period. To assess the number and growth of commoning projects (Part 4) we use online databases, verifying data where necessary with telephone interviews.[5] In addition, we conducted 18 semi-structured, in-depth interviews with leading participants in projects (ten male, eight female), and two group interviews. The information from interviews is contextualized through six months of formal fieldwork and participant observation by the first author, in six commoning projects, where he observed, participated in, and contributed to general assemblies, events, and collective actions.

---

[5] The databases used (Solidarity4all.gr, Enallaktikos.gr, Omikronproject.gr, www.enasalloskosmos-community.net and kolektives.org) have several limitations. First, projects were systematically recorded only after mobilization in the squares, so it is very difficult to quantify the evolution of projects before and after, other than through our own or our interlocutors' estimations. Second, the databases do not include new projects established over the last six months and are not updated to remove projects that may have faltered. Third, they include several state, private, or church solidarity projects that do not fall under our definition of commoning projects. The "solidarity4all" database might be more accurate, because it does not include such projects, but it has the drawback of association with the political party of SYRIZA, which makes some more radical projects unwilling to report to it. Our reports therefore on the number of projects are only an indicative approximation.

Part 3:   The liminal commons of the indignant squares

That the movement of the occupied squares, the movement of the "Aganaktismenoi" (Indignants), catalyzed the emergence of commoning projects is a sentiment shared by most of our interviewees (see also Hadjimichalis 2013; Kaika and Karaliotas 2014; Kioupkiolis 2014). The Time Bank of Syntagma Square, founded during the occupation, counted 2,000 new members within its first days and today has more than 3,000 members (Interview 1; Interview 5). A self-managed medical center at the occupied square gave birth to the permanent metropolitan solidarity clinic and pharmacy for those without access to public health (Interview 16; Enallaktikos.gr 2013). Before the occupation, there was only one self-organized clinic in Greece. Today there are 47. After an information event held in Syntagma by people experimenting with cooperatives, several workers cooperatives were conceived (Interview 1; Interview 9). New eco-villages and "back-to-the-land" initiatives started in the square, such as the "*Spithari waking life*" project in the countryside of Athens. Commoning projects organically connected with the squares presented the faster rate of growth, while the fate of projects developed independently from the occupation – "black holes" as some interviewees called them – is unknown (Interview 16; Interview 1). The model of the popular assembly, also first practiced in occupied Syntagma, moved to several neighborhoods, becoming the organizational mode for commoning projects (Interview 1; Interview 3; Interview 6; Interview 7; Interview 16).

The squares movement was rhizomatic. It was organized primarily through social media and there was no recognizable structure that defined the place, time or form of protests (Douzinas 2013; Hadjimichalis 2013). The first mass rally was held in Syntagma Square on May 25, organized spontaneously through social media as a response to a post placed by the Spanish Indignados on Facebook asking "*why are Greeks asleep?*". "We are awake" was the answer (Tsaliki 2012). Around 200,000 people attended, without any central organization (Hadjimichalis 2013). Some three million people passed through the square in the three months that it remained occupied. Protests first were organized through anonymous communications on social media. Later on, this evolved into a decentralization–recentralization model via neighborhood assemblies that would gather independently and then share their conversations and outcomes in the general assembly of the occupied square. Reciprocally the outcomes of the general assembly fed back to the next neighborhood assembly, without bounding it. As the occupation continued, more people and micro groups joined the square, leaving with more members. Nodes were added to the rhizome, as new projects were born that span off to neighborhoods and sectors of the economy.

Liminality was central in catalyzing this rhizome. The open access character of the public square conditioned the liminal openness of the mobilization. The December 2008 uprising was also rhizomatic and it also campaigned for reclaiming urban space, but after the initial clashes, it abandoned its open urban or digital spaces. Activists entrenched themselves behind the gates of three occupied universities. The gates acted literally and symbolically as check points for who could be included in the movement, an identity closure around the militant leftist and anarchist groups that defended the buildings against the police. In comparison, Syntagma, the central square of Athens was *de facto* a porous, open-access space. No single group could enclose it. A negotiation between diverse and heterogeneous groups and people was not only possible; it was *necessary* for the continuation of the movement.

Liminality was not only an outcome of space. The crisis ruptured identities, with many Greeks living "between a present yet to pass and a future still to come" (Vradis and Dalakoglou 2011). Austerity and economic destitution dismantled certainties and regularities. The perceived humiliation of a country governed by international institutions, its people portrayed as "lazy" or "corrupt," ended violently previous identities framed around a consumerist dream (Douzinas 2013). This liminal loss of identity was manifested in placards in Syntagma Square declaring "we are nobody" or "we don't know where we are going but we don't go back." People in Syntagma were wearing, symbolically, white masks declaring their intention to remain anonymous, or else, "de-identified." Emptiness means also possibility (Brighenti 2013), and the opening of the borders of a fixed identity made possible acting in common (Stavrides 2013b), by different people from diverse backgrounds, many of whom participated for the first time in protests.

The movement did not only unfold in urban space; it produced new, common space. The occupiers of Syntagma did not just protest toward the Parliament, but established a tent city where protesters slept; a direct democracy assembly held every day at 9:00 p.m.; a technical support space; centers for translation, administration, health, food, artistic and free expression; and transport and postal services. They set up a cleaning and care team, a time bank for service exchange, a solidarity bazaar, and a citizens' Debt Audit campaign, with more than 60,000 participants (Tsaliki 2012; Interview 1; Interview 2; Interview 5; Interview 11). These groups held assemblies every day at 6:00 p.m., open to everyone. The labor that went into these forms of cooperation, defining *what* is to be shared and *how*, transformed the square from a public space into a temporary commons. It is this commoning process that gives the Indignants movement its specific "materiality" (De Angelis 2013a) compared to previous political or protest movements, such as those of the 1960s or the anti-globalization movement. While the majority of social movements unfold in urban space and are organized around a set of demands, the Indignants movement re-invented urban space and prefigured alternative forms of production and reproduction.

Although there was a difference between the "lower" part of Syntagma Square where commoning projects concentrated, and the upper part in front of the Parliament where protests were held, with the presence of nationalists or xenophobes (Hadjimichalis 2013; Kaika and Karaliotas 2014), the two spaces were not distinct and separate but porous (Stavrides 2013b). The distinction between the "two squares" was not one of the identities of the participants (commoners down, nationalists up), but the different function of each zone. The upper part, composed of pavement and a street in front of the Parliament, assumed the function of demonstrating "against" the government and confronting the police, which protected the Parliament. The lower part, with its benches, trees, and small park, functioned as a space for settlement, discussion, and creation. Previous identities affected whether people would opt more for confrontation or commoning. But the innovation of Syntagma was precisely that many people transcended pre-established identities (Douzinas 2013; Stavrides 2013b). People from the lower square screamed and expressed their anger in the upper part, while even xenophobes or conservatives from the upper square took the floor and expressed their opinions in the lower part (Interview 3; Interview 7).

The liminal character of the new commons was manifested not only as a mass de-identification of the subjects but also in the performance of liminal institutions. First, assemblies and groups did not have stable membership. People would come and go, everyone having the right to participate at any moment (Tsaliki 2012; Stavrides 2013b). The assemblies and the collectively organized events were not the same every day; they were changing according to one's or to one's micro-group's emerging ideas. The characteristic phrase "make your statement! Find your room in Syntagma Square and express yourself" (a call from the artists' team) was not a mere encouragement for a

138

"public expression of the self." It expressed the openness and willingness to participate in and organize collectively and spontaneously all these micro-activities, which emerged unexpectedly. Collective invention flourished in Syntagma and gave birth to innovative practices of direct democracy, artistic events, and commoning projects. Some of those appeared for the first time in Syntagma Square while others were imitations of practices which appeared in other occupied squares, especially the ones in Spain.

Second, there was an explicit discouragement for people to identify themselves in assemblies as members of a specific collective. Representatives of political parties were prohibited from joining. This does not mean that there were no members of political groups or parties, or no people with pre-fixed political identity. However, they gradually had to learn to step back and negotiate their opinion or practice, something unprecedented for a social mobilization in Greece. Characteristically, during the assemblies, some Marxists, who initially perceived their role as one of an "avant-garde" with a concrete agenda, faced gestures of disapproval and had to step back (Stavrides 2013b). Mass de-identification allowed a negotiation in the production of the common among individuals who were not connected by a common ideology or identity. Stopping specific political groups from conquering the processes constituted a precarious institution or mechanism for preventing the accumulation of power by a single formation within the movement. This opened space for expression and participation to people who did not identify with pre-established political or ideological formations. Like the Spanish Indignados, "by joining an occupied site, citizens could be part of the movement without adhering to any ideology or organization, just by being there for their own reasons" (Castells 2012: 10). There were unifying slogans and demands such as the claim for "*real democracy*" or the rejection of the Troika memorandum. Yet these served mostly as "*empty signifiers*" (Laclau 1996a, 1996b), meaning different things to different people, allowing a degree of unity without homogenization against a common enemy.

Third, the resolutions of the assemblies did not aim at producing unifying proposals (Papadopoulos et al. 2012) but to check the limits of a possible consensus (Stavrides 2013b). Different opinions were allowed to co-exist. When authorities or the media asked for a representative, spokesperson, or coherent political program by the movement, the assembly refused to provide any (Papadopoulos et al. 2012). The S11 protest in Melbourne also had no spokesperson, primarily due to a generalized personalization which emphasized individual responsibility (McDonald 2002). In Syntagma, in comparison, this was a conscious mechanism for the prevention of the accumulation of power as made explicit both in our interviews and the square's assembly resolutions when activists often stressed that "we will not allow anybody to put his own hat upon our movement."

Liminality was catalytic in spreading the rhizomatic movement. First, openness in the square allowed a popularization of commoning practices that otherwise could not have been possible. Some 28 percent of all Greeks passed through the squares during the protests and occupations (Solidarity4all). Practices seen as "alternative," marginal, and ideologically loaded before were now communicated to wider parts of the Greek society. Newcomers could collectively perform actions and identities that they hadn't experienced before. Comparing collective actions, as simple as just cooking together, with previous habits was liberating for many and this is plausibly linked to the subsequent explosion of commoning projects.

Second, while many of these projects were initiated by politically motivated individuals or groups, with an agenda, such groups too changed through their participation and interaction with newcomers, redefining the content of their politicization and opening their political identities to new experiences, transforming their habits and ways of doing politics. Unlike Catalonia (Conill et al. 2012), commoning was marginal in Greece before the movement of the occupied squares, and was looked upon with suspicion by political parties, including anarchist or autonomist groups more keen on direct confrontation than on "creating a new world within the cracks of the old." Instead, after the squares movement, SYRIZA, the left-wing party that now governs Greece, founded and funded Solidarity4all, a network dedicated to the promotion of commoning projects. The "Antiauthoritarian Movement" (*Antieksousiastiki Kinisi*), a leading anarchist group, and "Antarsya," a far left party, also got heavily involved in commoning initiatives (Interview 14; Interview 15; Interview 16).

Third, the experience with commoning in Syntagma helped to deconstruct and de-stigmatize poverty. People who previously might have felt personally responsible for their loss of income, their failure to find work or their inability to provide for their dependents, found a space to share and transform their desperation. Eating in a communal kitchen, getting clothes for free from a bazaar or medicines from a free pharmacy was no longer a shame. Importantly, the projects initiated in Syntagma were not only symbolic; many people got engaged precisely because they addressed concrete needs for food, health, housing, or employment (Interview 1; Interview 2; Interview 3), while allowing them to *"take our lives in our hands,"* as a placard at the square read.

Part 4: The rhizomatic spread of commoning

As participation subsided, the square was evacuated violently in August 2011, and riot police defended it from occupiers for subsequent months (Hadjimichalis 2013). For some, the movement failed since it did not stop austerity (Kaika and Karaliotas 2014). However, the deterritorialization of power structures (Kioupkiolis 2014) and the complex political-economy of Greece's indebtedness within the Eurozone make such political reversals extremely difficult. The indignant movement was not only about negation and disdain, but also bringing forth *commoning* as an emancipatory project. Like in Spain, "the movement did not disappear; rather it spread out into the social fabric, with neighborhood assemblies ... spreading ... alternative economic practices such as consumer co-operatives, ethical banking, exchange networks and many other such forms of living differently so as to live with meaning" (Castells 2012: 1). As one of our informants argued: "people after Syntagma spread the occupation in their neighborhoods by creating hundreds of micro-squares." In most cases this happened in a rhizomatic, unstructured and invisible way (Insurgenta Iskra 2014; Vathakou 2015), while in others it took from the beginning the form of a more stable and cohesive network, as in social clinics and direct producer-to-consumer networks. Active commoning projects today include social clinics and pharmacies, workers' cooperatives, occupied urban spaces, time banks and alternative currencies, neighborhood assemblies and solidarity exchange networks, urban gardens, farmer or consumer cooperatives, farmer markets without middlemen, artist and publishing collectives, and single-occupied factories. Let us present each in more detail.

The metropolitan solidarity clinic was conceived in Syntagma and started operating in December 2011. Today it has more than 250 volunteers, having treated 33,000 patients in its three years of life (Interview 15; Interview 16). The clinic does not accept funding but only donations of medicines, materials, and services. Volunteers govern the clinic horizontally and democratically. Patients are encouraged to participate by providing services themselves (Interview 15; Interview 16; Solidarity4all), whereas work is exchanged between doctors, nurses, and patients through a time bank. Athens' metropolitan clinic

141

has served as a national model. From only three projects in September 2012, by March 2015 there were more than 50 functioning clinics in Greece (Interview 15; Interview 16; Solidarity4all). All provide free services, accept only in-kind donations and are governed by doctors, nurses, and volunteers. Many of them have as a guiding principle that health is a commons from which nobody should be excluded. The clinics spread rhizomatically and respond to local crises in health services, but within the first months of their operation they formed a relatively stable organization, networking via the "Nationwide Cooperation of Solidary Dispensaries and Pharmacies." Their organization can no longer be considered rhizomatic, a point to which we return later in the chapter.

Urban space commoning initiatives included the project in "Plato's Academy" (an area in Athens next to where Plato established his famous philosophy academy), where local citizens, in an effort to transform an abandoned 13-hectare public area, formed after the squares movement an assembly, frequently organized parties, collective kitchens, exchange bazaars, public lectures, and free educational initiatives and solidarity festivals. These events were part of protests and civil disobedience against the building of a shopping mall (euphemistically named "Academy Gardens") close to the archaeological site. Residents also founded two cooperative social centers next to the park, acting as meeting and organization points (Interview 2).

Notable occupations in Athens include the closed private theater "Empros," settled by artists who organize free performances and concerts, parties, and political events; the occupied social center of "Vox," previously a bookshop café and cinema; and "Sholeio," a free social center in Thessaloniki similar to Plato's Academy. These social centers serve as nodes, organizing and hosting various commoning activities such as solidarity clinics and pharmacies, urban gardening, political gatherings, and solidarity educational programs.

Another symbolic occupation is that of an urban garden in a small corner of the old Athens airport in Helleniko, with a self-organized camp on the nearby beach. This serves as a coordinating center for the mobilization against the privatization of the 620 hectares of the airport, worth an estimated €3 billion. Protesters want to reclaim the space as a commons and turn it into a metropolitan park. There are more than 23 urban gardening/agriculture projects such as this all over Greece, 13 of them in Athens alone (Solidarity4all; Enallaktikos. gr; Omikron Project).[6]

---

[6] These projects are taking place in abandoned or occupied spaces in various cities. In

Neighborhood assemblies act as hubs of urban commoning. They were the engines of the decentralization–recentralization process during the occupation of Syntagma; conversations and actions were decentralized in the neighborhoods before they were recentralized at the squares. Some of them remain popular and active. For example, the popular assembly of "Koukaki-Thisio-Petralona" occupied an abandoned public building, which had been offering health services previously, and transformed it into a social clinic and kindergarten. A different initiative is that against the privatization of the water utility of the city of Thessaloniki. Fifty citizens' groups together with the trade union of the utility organized a public referendum. Of the 218,002 citizens who voted, 98 percent were against water privatization. Initiative 136 in turn is a citizens' initiative to buy the water utility and turn it into a cooperative governed by municipal councils. "136" refers to the estimated cost per household of buying the company, allegedly an idea conceived on the back of an envelope during the square occupation in Thessaloniki.[7]

After the squares movement, and facilitated by a 2011 law for the social economy, 415 new workers cooperatives started operating by March 2014 (Koinsep.org 2014). Greece had seen an agricultural cooperativist movement in the past, which decayed as a result of political patronage, indebtedness, and corruption. Most of the new cooperatives now are dedicated instead to small services, especially cafés and restaurants, though there are also cooperative publishing houses, engineering and construction cooperatives, a cooperative newspaper, and several groceries and coop markets (such as Bioscoop in Thessaloniki, which covers the needs of more than 400 families per day; Interview 18), renewable energy cooperatives, collective couriers and manufacturing cooperatives. At least 150 of those cooperatives were functional and operating at the time of this writing, and at least 100 of them are, according to our own estimations, genuine social cooperatives (compared to opportunistic enterprises taking advantage of the exemptions of cooperatives from social security taxes). These are part of an emerging, still small, cooperativist movement in Greece espousing values of democratic self-management, confederation, and association (PASEGES 2011; Kioupkiolis and Karyotis 2013). Following their rhizomatic expansion, the cooperatives now seek a

addition, there are dozens of other urban gardening projects primarily organized by municipalities, but we do not refer to them as they do not constitute commoning projects.
[7] We owe this information to Maria Kaika.

more stable network structure and a shared building in the center of Athens to coordinate efforts, funding, and legal support.

There are also several projects that target needs directly without the intermediation of money: time banks, free-share bazaars, direct exchange networks, and local alternative currencies. While only three time banks and alternative currencies existed before 2011, at the time of writing there are 37 projects (or 110 according to estimates of others; Solidarity4all). While some are primarily interested in meeting everyday material needs, others, such as the time bank in the Holargos-Papagou neighborhoods of Athens, conduct political and solidarity campaigns, theatrical or musical performances, and popular assemblies (Interview 7).

In agriculture and food, direct producer-to-consumer networks were launched after February 2012, when potato producers in Northern Greece bypassed intermediaries and distributed their products to consumers directly, at a low price. This practice of circumventing middlemen spread across the country, expanding to other items besides potatoes. Collectives were set up to organize and inform members and the public about the days of direct distribution. From 12 initiatives in September 2012, there were 47 active networks in December 2014, supporting some 2,169 households and distributing more than 5,000 tons of food in metropolitan Athens alone (Solidarity4all). Like Solidarity Clinics, the alternative food networks quickly formed their formal network that coordinates action.

Solidarity kitchens existed before the crisis, but from three known ventures before 2011, there are now more than 21 all over Greece. In solidarity kitchens one can eat for free or for a small amount of money and participate in the cooking process if one so wishes (Vathakou 2015). Most operate weekly. Some are organized permanently at the same place. Others are "nomadic," moving from neighborhood to neighborhood or even city to city to spread the practice. There are no professional cooks and foodstuff is provided by donations or by participants who can afford it. There are several local associations which also organize "solidarity food parcels," which are collected from donations by shoppers or producers, and are distributed to those in need. A total of 1,987 parcels were distributed in February 2013, and more than 4,318 in September 2014 all over Greece (Solidarity4all). Initially, parcels served as nutrition complements, but as the system developed, they included deals with suppliers of fresh vegetables and meat, making it possible to cover the full dietary needs of the recipients (Interview 16). Even though such projects are mostly organized by people who are not directly in need themselves, in many cases the recipients are involved in the organization and the distribution of the parcels (30 percent of all recipients according to Solidarity4all), or they participate in other projects organized by the local associations. This distinguishes such "commoning" initiatives from charity.

Education initiatives cater to those excluded from the public system or to those who want to continue education but cannot afford it. Established for less than a year, the People's University of Social Solidarity Economy (UnivSSE) in Thessaloniki gives online lectures to thousands of visitors (Vathakou 2015). The Network of Solidary Knowledge "Mesopotamia," which emerged from the time bank of the Moschato neighborhood in Athens, offers tutorials to high school students, seminars for people of all ages, and tries to establish what organizers call a "community of knowledge." "Solidarity schools" provide free tutorials to schoolchildren who cannot afford private tuition (90 percent of all schoolchildren in Greece pay for private lessons for the national university exam). In "alternative schools" families come together to establish self-organized kindergartens (Vathakou 2015). As in the case of social clinics, they have also established a national network for a more effective collaboration between them.

Different projects do not operate in silos. Often a single collective develops different projects for different functions or at different scales. As commoning projects grew rhizomatically, stronger connections were forged between projects operating in different domains or locations. For instance, the old airport of Helleniko now hosts not only urban gardens and social centers but is closely related with the metropolitan social clinic and pharmacy which operates in the proximity of the airport. The patients of the clinic in turn developed a local time bank to exchange services with doctors. At the time of writing, the intention of the group was to start a worker cooperative as well (Interview 16). Likewise, in the neighborhood of Galatsi, the self-managed social space "Abariza" cooperated with the local food network without intermediates to start a consumers' cooperative (Interview 16).

Are these projects "successful"? This begs for a definition of success. Most projects do sustain and reproduce themselves. Yet they remain marginal, providing for a very small part of the needs of Greek society. In that sense they are very far from materializing a systemic change. Following De Angelis (2013b), however, the important question is not whether there is an alternative feasible model ready to substitute that of a faltering capitalism, but how

145

existing social experiments contribute to the – endless – process of pursuing emancipation. Experimentation with new forms of life leads to what Castoriades (1975) and Latouche (2009) have called the "decolonization of the imaginary," an essential act for the opening of a new spectrum of possible alternative futures.

Relatedly, an important question is: do participants change as a result of their participation in these practices, and how? First, participants redefine their needs. Many of our interviewees argued that those who wanted to fulfill the same desires in the same way either changed or had to leave the projects (Interview 2; Interview 3). Values such as equality, sharing, joy, and meaningful relations dominate in the projects compared to competition or aspirations of individualistic material affluence (Interview 2; Interview 3; Interview 4; Interview 6; Interview 16; Interview 17). Participation produces a totally different *habitus* that extends beyond the commoning project. Some participants, for example, ended up living in collective houses, or sharing work with others. This is why projects expanded in a rhizomatic way, as participants transferred the commoning experience from one terrain to another.

Second, our interviews and observations suggest that people accustomed to be "leaders" (sic), gradually learned to step back and leave room for others to express themselves. Those accustomed to "follow" or those uncomfortable with expressing themselves in public gradually found ways to contribute actively (Interview 2; Interview 3). The assemblarian decision-making processes and other institutions, which distribute time equally among participants, keep in check self-proclaimed "avant-gardes" and prevent the accumulation of power.

Third, whereas the majority of our interviewees were ecologically aware before the projects, they also emphasized how the decline of profit as a driving value allows ecological concerns to emerge more strongly. Projects such as urban gardening, seed sharing, battles against privatizations and enclosures, eco-villages and many (though not all) of the alternative food networks have a strong environmental component.

Whether these changes are permanent and sustainable, or whether the projects will perish if the economy recovers and people's needs are satisfied again through the market cannot be known in advance. What our fieldwork shows is that a return to the previous state is far from straightforward for participants. Our interviewees hardly knew of anyone who after committing to the projects returned to a conventional job or mainstream lifestyle. There is an assimilation of alternative values that is not easily foregone, though this depends on the level and kind of participation. Peripheral participants with lesser commitment are more likely to shift back to business as usual.

Part 5: Limits and challenges

Handling liminality

Syntagma's openness characterizes its spin-off commoning projects. The degree of ideological diversity differs among ventures depending on their origins, relations with political entities, and duration. Our research suggests that people with a leftist or broadly-defined alternative orientation constitute the backbone of most projects, but many projects also include people who claim they are not political or even self-identify as conservatives (Vathakou 2015; all 17 interviews). The only precondition for participation is commitment to solidarity and horizontality. This is manifested in the names and slogans of the majority of the projects, which do not declare a specific ideology or political affiliation, but rather their location and actions, like Plato's Academy, whose slogan is "building human relations," or the reclaimed Navarinou Park in Exarchia, whose members call themselves "the watering cans." These projects remain open to the public and to newcomers and by implication to continuous contestation and transformation. Exclusion is neither possible nor desirable.

On the other hand, there are also projects with registered members, such as the working cooperatives or the time banks. These remain open to new members, but also try to develop a collective memory and identity, open to transformation but with respect to past efforts and work. Liminality here seems to be approaching the end of a rite of passage, giving its place to more permanent structures.

There is, however, also the inverse situation, whereby groups that were homogeneous initially sacrifice a coherent identity in order to expand. For example, the time bank in Holargos-Papagou started by people affiliated with SYRIZA. The project attracted a diverse set of new people, and after several assemblies and negotiations between old and new members, it decided to become independent from the party (Interview 3).

How then do non-homogeneous groups manage to negotiate their unavoidable, internal differences? Unlike political groups, commoning projects do not constitute communities of opinion, but communities of practice, that is communities of producing the common. This is not just a matter of preference; for the majority of participants,

147

producing the common is essential for their livelihoods. Unlike communities of opinion, in communities of practice there is a tendency to bridge, rather than exaggerate differences.

Conflict is still present. Before the crisis and the squares movement, Greek society had virtually no experience with commoning, and there is, generally speaking, a weak culture of cooperation (Kioupkiolis and Karyotis 2013; Vathakou 2015). Liminality, initially an advantage, is meeting in some instances its limits, not only because of identarian mismatches, but also because of the inability of persons acculturated in an antagonistic environment to forge and sustain a common ground (Interview 2; Interview 6; Interview 7; Panagoulis 2013). Our interviewees emphasized the lack of tools for effective inter-personal communication (Vathakou 2015; Interview 1; Interview 2; Interview 3; Interview 7; Interview 17). The necessary openness becomes a weakness when every "passer by" can express an opinion and block a decision process (Panagoulis 2013). The non-mandatory character of assembly decisions, for example, allows minorities to dominate and creates fatigue and withdrawal. A problem for most dedicated interviewees is the uneven share of work between more and less active members, another side-effect of openness. New members often dedicate less time, with a self-exploitation and "burnout" of those most active.

Despite the recognition of these problems, there is a fundamental commitment to remain open. We have not noted any tendency toward fixed closure in the projects that we observed. Various interviewees told us that their projects, rather than setting rigid membership rules, experiment with novel interpersonal communication methods such as non-violent communication, world-cafés, "open space practices," or "assemblies of feelings." Educational and networking events on experiences from other parts of the world were also common. When disagreements persist, groups bifurcate and new projects are set.

After the rite of passage?

The liminal and rhizomatic spirit of the squares is still strong. If the occupation of the squares posed the question, the actual existing commoning movement is an open, precarious answer. All our interviewees saw in their commoning projects a continuation of the squares movement: "the time of the squares remain a reference point to the collective imaginary, defining the transformation process of solidarity networks," argues Insurgenta Iskra (2014), an organizer of the national Festival of the Solidarity Economy. However, there is a shift in the rhizomatic constitutions of the movement, though not in its rhizomatic attributes. Core participants with long-standing commitment now give a *strategic* character to their projects. Without formalization and strengthening of a network structure, we were told, projects and the movement risk stagnation (Insurgenta Iskra 2014; Interview 7; Interview 16). According to many interviewees, it is those projects that managed to associate, such as the social clinics, that increased their visibility and guaranteed the conditions for their success.

The nationwide "Coordination of Solidary Clinics and Pharmacies" was established in November 2013. Its Attika charter holds biweekly meetings (Interview 16; Solidarity4all), facilitating exchange of medicines and materials among projects, organizing collective publicity campaigns for medicine collection, coordinating support from the global solidarity movement, and intervening as a group in political struggles or policy processes such as the public consultation for the reform of the national health system (Interview 15; Interview 16).[8] Other associations include: a network of 15 working cooperatives in Athens that wishes to expand the sector and establish a common multi-space for the network, a common fund, and a common printing house (Interview 14; Interview 13; Kolektives.org; Interview 7; Interview 17); a network of 24 collectives for waste management at the national level established in March 2014; and the network of social cooperative enterprises of Northern Macedonia, established in July 2014 (Vathakou 2015).

Regarding connections across sectors, "Commons Fest" is a festival dedicated to the commons, organized since 2013, first in Crete and then Athens. The main umbrella for the movement, since 2012, is the Festival of the Solidarity Economy (#Festival4sce), where more than 200 commoning projects from all over Greece organize practical workshops, discussions, presentations, and collective events (Insurgenta Iskra 2014). These collectives adhere to minimal principles, namely, independence from political parties, no funding from private or public bodies, self-management, direct-democracy, horizontality, open processes, and openness to society (Insurgenta Iskra 2014). In the first edition of the festival, monetary exchanges were not allowed, but in subsequent events the sale of products was

---

[8] The association sees its role as complementary and not antagonistic to the public health system and it welcomes state or municipal support. This led to the divergence of a few projects with a more anarchist/autonomist orientation that have organized instead into a "network of self-organized health structures." These envision a non-state self-organized health system and refuse any aid from government entities (Interview 15; Interview 16; Interview 17).

permitted, allowing in enterprises from the broader "social economy" (Interview 7; Interview 1). The third festival in 2014 focused on networking and integration, inviting activists from the Cooperativa Integral Catalana[9] (CIC). The Cooperativa has an integrated structure aspiring to cover all needs of its members within its auspices, a model that inspires Greek counterparts as a structure for the commoning movement. The fourth festival in 2015 intended to develop a concrete agenda for setting up an Integrated Cooperative adopted to Greek reality.

A parallel, different networking approach is Solidarity4all, founded in 2012 and financed by a 20 percent donation from the salaries of SYRIZA's parliamentarians. The members of Solidarity4all are in their majority members of SYRIZA but, according to their own words during a group interview, do not seek to "provide solidarity" as a political party to those in need, but to facilitate networking, respecting the autonomy of projects. The association is divided on a sectoral basis. It keeps a national database of projects, and seeks to forge permanent bonds with and between projects via personal relations, campaigns, and direct support. In 2014 Solidarity4all facilitated a nationwide meeting of food collectives (Solidarity4all; Interview 16). Solidarity4all members claim that they do not intend to substitute grassroots movements or represent them politically (Interview 16). Yet several interviewees from the projects expressed skepticism, and no wish to relate to a political party, even a leftist party, that many of them happen to vote for. They did see as positive, however, the fact that SYRIZA founded an organization to support commoning, and have no problem participating in events organized by Solidarity4all.

Between state and the market

The relationship between the commoning projects and the state is complicated, and depends on which forces occupy the state, and their policies. The coalition of conservatives and social democrats that governed until 2015 was initially indifferent to the commoning movement. As the movement grew, threatening capitalist interests (e.g. by

---

[9] CIC is a well-known cooperative in Catalonia with thousands of active members. As they declare about their own initiative, "It is a constructive proposal for disobedience and widespread self-management to rebuild our society in a bottom-up manner (in every field and in an integral way) and recover the affective human relationships of proximity based on trust." Their objective is to bring together all the different elements of the social life such as production, reproduction, financing, currency, housing, health, and education, and to try to reconstruct them in an egalitarian and sustainable way.

occupying the lucrative old airport), the state intervened with force, including the intervention of police in the Metropolitan Social Clinic of Helleniko on October 24, 2013 with the excuse of illegal drug trafficking (Left.gr, 10/24/2013), announcements of regional "Doctors Organizations" against local social clinics (ixotisartas.gr, 4/29/2015), and crucially a 2014 law which prohibited direct producers-to-consumers networks (syn-kinisis.gr, 11/17/2014). Police used violence in protests against privatizations and public land enclosures or for the eviction of occupied social centers.

The left-wing government of SYRIZA provided a more favorable, at least initially, environment, with the institution of a ministry for "social solidarity" and stated intentions from high cadres in support of the solidarity economy. The question that commoning projects faced was whether they should try to remain totally autonomous, trying to create "a new world within the old" as in their liminal phase or whether to turn into nested forms of cooperation under the coordination of a progressive state.

Our interviews suggest ambivalence (see also Petridis and Varvarousis 2015). Many commoners hoped that a left-wing government would improve the legal framework, and remove its obstacles (Interview 1; Interview 8; Interview 15; Interview 16) such as the prohibitions to form cooperatives for many professions or the lack of provisions for indebted, worker-occupied factories. However, the movement, given its lack of formalized networking, had no clear agenda of what institutional reforms to claim from the new government.[10] There was hesitation by some participants to claim financial support from the state, justified by the fact that €150 million granted by the EU in support of a Social Economy Fund were directed to other public expenditures by the conservative government (Dikaiologitika.gr, 10/20/2014). Some hoped that a left-wing government would provide institutional and resource support, while others were concerned that the lack of confrontation would weaken the grassroots, leading to "delegation" to the state.

In liminality terms, we might draw an analogy here between a left-wing government and the "trickster" (Thomassen 2014), the master of ceremony which facilitates the process of maturation and graduation. In the liminal phase of the movement the core slogan was to "take life in our hands," accompanied by a total negation of the political system. In its post-liminal phase, and with a left-wing party

---

[10] A first attempt to formalize a set of proposals was a three-day nationwide forum on "prosperity without growth" held in late February 2015 in Athens.

in government, big parts of the movement tried to articulate specific proposals and to negotiate their future with the state. This in turn precipitates the search for more permanent structures.

Ambivalence characterizes also the relation of commoning projects with the anti-austerity and anti-privatization movements. Some interviewees argued that their projects should remain absolutely autonomous and indifferent to such coalitions, insisting on a vision of creating a new world on the ruins of a collapsing old one. Others suggest that if the commoning movement is to develop it should join forces with others who also want to bring political change. Active collaborations with social movements include the national campaign of solidarity clinics and pharmacies during the general strike of doctors and nurses (Solidarity4all), or the collaboration between a cooperative publishing house, the trade union of workers in the publishing sector, and anti-authoritarian occupations and social centers (Interview 14).

The lack of an anti-capitalist identity and agenda, and the participation of some initiatives in the market economy or their negotiations with the state, does not necessarily make them a-political, co-optable or less transformative. Despite a dislike for political parties, the movement has a political orientation (Insurgenta Iskra 2014; Vathakou 2015). Indeed, some argue that the projects are over-politicized rather than non-politicized (Sotiropoulos and Bourikos 2014). From a survey in a digital database with 200 commoning ventures, we found that more than three-quarters employ a discourse which transcends material objectives, i.e. providing food, health, etc., referring to political goals and the transition toward a society of solidarity and equality (or of "degrowth," a keyword that all of our interviewees found speaks to their vision of change). The general sense from the interviews is that for our interlocutors, political action differs from militant tactics and a "what is to be done" type of analysis: social change is envisioned as the outcome of a creative action. As one of them put it, "to direct democracy one can go only through direct democracy and to self-sufficiency only through self-sufficiency." Abstract ideas such as equality, solidarity, or democracy are grounded in the real production of the common, which in turn checks the validity of these values.

As the movement evolved, several core activists have shifted their efforts to worker cooperatives that produce, at least partly, for the market. A 2011 European law for the social economy offered legal status to cooperatives which offer social care and care for vulnerable populations, and to a limited range of other activities. This included partial state support, tax and social security deductions (Nakou 2013). Many interviewees argued that while their project initially aspired to stay out of the market economy, over time they realized that they could not cover all their needs through them and had to work in conventional businesses to fund their volunteer commoning work in their spare time. These "double shifts" lead to self-exploitation, "burnout," and for some, withdrawal. Cooperatives provide an alternative that combines activism with making a living. Interviewees from cooperatives argued that many more people would be willing to participate in commoning projects, if they knew that they could pay for at least part of their basic needs. Rather than assimilation by capitalism, our interviewees see in their "realism" an opportunity to symbolically show that commoning is a viable alternative that can compete both within and against capitalism. They want to challenge the prevalent view that they can only be marginal, practiced only as ideological or lifestyle strategies by bourgeois who have basic needs secured by other sources of income.

There is a risk of co-optation, or what De Angelis (2012) calls a "commons fix," where successful commoning ventures create novel outlets for capital accumulation (see also Bauwens 2014). However, the working cooperatives we studied, even when producing for the market, maintain their core solidarity function: not only are they internally egalitarian, but after covering the very basic needs of members, they share their surplus with other commoning projects or return it to society. A restaurant and a publishing house that we observed in several instances offered what they regarded as surplus to other cooperatives. "Ekdoseis ton Sinadelfon," the publishing house, supported financially the trade union of workers in the publishing sector, the bicyclists' association, an association of parents starting a self-organized kindergarten, selected squats, and the Zapatistas solidarity movement.

Such sharing happens spontaneously and without formal organization. Conversations about networking and association aim to formalize this inter-solidarity, taking the lead from the network of 15 workers cooperatives, which as mentioned has set up a common fund. By being solidary to other commoning projects and the rest of the society, the new commons open a new cycle for the "accumulation of the commons," rather than capital (Bauwens and Kostakis 2014).

Conclusion

This chapter contributed to the literature on the commons, and more generally societal transitions, by showing how and why new commons are being constantly created and how they network and expand. We identified a rhizomatic dynamic, whereby liminality plays a catalytic role. We argued that as the network of commons expands, there is a tendency to keep its rhizomatic attributes, while foregoing its rhizomatic constitution, entertaining strategies of both internal association and innovative external interactions with state and the markets, facilitating in this way an accumulation of and for the commons.

Plan C&D – Commons & Democracy – has been proposed as an alternative to austerity and stimulus for a future without growth (De Angelis 2013a). Here we explained how and why new commons emerge. Benefiting from an ethnography of new commons in Greece, we argued that their exponential growth can be traced to the open-access character of the occupied squares and the shock of the crisis with the rupture of established identities. This favored the emergence of "liminal commons": projects of sharing without pre-fixed collective or individual identities. We proposed a direct and catalytic relationship between this liminality and the subsequent growth of the new commons: practices that were previously marginal were popularized, recruiting new members, while identarian political formations opened to take advantage of the new possibilities. C&D hence went together: the democratic assemblarian processes first tried in the squares became a crucial element of this liminality, making expansion of the commons possible; reciprocally, the new commons became the material embodiment of the new democratic spirit of the squares, transferring it to different spheres of life.

Projects in open-access spaces, such as occupied squares, continue to be liminal since by definition they cannot enclose a public space. Projects that had previously a more closed, political mission, by necessity open up as they want to engage new people. And yet, many other projects that formed in the squares and passed through a period of liminality try now to find ways to stabilize. Importantly, rather than closing themselves around fixed identities and memberships, or establishing hierarchical structures of organization, most projects experiment with novel forms of deliberative and conflict resolution processes, and new ways to train and incorporate newcomers.

Are the projects sustainable, can they be scaled up and will they avoid the short life or assimilation of similar mobilizations in the past, including the student and counter-culture movements of the late 1960s? We did not directly engage with these questions, as we were more interested in understanding the dynamics of take-off of new commons. But we can reflect on this question on the basis of our empirical material.

First, it is important to recognize the differences between different waves of mobilizations as movements learn from their predecessors, and adapt to their contexts. A distinctive characteristic of the indignant/occupy mobilizations is the attention to the pre-figurative transformation of the space, and their direct experimentation with actual ways of producing, consuming, and deciding differently. In Greece, for example, the 1972 students' movement focused on toppling the dictatorship and democratizing the political system, and only marginally with establishing new forms of cooperative production, education, or health.

Second, it is not only the direct effects and scaling up of the projects that should concern us but their "afterlives" and legacies (see Ross 2002). Our research suggests, as we showed, a fundamental transformation of the imaginaries of those participating in the new commons; for them there is no way back to the way things were. Further research is necessary to evaluate the effects of the new commons upon Greek society at large.

Third, one cannot rule out the assimilation of projects and participants by the mainstream capitalist economy or political party system; it will not be the first time. As our research indicated, however, movement participants are very aware and try to negotiate carefully their relationship with state and the market. Aware of the risks of a capitalist "commons fix," they attempt to develop structures that will allow an accumulation of the commons. They engage with the state strategically and selectively, to establish an institutional framework conducive to the flourishing of the commons. This is very hard, given the political economy of the Eurozone, and the very limited scope for national policies that diverge from the neoliberal norm.

At the time of this chapter's writing, commoning projects in Greece are concerned with how to stabilize networking, forming inter-sectoral associations at regional or national levels. These will allow, first, a more complete satisfaction of members' needs, without money, within their space; second, act as mechanisms of redistribution, collecting the surplus of individual projects and investing it for the expansion of others (an "accumulation of the commons"); and third, provide a common face for interacting with the government and negotiating institutional changes.

155

No doubt, despite their phenomenal growth, the scale of the new commons is still small if seen in the context of the Greek economy or the total needs of the population. Will they remain small and perhaps vanish over time? One can never predict the future. Secular stagnation and perpetual economic crisis might be the new norm (Kallis, this volume) and then the experience from the fate of past movements or other alternative economies cannot be a guide for the future. Perhaps, just perhaps, the importance of Greece's new commons is here to stay and grow.

Acknowledgments

The authors acknowledge the support of the Spanish government through the project CSO2014-54513-R SINALECO.

References

Abramovich, A. and Vázquez, G. (2007) Experiencias de la economía social y solidaria en la Argentina. *Estudios Fronterizos* 8, 15, 121–45.

Agrawal, A. and Gibson, C. (1999) Enchantment and disenchantment: The role of community in natural resource conservation. *World Development* 27, 4, 629–49.

Bauwens, M. and Kostakis, V. (2014) From the communism of capital to capital for the commons: Towards an open cooperativism. *TripleC* 12, 1, 356–61.

Bollier, D. (2014) The commons as a template for transformation. Available at: http://www.greattransition.org/publication/the-commons-as-a-template-for-transformation

Brighenti, A. (2013) *Urban Interstices: The Aesthetics and the Politics of the In-between*. Ashgate, Farnham.

Castells, M. (2012) *Networks of Outrage and Hope*. Polity, Cambridge.

Castoriadis, C. (1975) *The Imaginary Institution of the Society*. Kedros, Athens.

Conill, J., Castells, M., Cardenas, A. and Servon, L. (2012) Beyond the crisis: The emergence of alternative economic practices. In: Castells, M., Caraça, J. and Cardoso, G. (eds.) *Aftermath: The Cultures of Economic Crisis*. Oxford University Press, Oxford, pp. 210–51.

D'Alisa, G. (2013) Bienes comunes: las estructura que connectan. *Ecología Política* 45, 30–41.

Dalakoglou, D. (2013) The crisis before "the crisis": violence and urban neoliberalization in Athens. *Social Justice*, 39, 1, 24–42.

De Angelis, M. (2010) The production of commons and the "explosion" of the middle class. *Antipode* 42, 4, 954–77.

De Angelis, M. (2012) Crisis, capital and cooptation. In: Bollier, D. and Helfrich, S. (eds.) *The Wealth of the Commons: A World Beyond Market and State*. Levellers Press, Amherst, NY.

De Angelis, M. (2013a) Crises, commons and social movements: Problematizing the diffusion of alternatives. Paper presented at ISA-San Francisco.

De Angelis, M. (2013b) Commoning and radical transformation. *Occupy Wall Street*. Available at: http://occupywallstreet.net/story/commoning-and-radical-transformation

Douzinas, C. (2013) Athens rising. *European Urban and Regional Studies* 20, 1, 134–8.

Economou, M., Madianos, M., Peppou, L., Theleritis, C., Patelakis, A. and Stefanis, C. (2013) Major depression in the era of economic crisis: A replication of a cross-sectional study across Greece. *Journal of Affective Disorders* 145, 3, 308–14.

EL.STAT (2009) Labour Force Survey, 4th quarter. Available at: www.statistics.gr

EL.STAT (2012) Report on suicide rates 2012. Available at: www.statistics.gr

EL.STAT (2013) Labour Force Survey, 3rd quarter. Available at: www.statistics.gr

EL.STAT (2014) Hellas in Numbers-2014. Available at: www.statistics.gr

EL.STAT (2015) Hellas in Numbers-2015. Available at: www.statistics.gr

Fillipidis, C. (2011) The polis-jungle, magical densities, and the survival guide of the enemy within. In: Vradis, A. and Dalakoglou, D. (eds.) *Revolt and Crisis in Greece: Between a Present Yet to Pass and a Future Still to Come*. AK Press and Occupied London, Oakland, CA and London, pp. 59–77.

Gibson-Graham, J.K. (2008) Diverse economies: Performative practices for "other worlds." *Progress in Human Geography* 32, 5, 613–32.

Gritzas, G. and Kavoulakos, K. (2015) Diverse economies and alternative spaces: An overview of approaches and practices. *European Urban and Regional Studies*, doi: 10.1177/0969776415573778

Hadjimichalis, C. (2013) From streets and squares to radical political emancipation? Resistance and lessons from Athens during the crisis. *Human Geography* 6, 2, 116–36.

Hardin, G. (1968) The tragedy of the commons. *Science* 162, 3859, 1243–8.

Harvey, D. (2000) *Spaces of Hope*. Edinburgh University Press, Edinburgh.

Harvey, D. (2012) *Rebel Cities: From the Right to the City to the Urban Revolution*. Verso, London.

Hopkins, R. (2008) *The Transition Handbook: From Oil Dependency to Local Resilience*. Green Books, Dartington.

Insurgenta Iskra (2014) Transforming crisis to krisis. The #Festival4sce: A hub of networks towards the Alternative Route in Greece. *Revolution News*.

Jackson, T. (2009) *Prosperity Without Growth? Economics for a Finite Planet*. Earthscan/Sustainable Development Commission, London.

Kaika, M. and Karaliotas, L. (2014) The spatialization of democratic politics: insights from indignant squares. *European Urban and Regional Studies*, doi: 10.1177/0969776414528928.

Kaplanis, Y. (2011) An economy that excludes the many and an "accidental" revolt. In: Vradis, A. and Dalakoglou, D. (eds.) *Revolt and Crisis in Greece: Between a Present Yet to Pass and a Future Still to Come*. AK Press and Occupied London, Oakland, CA and London, pp. 215–29.

Kioupkiolis, A. (2014) *The Commons of Freedom*. Exarcheia, Athens (in Greek).

Kioupkiolis, A. and Karyotis, T. (2013) The commons in theory and practice: Self-management in contemporary Greece. Economics and the Commons Conference, May.

Laclau, E. (1996a) *Emancipation(s)*. Verso, London.

Laclau, E. (1996b) The death and resurrection of the theory of ideology. *Journal of Political Ideologies* 1, 3, 201–20.

Lapavitsas, C. (2012) *Crisis in the Eurozone*. Verso, London.

Latouche, S. (2009) *Farewell to Growth*. Polity, Cambridge.

Lichterman, P. (1996) *The Search for Political Community*. Cambridge University Press, Cambridge.

Matsaganis, M. (2013) *The Greek Crisis: Social Impact and Policy Responses*. Friedrich Ebert Stiftung, Berlin.

McDonald, K. (2002) From solidarity to fluidarity: Social movements beyond "collective identity" – the case of globalization conflicts. *Social Movement Studies* 1, 2, 109–28.

Nakou, V. (2013) Forest cooperatives in new roles – A green proposal in forestry. Speech at public event about Social Economy and Cooperativism, Grevena, April 23.

Olaveson, T. (2001) Collective effervescence and communitas: Processual models of ritual and society. *Dialectical Anthropology* 26, 2, 89–124.

Ostrom, E. (1990) *Governing the Commons: The Evolution of Institutions for Collective Action*. Cambridge University Press, Cambridge.

Panagoulis, H. (2013) Seeds have grown, experiences from the collective venture of "Sporos." Available at: Solidarity4all.gr

Papadopoulos, D., Tsianos, V. and Tsomou, M. (2012) Athens: Metropolitan blockade – real democracy. *Journal of the European Institute for Progressive Cultural Studies*. Available at: http://eipcp.net/transversal/1011/ptt/en

PASEGES (2011) Theses of the Pan-Hellenic Confederation of Unions of Agricultural Co-operatives on the framework for the reconstruction of agricultural co-operatives. Available at: paseges.gr

Petridis, P. and Varvarousis, A. (2015) Transformation or replication? On the aftermath of the Greek government shift. Available at Degrowth.de

PROLEPSIS (2013) Results from the survey on "Dietary Habits". Available at http://diatrofi.prolepsis.gr/en/what-we-do/the-need/food-insecurity/

Ross, K. (2002) *May '68 and its Afterlives*. University of Chicago Press, Chicago, IL.

Ross, K. (2015) *Communal Luxury: The Political Imaginary of the Paris Commune*. Verso, London.

Sotiropoulos, A. and Bourikos, D. (2014) *Economic Crisis, Social Solidarity and the Voluntary Sector in Greece*. Crisis Observatory, Athens.

Stathakis, G. and Hadjimichalis, C. (2004) Athens international city: From the desire of the few to the reality of the many. *Geographies* 7, 26–47.

Stavrides, S. (2013a) *The City of Thresholds*. Professional Dreamers, Trento.

Stavrides, S. (2013b) Re-inventing spaces of commoning: Occupied squares in movement. *QUADERNS-E* 18, 2, 40–52.

Stavrides, S. (2015) Common space as threshold space: Urban commoning in struggles to re-appropriate public space. *Footprint* 9, 1, 9–21.

Steins, N. and Edwards, V. (1999) Platforms for collective action in multiple-use common-pool resources. *Agriculture and Human Values* 16, 241–55.

Szakolczai, A. (2009) Liminality and experience: Structuring transitory situations and transformative events. *International Political Anthropology* 2, 1, 141–72.

Thomassen, B. (2009) The uses and meanings of liminality. *International Political Anthropology* 2, 1, 5–28.

Thomassen, B. (2014) *Liminality and the Modern Living through the In-Between.* Ashgate, Farnham.

Tsaliki, L. (2012) The Greek "Indignados": The Aganaktismenoi as a case study of the "new repertoire of collective action." Speech at the "In/compatible publics: Publics in Crisis- Production, Regulation and Control of Publics" panel, Transmediale Media Art Festival, Berlin.

Turner, V. (1977) *The Ritual Process.* Cornell University Press, Ithaca, NY.

Vaiou, D. (2014) Tracing aspects of the Greek crisis in Athens: Putting women in the picture. *European Urban and Regional Studies* 23, 3, 220–30.

Van Gennep, A. (1960 [1908]) *The Rites of Passage.* Routledge and Kegan Paul, London.

Vathakou, E. (2015) Citizens' solidarity initiatives in Greece during the financial crisis. In: Huliaras, A. and Clark, J. (eds.) *Austerity and the Third Sector in Greece: Civil Society at the European Front Line.* Ashgate, Farnham.

Vradis, A. and Dalakoglou, D. (2011) *Revolt and Crisis in Greece: Between a Present Yet to Pass and a Future Still to Come.* AK Press and Occupied London, Oakland, CA and London.

Wade, R. (1988) *Village Republics: Economic Conditions for Collective Action in South India.* Cambridge University Press, Cambridge.

Zibechi, R. (2010) *Dispersing Power: Social Movements as Anti-State Forces.* AK Press, Oakland, CA.

Information retrieved from the following websites/blogs/Facebook pages/data bases

Eurostat, http://ec.europa.eu/eurostat

Hellenic Statistical Authority, http://www.statistics.gr/portal/page/portal/ESYE

Koinsep, http://koinsep.org/

Kolektives, http://kolektives.org/

Left, http://left.gr

Networking Platform-Another World, http://www.enasalloskosmos-community.net/

Newspaper Vima, 10/04/2015. Roads and security, the victims of crisis in public infrastructure. By Avgenakis Lefteris (in Greek), http://www.tovima.gr/

NGO Klimaka, http://www.klimaka.org.gr/newsite/

NGO Prolepsis http://diatrofi.prolepsis.gr/en/what-we-do/the-need/food-insecurity/

Omikron Project, http://omikronproject.gr/

Solidarity4all, http://www.solidarity4all.gr

Chapter 7

Alternative Economic Practices in Barcelona: Surviving the Crisis, Reinventing Life

Manuel Castells and Sviatlana Hlebik

Introduction

The financial crisis that shook the economies and societies in the European Union and the United States in 2008–13 was met with different responses from institutions and firms. While governments tried to fix the system at a high social cost by imposing austerity policies and the retrenchment of the welfare state, many people decided that financial capitalism is the problem, not the solution. Instead, tens of thousands engaged in new forms of practices of production, consumption, and exchange that do not follow capitalist rules but instead emphasize the search for the meaning in their lives. This chapter presents the results of empirical research that assesses and explains the dynamics of these alternative economic cultures in Barcelona, one of the most innovative cities in the world, in a context of widespread unemployment at the time of our study (2010–11).

First, on the basis of interviews and analysis of focus groups, we present the emergence of non-capitalist economic practices among networks of individuals that consciously aim at changing their lifestyles. Second, we analyze the results of a survey of a statistically representative sample of the population of Barcelona to investigate the diffusion of these practices among people at large. We then proceed to a statistical analysis that shows the intertwined presence of two economic cultures: the culture of need, as a response to the deterioration of the economy, and the culture of meaning of life by developing new social relations. We identify the factors explaining the frequency and intensity of practices that embody these two cultures and their inter-relation. Finally, we reflect on the scalability and sustainability of these practices, in Barcelona and beyond.

The crisis of financial capitalism and the rise of a new economic culture

The financial crisis of 2008–13 undermined the trust of citizens in financial and political institutions around the world (Castells 2015; Mason 2015). Faced with dire economic prospects, as well as suffering the consequences of the crisis in their everyday lives, a growing number of people have engaged in alternative economic practices. As such, we understand these practices to be production, consumption, exchange, payment, and credit, which do not follow the usual rules of the capitalist market. That is: they do not originate from profit-seeking economic mechanisms. Many of these practices were already present in the daily workings of capitalism, usually disregarded in terms of their relevance and pervasiveness, but have re-surfaced with the crisis. Indeed, they have spread through many different sectors of the population, and in countries around the world. Some of these practices refer to survival strategies used to cope with the crisis. Yet, many others are rooted in alternative values that consciously challenge the commodification of everyday life. A growing stream of literature in recent years has shown the rise of these practices and explores the causes and consequences of the phenomenon, challenging traditional theories of economic behavior, based on ideological assumptions about the universal economic rationality of monetary transactions (Nolan 2009; Akerlof and Shiller 2010; Schor 2011; Zelizer 2011).

As the 2008 crisis unfolded over several years, the failure of traditional economic policies became clear for millions struck by unemployment, layoffs, cuts in social services, mortgage foreclosures, and loss of credit (Engelen et al. 2011; Castells et al. 2012). Thus, a number of practices that in the advanced capitalist context were confined to the margins of society, diffused both as a viable alternative to solve problems in everyday life and as a project of a new economy based on different sets of values than those underlying global financial capitalism. This has been known for some time as "solidarity economics," defined by Miller as "a view of the economy as a complex space of social relationship in which individuals, communities, and organizations generate livelihoods through many different means and with many different motivations and aspirations," other than maximization of individual gain (Miller 2006).

In recent years we have witnessed the rise of alternative means of payment and credit (Swartz 2015). Local currencies and currency networks have been created (North 2005; Swartz 2015). Ethical finance is redefining banking practice. Time banks have given new meaning to exchange networks. Multiple forms of barter are transforming social bonds into a new service economy (Benkler 2004). Self-help is decommodifying the production of goods and services. Urban farming and agro-ecological production, coupled with consumer cooperatives, are providing new forms of subsistence with paramount emphasis on ecological values (Conill et al. 2012). These practices, and the studies that reported and analyzed them, raise fundamental questions such as the reasons for the persistence, growth, and diffusion of these economic practices, their diverse manifestation in different domains of economic life, and the factors that predispose people to engage in these economic behaviors in spite of the structural prevalence of institutions of capitalist markets (Thompson 1998; Marks 2011). In this chapter we propose a typology of the different dimensions of these economic practices based on our ethnographic observation and suggest an analysis of the socio-demographic and cultural factors inducing these variegated practices.

Our field of study is the city of Barcelona, one of the most socially innovative urban environments in the world, where alternative cultures have been present, both historically and through the years of the recent financial crisis; a city that in 2008–11, during the time of our study, was hit hard by the economic crisis, reaching 20 percent unemployment and 45 percent youth unemployment. Our investigation, while starting from the observation of the most conscious alternative practices within a fraction of the population, will probe the extent to which these practices are present in the population at large as well as the factors inducing the frequency and intensity of these practices beyond the networks of the counter-cultures of the city.

Methodology

Our research relies on two different sets of data, which we will integrate in the analysis using both qualitative and quantitative methodologies. On the one hand, we have observed the networks, organizations, and individuals that, at least part-time, live apart from capitalist patterns of economic behavior according to values they personally find meaningful. On the other hand, we have investigated to what extent these practices are integrated into the behavior of the population at large

162

during the time of the crisis. Our findings suggest that there is more convergence than is usually acknowledged between a conscious alternative economic culture and the mainstream culture when the capitalist economy is called into question by the financial crisis. This research strategy is reflected in our methodology, which we will briefly describe here, referring to the methodological appendix for technical details.

First of all, we have studied the universe of conscious alternative economic practices in Barcelona by conducting three research operations:

1. We identified networks and organizations involved in these practices and interviewed 70 individuals, all selected with regard to their strategic role and knowledge of the practices.
2. On the basis of these interviews we made a documentary film (www.homenatgeacatalunyaII.org) that communicated our findings. We used the film to provoke a debate within eight focus groups, which provided the opportunity to understand the formation of the consciousness of an alternative economic culture, within the diversity of its expressions, and contrast it with individuals who do not share the culture.
3. Using qualitative content analysis from the focus groups and interviews, we elaborated a list of 26 alternative economic practices observed in a segment of Barcelona's population.

Secondly, using the results from the qualitative research, we elaborated a questionnaire and conducted a survey from a representative sample of Barcelona's population (800 interviews). The survey tried to measure the extent of diffusion of each of the identified alternative economic practices among the population at large, and to provide information on the socio-demographic characteristics of the people surveyed, their experience of the crisis, and their attitudes toward capitalism. This chapter focuses on the findings from the survey analysis of Barcelona's population at large.

Thirdly, we created an analytical typology of alternative economic practices found among the respondents to our survey by conducting a cluster analysis of the survey data.

Fourthly, we investigated the statistical relationship between socio-demographic variables, attitudinal variables, and the typology of alternative economic practices by conducting an analysis of correspondence on the basis of survey data.

Lastly, we discuss the analytical and theoretical implications of our statistical analysis.

Descriptive analysis

We will start by identifying practices related to organizations that existed in Catalonia at the time of our study. While our observations focus on the 2009–11 period, during the time of the economic crisis many of these organizations, and related practices, pre-date the crisis and seem to be related to the search for a more meaningful way of life. Thousands of people are engaged in this search; most, but not all, are college-educated young adults, with an average age of 35.

For the sake of clarity, we have grouped the diverse universe of these organizations and their membership in a typology presented in figure 7.1 and table 7.1.

On the basis of observation and interviews conducted with people in the networks and organizations of alternative economic cultures as well as in the focus group discussions, we identified 26 distinct practices. For the sake of clarity, we grouped these practices into three categories: self-sufficiency, altruistic, and exchange and cooperation. Self-sufficiency practices involve work people do themselves rather than relying on the market and paying for goods and services. The second category of activity is what we call altruistic practices. That is, the act of performing a service for others that is worth something in the market, but without receiving financial compensation in return. The last category, cooperation and exchange activities, involve the exchange of goods or services – bartering or similar – without using money as the medium of exchange.

Table 7.2 presents the percentage from the representative sample of the Barcelona population that has engaged in each of the practices at some point since 2008, the year in which the financial crisis began.

We would like to call attention to some significant findings. About 20 percent of respondents grew vegetables for their own consumption in spite of living in very dense urban areas. Over 50 percent repaired their own homes, one-third repaired their own household appliances, and another third made or repaired their own clothing. Others have repaired their own car, motorcycle, or bicycle (21.5 percent). Another 16 percent picked up useful objects or food from the street. Furthermore, 21 percent of respondents repaired another person's home without the mediation of money and 11 percent repaired another person's car, motorcycle, or bicycle without the mediation of money. Additionally, 16 percent of respondents cared for children, elderly or sick persons and *over one-third had lent money without charging interest, during the time of the crisis, to people who were not family members*; 65 percent of

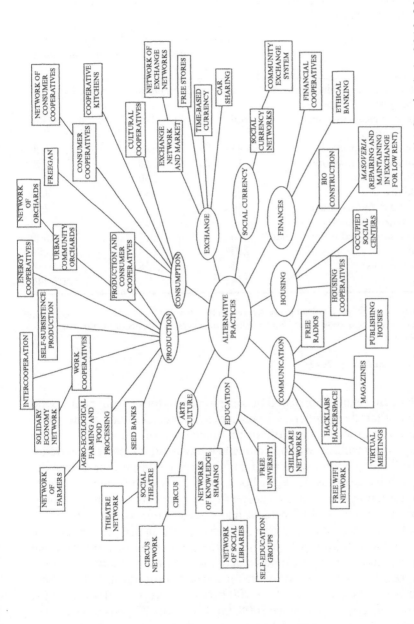

Figure 7.1: Structure of the alternative economic practices that are most pervasive in Catalonia in 2010–2011

Source: Conill et al. (2012)

Table 7.1 Typology of most active organizations and networks involved in alternative economic practices in Catalonia. Estimation of organizations and participating persons

	Number	Average number of persons	Total number of persons involved
Agro-ecological production networks	12	22 families	$264 \times 4 = 1,056$
Agro-ecological consumer cooperatives	120	30 families	$3,600 \times 4 = 14,400$
Exchange networks	45	120	5,400
Social currency networks	15	50	750
Free universities	3	200	600
Hacklabs	1	150	150
Shared parenting cooperatives	10	25	250
Seed bank networks	4	20	80
Community-based urban orchards	40	15	600
Total[a]	250		23,286
Ethical banks[b]	4	71,138	284,554
	254		307,840

[a] Some of the people involved in these practices may overlap.
[b] Numbers of persons in ethical banks indicate members and clients of the financial cooperatives.

Source: Conill et al. (2012)

respondents lent or borrowed books, movies, or music from people who were not family members; 22 percent exchanged clothing, home appliances, and other goods without the mediation of money; 24 percent engaged in teaching without monetary payment; 17 percent shared a car with people who were not family members; 34 percent shared the use of video cameras, tools, or home appliances with people who were also not family members; 97 percent of respondents had engaged in at least one activity and 83 percent had engaged in three or more activities. The average surveyed person had engaged in six practices. Since this sample is fully representative of the population of Barcelona, we may conclude that non-capitalist activities and the solidarity economy are a regular part of everyday life for a sizable proportion of Barcelona residents. In fact, only 22 of the 800 persons surveyed had not engaged in any of these practices since 2008. Of this group, 77 percent were over the age of 64. Many respondents reported that age-related health issues have kept them from doing more.

Table 7.2:   Data on a representative sample of the population of Barcelona that has engaged in each of various practices at some point since 2008

DATA ON A REPRESENTATIVE SAMPLE OF THE POPULATION OF...

	Percentage of the total population that has done the following practices in the period 2008–2011	Absolute Numbers
Self-sufficiency Practices		
Has painted or performed their own home repairs.	55.6%	445
Has repaired or made their own clothing.	39.0%	312
Has repaired their household appliances themselves.	34.6%	277
Has repaired their own car, motorcycle, or bicycle.	21.5%	172
Has picked up food or useful objects found on streets or markets.	16.1%	129
Has planted tomatoes, vegetables, or other products for self consumption.	18.8%	150
Has raised chickens, rabbits, or other animals for self-consumption.	1.9%	15
Altruistic Practices		
Has lent or has borrowed books, movies, or music from people who are not family members.	64.5%	516
Has lent money without charging interest to people who are not family members.	34.0%	272
Has repaired the house of others without the mediation of money.	21.3%	170
Has taken care of children, elderly people, or sick people without the mediation of money.	16.1%	129
Has repaired the car, motorcycle, or bicycle of others without the mediation of money.	11.1%	89
Exchange and Cooperation Practices		
Has legally downloaded software from the Internet.	39.8%	318
Knows an agro-ecological farmer.	29.5%	236
Uses free software.	24.6%	197
Has engaged in teaching exchanges without the mediation of money.	23.8%	190
Has exchanged products, clothing, home appliances, and other goods without the mediation of money.	21.9%	175

167

Table 7.2: (continued)

DATA ON A REPRESENTATIVE SAMPLE OF THE POPULATION OF...

	Percentage of the total population that has done the following practices in the period 2008–2011	Absolute Numbers
Has shared the use of a car with people who are not family members.	17.6%	141
Has engaged in service exchanges without the mediation of money.	16.9%	135
Is or has been a member of a food cooperative.	9.0%	72
Has participated in a community garden.	6.9%	55
Lives with two or more adults who are not family members nor employees.	6.0%	48
Has taken care of other people's children in exchange for having others take care of their children.	5.3%	42
Has used social currency.	2.3%	18
Has participated in an ethical bank credit cooperative.	2.0%	16

	Percentage of the total population that did this practice for the last time before the year 2008	Absolute Numbers
Self-sufficiency Practices		
Has painted or performed their own home repairs.	8.4%	67
Has planted tomatoes, vegetables, or other products for self-consumption.	4.5%	36
Has raised chickens, rabbits, or other animals for self-consumption.	2.6%	21
Has picked up food or useful objects found on streets or markets.	2.4%	19
Has repaired their own car, motorcycle, or bicycle.	2.3%	18
Has repaired or made their own clothing.	2.1%	17
Has repaired their household appliances themselves.	0.5%	4

Table 7.2: (continued)

DATA ON A REPRESENTATIVE SAMPLE OF THE POPULATION OF...

	Percentage of the total population that has done the following practices in the period 2008–2011	Absolute Numbers
Altruistic Practices		
Has lent money without charging interest to people who are not family members.	6.1%	49
Has repaired the house of others without the mediation of money.	3.0%	24
Has taken care of children, elderly people, or sick people without the mediation of money.	2.4%	19
Has lent or has borrowed books, movies, or music from people who are not family members.	1.5%	12
Has repaired the car, motorcycle, or bicycle of others without the mediation of money.	0.6%	5
	0.3%	2
Exchange and Cooperation Practices		
Knows an agro-ecological farmer.	29.5%	236
Lives with two or more adults who are not family members nor employees.	6.0%	48
Is or has been a member of a food cooperative.	3.1%	25
Has engaged in teaching exchanges without the mediation of money.	2.1%	17

We also asked people if they had been affected by the economic crisis, and if so, how? *The majority of survey respondents, 62 percent, indicated that they were negatively affected by the economic crisis.* More than half reported that the crisis has adversely affected their spending and income, and had caused them to worry about their future and the future of their families. Nearly one-third of respondents indicated that their employment had been negatively affected and more than 29 percent told us that their health suffered as a result of the crisis.

We also collected data on the range of attitudes toward capitalism and social change from survey respondents. The survey results point to broad disenchantment with the capitalist system. Over half of respondents answered "bad" or "very bad" to the question: "What do you think about capitalism?" Only 2.5 percent answered "very good." Despite this negative attitude toward capitalism, the vast majority of respondents, 77.4 percent, believed that society could change for the better and 67.8 percent believed that they could personally contribute to this change.

Nearly 60 percent of respondents reported that they would like to work less and make less money, if such an option were possible. This finding, coupled with the engagement of a large segment of the population in non-capitalist practices, expressed dissatisfaction with the capitalist system and a desire for other ways to organize their work lives as well as for greater control over their time. Those who said they would like to work less indicated that they would spend more time with their friends and family and pursue other activities they enjoyed with their newly available time.

Having observed the pervasiveness of different kinds of alternative economic practices among the respondents of our survey, we will now turn to the analysis of the determinants of these practices. To do so, we first need to create a statistically grounded typology of alternative economic practices to be able to reason on a synthetic representation of this universe of practices beyond the maze of relationships that result from a list of 26 different practices.

An empirical typology of alternative economic practices

In order to build a typology of practices resulting from our data, we have conducted a cluster analysis from the responses to our survey. Due to an insufficient number of responses to certain questions, we excluded five practices from our data set.

The investigation of relationships among the remaining 21 practices was achieved through a variable cluster analysis which:

- by determining clusters of variables, finds similarities (variables in the same cluster) and differences (variables in different clusters) among the basic alternative practices;
- by giving meaningful interpretation to each set of practices which fall into a cluster, discovers general "types" of practices driven by different logics;
- simplifies the further analysis of the relation between practices and socio-demographic variables and attitudinal variables by using a limited number of significant clusters instead of the whole set of practices.

170

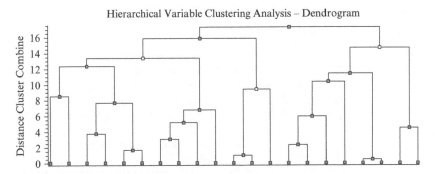

Figure 7.2: Hierarchical variable clustering analysis

Figure 7.2 presents the hierarchical clustering made with the assistance of the Tanagra statistical free software. The technique finds three clusters by optimizing the variance explained (for a description of the technique, we refer to sources in the methodological appendix), but two of them have been successively divided into two sub-clusters due to the significant characteristics they assume. Ultimately, there are five clusters considered in our analysis, which are described in the following sections.

Clusters 1a "Goods Economy" and 1b "Agricult Economy"

Originally grouped into one cluster by the VARCHA technique, we preferred to split the cluster into two sub-clusters as they had different meanings.

"Goods Economy" is a sub-cluster made by six practices. Table 7.3 shows the practices that are components of this cluster. Observing the entire sub-cluster, the percentage of positive respondents is 27 (i.e. 27 percent is the average percentage of positive responders to each of the six practices in the cluster). Practices in this sub-cluster are characterized by:

- the purpose to "save" money by doing domestic services by themselves;
- the attention to domestic necessities;
- the lack of strong relations or involvements with non-family individuals.

This sub-cluster can be defined as that of practices that focus attention on saving money and optimizing domestic free time, but

171

Table 7.3   Goods Economy cluster

CLUSTER	PRACTICES
GOODS ECONOMY	Has repaired their household appliances themselves
	Has painted or performed their own home repairs
	Has repaired the house of others without the mediation of money
	Has repaired their own car, motorcycle, or bicycle
	Has repaired the car, motorcycle, or bicycle of others without the mediation of money
	Has taken care of other people's children in exchange for having others take care of their children

Table 7.4   Agricult Economy cluster

CLUSTER	PRACTICES
AGRICULT ECONOMY	Has planted tomatoes, vegetables, or other products for self-consumption
	Has raised chickens, rabbits, or other animals for self-consumption

don't particularly involve people in strong social relations. The only practice more relational in the cluster – the care of non-family babies in exchange for analogous service when necessary – remains more oriented toward receiving a service rather than creating a social relation.

"Agricult economy" is the residual cluster made by only two practices. Table 7.4 shows the practices that are components of this cluster. Observing the entire sub-cluster, the percentage of positive respondents is 14 (i.e. 14 percent is the average percentage of positive responders for each of the two practices in the cluster). The two practices in this cluster represent the attempt to get a sort of "food sufficiency" by recovering auto-sustainment practices.

Clusters 2a "Social Relational" and 2b "Relational Exchange"

In this case as well, the two sub-clusters were grouped by the VARCHA technique into one cluster, but we preferred to split the cluster into two sub-clusters as they had different meanings.

"Social Relational" is a cluster made up of six practices. Observing the entire sub-cluster, the percentage of positive respondents is 18. Practices in this cluster are characterized by:

172

Table 7.5   Social Relational cluster

CLUSTER	PRACTICES
SOCIAL RELATIONAL	Has taken care of children, elderly people, or sick people without the mediation of money
	Has used social currency
	Has picked up food or useful objects found on streets or markets
	Has exchanged products, clothing, home appliances, and other goods without the mediation of money
	Has engaged in teaching exchanges without the mediation of money
	Has engaged in service exchanges without the mediation of money

- the necessity to involve a large network for activating the practice (especially in the case of "social_currency" and "food_collector");
- the "outside the family context" in which the practice has been made;
- the interest in social aspects, more than the opportunity to save money;
- the focus on social advantages, more than personal advantages;
- an "exchange-logic" not strictly related to gain direct "credits."

Table 7.5 shows the practices that are components of this cluster. This sub-cluster can be defined as that of practices that focus attention on social aspects and involve large relations. It seems that the advantages of the activation of these practices is not immediate and personal, but remote and social.

"Relational Exchange" is a cluster made up of four practices. Observing the entire sub-cluster, the percentage of positive respondents is the highest at 40. Practices in this cluster are characterized by:

- the presence of a non-family network in which exchange of things is activated;
- even if practices take place in a social context, the purpose of practices remains concrete as it is finalized to exchange "things" (cameras, videos, books, money, cars, etc.);
- the interest is on obtaining things, but in a social context of interaction to achieve that purpose.

Table 7.6   Relational Exchange cluster

CLUSTER	PRACTICES
RELATIONAL EXCHANGE	Has shared the use of video cameras, tools, home appliances and similar objects with people who are not family members Has lent money without charging interest rates to people who are not family members Has lent or has borrowed books, movies, or music from people who are not family members Has shared the use of a car with people who are not family members

Table 7.6 shows the practices that are components of this cluster. This sub-cluster can also be defined as that of practices that focus attention on the sharing of goods involving large relations. The advantages remain immediate and personal even if they are gained in a social network.

Cluster 3 "No Relational"

"No Relational" is a cluster made up of three practices. Observing the entire sub-cluster, the percentage of positive respondents is 36. Practices in this cluster are characterized by:

• practices that do not require a social network nor a direct relation with people;
• even if the practice involves intellectual and technological components, it remains a "stand-alone" practice.

Table 7.7 shows the practices that are components of this cluster. This cluster can be defined as practices that do not facilitate the construction of a social and "physical" network.

In sum, variable cluster analysis helped us understand that these practices can be distinguished into two very distinct types. On the one hand, practices involving strong social motivation (Social Relational) or a concrete purpose can only be pursued in a social context (Relational Exchange). On the other hand, practices oriented to solve economic problems, with a direct personal and familiar purpose can be performed in a domestic context (Goods Economy, Agricult Economy) or alone (No Relational). In general, practices with the specific purpose of problem solving are more frequently adopted. Yet, what is meaningful is that different people engage in different types of

174

Table 7.7   No Relational cluster

CLUSTER	PRACTICES
NO RELATIONAL	Uses free software Has legally downloaded software from the Internet

practices. Below, we study the factors conducive to each of the types of practices.

Who practices what: socio-demographic, attitudinal and cultural determinants in the activation of alternative practices

We will now investigate which category of subjects, defined by their socio-economic attributes or attitudes, engage in one or more clusters from the practices we have identified in the previous cluster analysis. As socio-economic conditions, attitudes, and practices are expressed by categorical variables, the useful technique that can explore the associations between these variables is correspondence analysis, which is basically a factorial analysis based on contingency tables that report the number of concomitant occurrences from each socio-economic or attitudinal category with each cluster of practices.

In the following paragraphs, we summarize the results of the analysis of correspondence between significant groups of socio-demographic factors, attitudes and clusters of practices. To facilitate the reading of this chapter, we have placed the results of the correspondence analysis in the methodological appendix, while summarizing the content of our findings in the text of the chapter.

1. *Correspondence analysis between five clusters of practices and socio-demographic variables: "education," "income," and "marital status"* (figure 7.3)
Practices that involve a strong "social" and "relational" component ("Social Relational" and "Relational Exchange") are more frequent among the "unmarried" than the married. Instead, those who are married engage in "practices" that do not require strong social commitment and are primarily directed toward savings ("No Relational" and "Goods Economy").

"Marital status" is the strongest "predictor" of the type of practice engaged in. Unmarried people are more likely to be involved in relational practices while married people will be predominant in practices

175

oriented toward obtaining economic goods, agricultural practices, or practices with no relational component. However, education and income also add their own causal effect, increasing the likelihood that people will focus on relational practices over less relational or non-relational practices.

2. Correspondence analysis between five clusters of practices and attitudes: "opinion on capitalism" and "influence of crisis" (figure 7.4)
Those who have a negative view of capitalism (cap_bad) coincide with the area of "relational practices," that is "Social Relational" and "Relational Exchange" clusters of practices. They were defined as "social and relational" as they require a strong collaboration with other people in the performance of the practice. Those who have a positive view of capitalism (cap_good) and practices in this area are "economic" or "non-relational." One can say that the inclination to carry out the practices which are oriented toward a change in social relations is influenced by a negative attitude toward capitalism, while those with a more favorable attitude toward capitalism tend to engage in practices with the purpose of saving money. Interestingly, the more "advanced" practices ("Social Relational"), i.e. the social practices that have primarily "relational content," are made largely by those who not only have a negative opinion of capitalism, but state that they have been adversely affected by the crisis.

3. Correspondence analysis between five clusters of practices and attitudes: "opinion on capitalism" and "motivation to carry out the practice" (figure 7.5)
Our findings show a very strong correspondence between the "relational" practices and the motivation to act for "social reasons" (mot_soc). It seems that attitudes that are defined by the search for solidarity in society, and the goal of doing something useful for society, are also inductive of relational practices, regardless of the opinion toward capitalism, be it good or bad. Instead, the cluster of practices that have an immediate practical and personal reason such as saving (mot_money), or personal pleasure (mot_like), are less oriented toward relational economic practices and are more inclined to solve economic problems with little or no relational component.

4. Correspondence analysis between five clusters of practices and attitudes: "influence of the crisis" and "motivation to carry out the practice" (figure 7.6)

This analysis confirms that the preceding observation relates to the importance of motivation in determining the content of the action. The reason why it works (mot_soc) is an even stronger factor than the influence the crisis has had on the respondents. It may indicate that the development of alternative practices with connotations of "social" and "relational" prior to the crisis is dictated by a strong motivation to act for the purpose of social change.

5. *Correspondence analysis between the combination of socio-demographic factors "income" and "education" and the combination of attitudes "influence of the crisis" and "opinion on capitalism"* (figure 7.7)
The negative opinions about capitalism and the feelings of having been hit by the crisis are most prevalent among those who have both a low average income and low average education. On the other hand, those who believe that they were hit by the crisis and still maintain a positive view of capitalism have a higher family income and a good level of education.

6. *Correspondence analysis between the combination of socio-demographic factors "income" and "education" and the combination of attitudes "motivation to carry out the practice" and "opinion on capitalism"* (figure 7.8)
Respondents with medium-to-low education and income level view capitalism in a negative light. Interestingly, the different motivations to act, in particular social motivation (mot_soc), are distributed transversally with respect to different categories of income and education. Consequently, the drive to act and carry out a certain kind of practice is not reserved to a particular category of economic level (and, in fact, we did not find a strong connection between education, income, and type of practices). In conclusion, everyone can potentially carry out practices, particularly practices with strong "relational" connotations if they have the motivation to act based on social goals useful to society. On the other hand, those essentially motivated by practical or personal reasons are more oriented toward purely economic practices, although this association is not as strong as the preceding one in statistical terms. Socio-economic status affects attitudes toward capitalism, but it does not as strongly affect the attitude toward relational or non-relational practices. The key factor in inducing involvement in practices that are relational or non-relational is the motivational factor of seeking social change. And this motivation is not determined by socio-economic status

or by the opinion toward capitalism. The desire for social change appears to be a stronger cause of engaging in relational practices than the suffering of the crisis or the position in the social structure. However, there are certain socio-demographic conditions that favor the intensity of a social change motivation, according to the analysis presented below.

7. Correspondence analysis between the combination of objective factors "income" and "education" and the "motivation to carry out the practice" attitude (figure 7.9)

According to our analysis, the social motivation to act is even stronger among: those who have a lower-to-middle level income associated with higher-level education (bottom, right area of the graph), i.e. those that seem to be in the right condition to form an emerging and critical social group who can challenge the dominant socio-economic system. This analysis is based on three observations:

1. "Relational practices" are practiced by those having a strong social motivation.
2. Those who have a strong social motivation mainly correspond to those having a higher level of education and a lower-to-middle level income. We may define this group as formed by those who have high intellectual capacity, but are "frustrated" in their economic expectations. Those who are more committed to practicing social or relational practices have high education but not a high income level.
3. People who just exercise practices for their pleasure seem to not favor a particular kind of practice, as it is selected by personal choices.

Two alternative economic cultures: survival and the meaning of life

Our data show that in spite of their diversity, alternative economic practices, as observed in Barcelona in the midst of the 2008–10 economic crisis, can be divided into two main categories. On the one hand, there are practices whose primary aim is to remedy economic distress by obtaining necessary goods and services needed, in a time of scarce resources, at a low cost or no cost at all. On the other hand, there are practices aimed at generating new social relationships, based on solidarity and mutual support, or that can only deliver goods and services by constructing a large social network of solidarity. The former category embodies a strategy for economic survival and the latter is a project for social change.

It is critical that both practices take place simultaneously and are intertwined within the context of a major economic crisis. As is often the case through history, it is in the connection between the need to survive and the desire for a more meaningful life that major processes of social change occur.

Who would be the likely actors of such a process? In this regard, our research provides several significant answers. Motivational attitudes are more important than socio-demographic variables in explaining the predominant orientation toward relational/social practices. Those who want to be useful to society and to find meaning in their lives are the most active in constructing alternative practices with a strong relational content. This holds for all socio-demographic categories. However, there are certain conditions that predispose this kind of attitude: those persons who have a higher level of education and a low or medium income. It is the combination of economic depriva-tion and cultural capacity that favors mobilization for social change in the form of alternative economic practices with relational content. This statistical finding in our survey coincides with the observation from the most active group of actors in the networked social move-ments that arose in many countries during 2011 in response to the economic crisis (Castells 2015).

Another empirical observation must be interpreted. We found that those who are unmarried, while living together, are keener to engage in relational practices than those who are married. This is the most potent socio-demographic variable in inducing certain types of practices, and its influence holds when controlled by education, income, and age. We interpret this finding as an indicator of cultural autonomy. It reflects on persons who do not bow to social pressure, in terms of the institution of marriage, and thus build their lives accord-ing to their own norms of conduct. Again, it is a cultural value rather than a socio-demographic status that defines the type of alternative practice in which people engage.

Furthermore, attitudes toward capitalism and the feeling of having been hit by the crisis are also determinants of the engagement in relational or social practices. These factors are particularly strong in their influence when they converge. This is not an obvious finding. Although people of higher socio-economic status are less critical of capitalism, low socio-economic status does not predispose people to relational practices, but to survival practices. In other words, it is the

179

fact that people are critical of capitalism and feel like they have been hit by the crisis that favors relational practices regardless of socio-economic status. We must differentiate how people become critical of capitalism from how people feel predisposed to social change, even if being critical of capitalism does predispose people to social change.

Conclusion: Are alternative practices sustainable?

The meaning of these findings cannot be overstated. Our research was conducted in early 2010 at a moment when Europe was under the impact of a major economic crisis, but without social movements that would respond to it. Yet, in the daily practice of a large proportion of the population, new economic practices were emerging at an individual level, often forming alternative networks of survival. These practices represented embryos of a new economy, out of the necessity of replacing dysfunctional capitalism, but were also motivated by a search for a meaningful life; a meaning that was rooted in alternative economic practices that would later spring up as social movements in search of new democracy (Castells et al. 2012; Castells 2015).

However, the question arises about the sustainability of these practices. Will they fade away as the mechanisms of financial stabilization restore capitalist markets as usual? Will they remain in the daily lives of people? Have they raised the level of social consciousness of citizens at large so that they are capable of reinventing life beyond surviving the crisis?

First of all, what our research shows is that a considerable proportion of economic activity (with or without crisis) does not follow market rules dominated by profit seeking and consumerist ideology. They are simply ignored by most mainstream economists and policy makers because they are more interested in capital circulation than in brain circulation.

Second, the notion that the economic crisis has been superseded in Barcelona and in many areas in Europe is belied by observation of the living conditions of large segments of the population, at the time of this writing, in the spring of 2016. There has been a substantial shake-up of the model of informational financial capitalism that came near collapse in 2008. The consequences of the crisis for producers and consumers are extremely different for those at the top of the social scale and for the rest of the population. Thus, for many the practices of survival that we observed in 2010–11 continue to be a daily way out of their dire economic situation. And for the population at large, the impact of the crisis and their experience of solidarity networks were at the source of powerful social movements that ultimately transformed the political landscape of Barcelona in the municipal elections of May 29, 2015. The leader of the movement against housing evictions, a key component of the social movements against austerity policies, Ada Colau, was elected Mayor of Barcelona, without the support of any political party. She immediately went on to transform municipal policy, emphasizing the fight against poverty, and helping cooperative movements and social experiments in occupied buildings, while dismantling the special riot police that had been haunting squatters and alternative communities. Multiple initiatives of a locally shared economy, including barter networks and consumer and housing cooperatives, blossomed under the protection of new municipal legislation and some targeted funding to support their self-improvement initiatives. Furthermore, a broad citizen participation program was designed by those who had been the activists in the social movements, both in the neighborhoods and over a special web of the City of Barcelona. Experiences were exchanged, proposals were debated and voted upon, and without fear of repression multiple initiatives took place, expanding the social base of the alternative economy that had been nurtured in Barcelona during the crisis. In fact, the previous mayor of Barcelona, from the Catalan nationalist party, lost the favor of a critical group of the electorate (the youth) after he ordered the violent eviction of one of the oldest occupied buildings in Barcelona, Can Vies, a symbol of alternative communities.

It could be said then that the condition for sustainability of these alternative practices would be political change in the institutions of governance. In reality, it is more appropriate to see it as a dialectical process. The creation and expansion of alternative practices transformed the consciousness of a segment of the population whose mobilization in the political realm led to the emergence of new political conditions that consolidated alternative practices and opened new perspectives, ushering in a solidarity economy. Moreover, Barcelona was not an exceptional case. Similar political victories inspired by social movements in the cities of Madrid and Valencia multiplied the demonstration effect, showing to society at large that another economy could be possible.

Methodological appendix

Characteristics of the survey of alternative economic practices in the population of Barcelona

We administered a questionnaire containing 43 questions to a statistically representative sample of Barcelona's population. A total of 800 telephone interviews were conducted between February 9 and February 10, 2011. The questions focused on a list of 26 alternative economic practices, on attitudes toward capitalism and social change, and on the socio-demographic characteristics of the respondents. The questionnaire was elaborated by our research team.[11] The design of the sample, the pre-test of the interviews, and the interviews were carried out by the technical team of Instituto Opina, one of the leading private survey research organizations in Spain (www.opina.es).

Definition of variables, codification and data manipulation of the cluster analysis and the correspondence analysis

In the interest of simplicity, we have omitted a detailed presentation of the selection of variables, data coding, and statistical manipulation underlying the analysis presented in this chapter. Full technical details can be found in Conill et al. (2012).

We present in Figures 7.3–7.9 the results of the correspondence analysis as presented in the text of the chapter. Identification of the figures corresponds to the text in the main body of the chapter.

---

[11] We specifically analyzed people who have engaged in non-capitalist economic practices since 2008 in order to focus on the period following the economic crisis. This group respects the representativeness of the survey and constitutes 88 percent of the entire population surveyed.

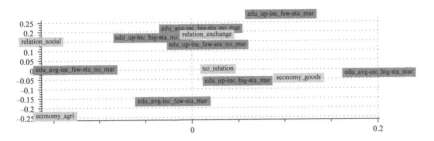

Figure 7.3: Correspondence analysis between five clusters of practices and socio-demographic variables: "education," "income," and "marital status"

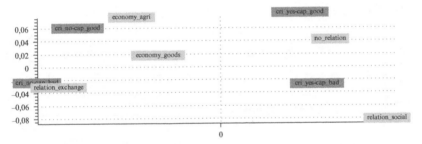

Figure 7.4: Correspondence analysis between five clusters of practices and attitudes: "opinion on capitalism" and "influence of crisis"

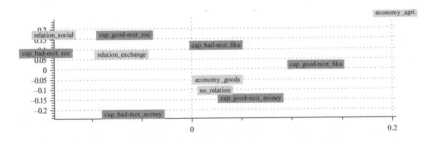

Figure 7.5: Correspondence analysis between five clusters of practices and attitudes: "opinion on capitalism" and "motivation to carry out the practice"

183

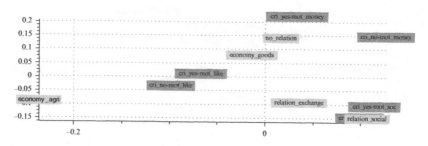

Figure 7.6: Correspondence analysis between five clusters of practices and attitudes: "influence of the crisis" and "motivation to carry out the practice"

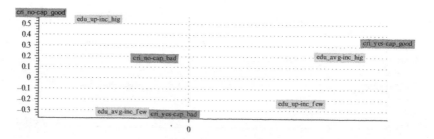

Figure 7.7: Correspondence analysis between the combination of socio-demographic factors "income" and "education" and the combination of attitudes "influence of the crisis" and "opinion on capitalism"

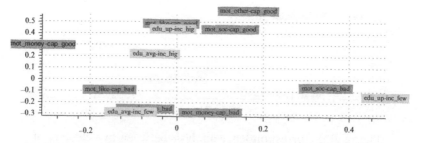

Figure 7.8: Correspondence analysis between the combination of socio-demographic factors "income" and "education" and the combination of attitudes "motivation to carry out the practice" and "opinion on capitalism"

184

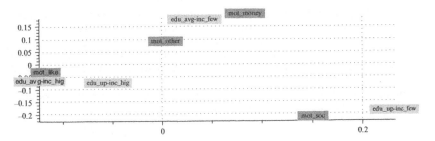

Figure 7.9: Correspondence analysis between the combination of objective factors "income" and "education" and the "motivation to carry out the practice" attitude

References

Akerlof, G.A. and Shiller R.J. (2010) *Animal Spirits: How Human Psychology Drives the Economy and Why It Matters for Global Capitalism*. Princeton University Press, Princeton, NJ.

Benkler, Y. (2004) Sharing nicely: On shareable goods and the emergence of sharing as a modality of economic production. *Yale Law Journal* 114, 2, 273–358.

Castells, M. (2015) *Networks of Outrage and Hope*, 2nd edn. Polity, Cambridge.

Castells, M., Caraça, J. and Cardoso, G. (eds.) (2012) *Aftermath: The Cultures of the Economic Crisis*. Oxford University Press, Oxford.

Conill, J., Cardenas, A., Castells, M. and Servon, L. (2012) *Otra vida es posible: prácticas alternativas durante la crisis*. UOC Press, Barcelona.

Engelen, E., Ertürk, I., Froud, J., Johal, S., Leaver, A., Moran, M., Nilsson, A. and Williams, K. (2011) *After the Great Complacency: Financial Crisis and the Politics of Reform*. Oxford University Press, Oxford.

Marks, N. (2011) *The Happiness Manifesto: How Nations and People Can Nurture Well-being*. TED Books, New York.

Mason, P. (2015) *Postcapitalism: A Guide Tour to Our Future*. Allen Lane/ Penguin, London.

Miller, E. (2006) Other economies are possible! Organizing toward an economy of cooperation and solidarity. *Dollars & Sense* 266, July–August.

Nolan, P. (2009) *Crossroads: The End of Wild Capitalism and the Future of Humanity*. Marshall Cavendish, London.

North, P. (2005) Scaling alternative economic practices? Some lessons from alternative currencies. *Transactions of the Institute of British Geographers* 30, 221–33.

Schor, J.B. (2011) *True Wealth: How and Why Millions of Americans Are Creating a Time-rich, Ecologically Light, Small-scale, High-satisfaction Economy*. Penguin, New York.

Swartz, L. (2015) Money as communication: culture, means of payments, and new currencies. PhD Dissertation, University of Southern California, Annenberg School of Communication and Journalism, Los Angeles.

Thompson, G. (1998) On networks and trust. Paper presented at the European Association of Evolutionary Economics Conference, Technical University of Lisbon, Portugal.

Zelizer, V.A. (2011) *Economic Lives: How Culture Shapes the Economy.* Princeton University Press, Princeton, NJ.

Chapter 8

Imagining and Making Alternative Futures: Slow Cities as Sites for Anticipation and Trust

Sarah Pink and Kirsten Seale

Introduction

The "future" is a contested concept – both in scholarship and in how different stakeholders invest in it as real-world situations play out. In this chapter we put the notion of future-making at the center of an analysis of how alternatives are constituted by groups of activists in contexts of crisis or external threats. We propose that by interrogating how futures are conceptualized and situated in contexts of crisis, new insights are gained into how future-oriented forms of resilience are constituted.

The concept of resilience has recently been appropriated within risk-averse anticipatory institutional logics of defense and policy and planning (Anderson 2015). Here we re-engage it to understand how local communities might live with and recover from the crisis of natural disaster or the threat of global capitalist enterprise. This advances Pink and Lewis's earlier proposal that resilience can be beneficially engaged as a future-oriented concept, in that "as a category and objective for policy and planning, resilience needs to be re-thought ... [with] ... attention to its qualities as processual, as happening where different scalar realities meet and as part of the sensory and affective ways that people engage with others and with their environment" (Pink and Lewis 2014: 707). Here we take contexts of crisis or external threats as a starting point through which to investigate the mundane and celebratory ways that people make, or seek to make resilient futures. We examine how people imagine, shape, and create alternative local futures in which they can live *with* rather than *against* that which they contest.

We explore this through the example of the global Slow City movement, which advocates for and disseminates a model for locally rooted sustainable development. The Slow City movement practices "indirect activism" (Pink 2012), which we argue can generate a locally based but globally connected form of resilience. Based on our research with the movement's Australian network, and comparable examples from earlier research with Slow Cities internationally in the United Kingdom and Spain, we compare the logics of modes of resilient, resistant and capitalist growth-based future-making through the concepts of temporalities, anticipation, and trust. We now briefly introduce these concepts through a series of binaries. This we emphasize is not intended to create "opposites" but is used as a methodological device through which to conceptualize resilience as a departure from existing dominant strands of ways of thinking about change.

Temporalities of resilience v. resistance: The temporalities of resistance and resilience work differently. While resistance can persist over long periods of time, it implies a linear temporality in that it must fail or succeed. If we take this view of resistance, we can arguably see resistance as pushing up against that which is more powerful and seeking to overcome it. Resilience in contrast challenges this narrative sequence. It creates a time-space that is ongoing and tends to be rooted in a powerfully nostalgic sense of what has "always been" and does not need to end. Rather than making a splash or a dent in what it is "against," resilience thus winds its way around that which it is opposed to, puts down roots and becomes embedded.

Anticipation of resilience v. economic growth: Processes that generate resilience are associated with ways of anticipating narratives of crisis and future recovery and wellbeing that differ from predictive forecasts of economic growth. By interrogating the forms of anticipation that participate in how the Slow City movement anticipates future scenarios through the movement's discourses and through their accreditation processes, we explore how anticipatory logics related to local processes exist in tension with predictive modes of capitalist growth, and potentially subvert them.

Trust as a form of resilience: The types of resilience we are concerned with involve modes of care, responsibility, volunteerism, hospitality, and sociality, and the forms of wellbeing these generate. These modes represent core Slow City principles, which are represented in its membership criteria, and are characterized by particular moralities, forms of trust and feelings of certainty and uncertainty. They are also associated with particular temporalities of future-making and anticipation. For instance, while Slow Cities are not degrowth models, they have some characteristics in common with the social elements that Kallis (this volume) argues are integral to a degrowth economy.

To undertake this analysis, we draw on our ethnographies of mundane tasks undertaken by Slow City activists, which we interpret as being directed to making the future in the present. These tasks – planning, meeting, preparing materials, translating, and documenting – produce a form of activism that celebrates the local and generates possible future ways of being and the potential for resilience. They stand in contrast to both the resistance of direct action against corporate capitalism and the growth-based model of capitalism. Thus they offer activists an alternative way through what is often the impasse of directly challenging powerful global or environmental forces. As we show, routes to making resilience are at least partially constituted through the mundane, and embedded through activities that are generative (e.g. involving incrementally compiling, contemplating, and learning) and self-defining. Their making has little of the glamour or heroism of direct action campaigns. They are, rather, concerned with building global and local frameworks through which to endorse their work; networks of trust and collaboration, and a sense of hope and wellbeing.

Below we first outline a concept of resilience and explain how it can be appropriated as a future-oriented concept, conducive to the making of collaborative processes of imagination and consolidation. In doing so we discuss how theories of the future can be mobilized to understand the making of alternatives. We then compare how Slow City futures are envisioned through activities that generate resilience. We next examine two ethnographic examples which have informed the insights discussed in this chapter, to demonstrate how these forms of future-making are played out – these are portrayed as two stories concerning how the Slow City movement translates its global criteria to be locally relevant, and the mundane processes through which cities join the Slow City movement. Finally, we outline the implications of re-working the notion of making alternative futures through a concept of resilience.

Resilience as a future-oriented concept

There has been a surge of research in the social sciences that is explicitly engaged with the notion of futures. This includes sociological work about hope (Castells 2012), geographies of anticipation (Anderson 2010), and the work of Adam and Groves (2007), which critically reviews how futures are constituted in culture and society. Collectively these literatures call on us to account for how corporate enterprises, activists, and neoliberal regimes go about envisaging and planning for futures.

Some existing research has systematically mapped different future-oriented logics. Adam and Groves (2007) suggest five historical and contemporary ways that the future has been conceptualized: through prophecy, which accounts for fate and destiny, and assumes that the future already exists to be "discovered and told," but might be changed (Adam and Groves 2007: 6); through rituals, rhythms and routines – routinized actions or "knowledge practices," which create a sense of security and certainty for the future; through capitalism and futures trading, which they suggest is a way of commodifying the future into something that "can be calculated, traded, exchanged and discounted without limit" (Adam and Groves 2007: 10); through the idea of a transformable future; and finally, through the argument that the present is the outcome of the ways that the future was imagined in the past, which gives us the responsibility (also as researchers) to be conscious of how the current present is shaping the future (Adam and Groves 2007: 14). Anderson has developed a system for understanding the anticipatory logics involved in notions of future. He argues that "an analytics of how anticipatory action functions should attend to: styles, consisting of statements that disclose and relate to the form of the future; practices, consisting of acts that make specific futures present; and logics, consisting of interventions in the here and now on the basis of futures" (Anderson 2010: 793). As Anderson shows, practices of calculating, imagining, and performing, and logics of precaution, preemption, and preparedness, differ from "social movements that may welcome, enact and live radically different futures that genuinely surprise" whereas "anticipatory action aims to ensure that no bad surprises happen" (2010: 782).

The typologies developed by Adam and Groves and Anderson offer a view that abstracts future-making through a set of already familiar sociological concepts, which are attached to particular activities, social formations, and structures already found in society. They point to the existence of different futures, or anticipatory logics of resistance, neoliberal contingency planning, and capitalist growth, and begin to explain how these are articulated and materialized as part of society and forms of governance. However, they also leave a gap: the question of how these concepts are actually mapped onto/over what is always in actuality a much more messy everyday social and experiential reality, where logics tend to get mixed up, might be inconsistent,

190

and people's aspirations, priorities, beliefs, and actual activities are always navigated, situated, and contingent. Here we acknowledge the utility of these mappings but we advance the question of future-making by examining how alternative futures are carved out through and in relation to ideologies, structures and forms, *and* through the improvisory and often meandering routes that people take through the world (Ingold 2007).

Therefore, whereas Anderson sees the anticipatory logics of social movements and the risk averse anticipatory logics of neoliberal policy agendas to be rather different, we consider how these different strands of social and political action and imagination are part of the same world, and become entangled in messy ways. The world, when researched ethnographically, is never as straightforward as it is theoretically. For instance, the concept of resilience, originally developed as an ecological concept, and often seen as a form of bouncing "back" or maintaining of a balanced ecosystem, has been appropriated for multiple future-oriented agendas across policy, development, and other institutional ambitions. As it has been articulated and mobilized across a range of agendas, resilience cannot be seen as just one thing, but as Anderson points out "resilience may not only be empirically multiple but can also be very different types of things, then we need to think again about how resilience enacts, reflects, and reproduces other ways of governing and organizing life" (2015: 62). Resilience has recently been appropriated as a concept for planning in neoliberal regimes, and correspondingly the resilience discourse has also been critically interpreted as part of the ways in which race and gender become more deeply entrenched as forms of difference through neoliberal agendas (James 2015). However as Pink and Lewis (2014) have shown, to approach the resilience as a concept through which to understand the alternative futures that Slow City activists are making means seeing resilience rather differently; it is not necessarily an objective state that can be arrived at, balanced, or maintained, but rather it needs to be seen as processual. Therefore we can understand being resilient as part of a process of weaving one's way through the world, and thus as pertaining to alternative ways of living that are adaptive and relational rather than resistant to others (in the case discussed below through forms of humility, caring, respect, and trust).

By separating out the generation of "bottom up" forms of resilience as associated with social movements from the "top-down" ways of securing safe futures developed by frameworks like those of regulatory regimes, we can see how different logics are active in shared worlds. This unlocking of the association between neoliberalism and

191

resilience is important since: "resiliences, rather than an ideal type 'resilience,' are always connecting up to a range of economic-political logics that exceed their designation as neoliberal. The multiplicity of resiliences (not to mention neoliberalisms) confounds any simple connection between resilience and neoliberalism" (Anderson 2015: 64). Thus we can situate resilience as processual, as relational to the neoliberal structures of governance with which it tends to share the same localities and bureaucratic domains in a context where "local forms of resilience may be understood as emergent from their entanglements with global and regional flows" seeing "resilience as processual, affective and as part of place" (Pink and Lewis 2014: 696). Resilience thought of as such is different from, and indeed is an alternative to, resistance. As Pink and Lewis argue "through a notion of resilience as emergent – in the making – we can re-think how forms of indirect activism become 'active' in the world, beyond the binaries associated with theories of resistance" (2014: 696). It involves a weaving through, and a way of living with, those things with which one might not be comfortable but that are inevitably and seemingly indestructibly present.

The Slow City movement

The Slow City (Cittaslow) movement was born in Italy in 1999 when Carlo Petrini, leader of the Slow Food movement, and a group of Italian mayors decided to apply the principles of Slow Food to infrastructure and communities in small towns. The movement's predominant concentration of member towns remains in Italy; however, it is now firmly established as a global movement. Since its inception it has expanded to encompass in 2014 "187 cities present in 28 countries in the world" (Cittaslow 2014). Slow Food and Slow City are separate organizations, yet are inextricably linked to each other; all Slow Cities have a relationship to Slow Food groups, and local produce remains at the core of the Slow City movement's values and accreditation criteria. Our research has focused on the development of the movement internationally, and specifically we have undertaken ethnographic and interview-based studies of Slow Cities in the UK (Pink 2012), Spain (Pink and Servon 2013), and Australia (Pink and Lewis 2014).

The Slow City movement's requirements for excellence involve criteria set across seven categories: energy and environmental policy; infrastructure policies; quality of urban life policies; agricultural, touristic, and artisan policies; policies for hospitality, awareness, and training; social cohesion; and partnerships (Cittaslow 2014). The people who develop Slow City accreditation applications for their towns are, in our experience, mainly active, middle class, competent, and accomplished professionals. They are sometimes recent (and not so recent) retirees, and in several towns researched in the UK and Australia (although not in Spain) often incomers. While the association of the Slow movement with middle-class tastes and aspirations, which has been made by some scholars, is in this sense understandable, they are not the elitist movements that some would suggest (e.g. Tomlinson 2007). The success of Slow City leaders doubtlessly depends on their leadership, networking, and practical skills in completing a complex application and accreditation process and setting up and administering a local organization, often derived from professional trajectories in leadership roles in business and government. However, Slow City leadership groups draw on, and draw in, diverse elements of local communities, ensuring that the work of the movement is connected to socially and economically diverse groups including involvement in skill building with teenage students, with the elderly, and with alternative and regional food groups. Here we draw on the criteria and values expressed by the movement's discourses and criteria, and examples of its work. However, we note that Slow City leaders, in terms of national politics, are not necessarily a politically and economically homogeneous group.

Finally, it is important to note that the notion of Slow, as defined by the Slow City and its sister movement, Slow Food, is not simply a reaction against a "fast world" or cultures of speed. As cultural studies scholars are increasingly accounting for, the notion of speed does not so much characterize, as Sharma has put it, "a larger temporal order" (2014: 8). Indeed, the idea that we live in a culture of speed is to a certain extent a construct of cultural studies theory, rather than something that emerges in ethnographic studies of everyday experience. As Sharma suggests: 'Temporalities do not experience a uniform time but rather a time particular to the labor that produces them" (Sharma 2014: 8). Yet, while Sharma would understand the Slow in Slow Cities in relation to forms of speed-related temporality, the ethnographic studies undertaken by Pink and her collaborators suggest that for the leaders of Slow Cities themselves, the key concern is not a slow/fast dichotomy. Instead, concerns for them have focused around questions related to how they are already aligned to the movement's principles for local urban environmental sustainability, economy, and sociality. Therefore, in order to understand how the movement is actually engaged with local temporalities, we need to look beyond an analysis of its discourses, to instead ask how it is actually manifested in the processual and material realities of member towns. Thus our interest in temporality is in how past-present-future become entangled in defining Slow and its alterities, rather than in speed.

The Slow City movement has recently become implicated in town-based narratives about recovery from crisis, which reveal how the movement expounds alternative routes to recovery from crisis that evade both resistance and growth models, and suggest how Slow City membership may generate forms of resilience. The Australian network of the movement, with whom we undertook research, offers an ideal example. Crisis and recovery were at the center of Slow City leaders' narratives in their discussions with us and in their more formal engagements with the movement and other members. For example, Adele Anderson, who was in 2013 Vice-President of Cittaslow Australia (CSA), explicitly positioned her town Yea's bid for Slow City status as an attempt to rebuild the town after it was physically and psychologically devastated after deadly bushfires in 2009. In 2013, Katoomba, Blue Mountains, another member town, suffered serious bushfire damage, while the CSA Annual conference was taking place in the town of Goolwa, and Adele suggested the network could act as a support to Katoomba in the aftermath of bushfires. These narratives of crisis, trauma, and recovery were told around a range of issues. Goolwa itself had also undergone collective emotional and economic hardship as a consequence of years of drought and national and state water management policies that drained its Murray River system and decimated local tourism and fishing industries. Margaret Gardner (member of Alexandrina Council and member of Cittaslow Goolwa) described the town as "depressed" during the drought. Goolwa was, moreover, recovering from the effects of The Hindmarsh Affair – a dispute relating to Indigenous beliefs and property rights – which caused deep, ongoing social and political divisions in the town (Simons 2003). While the CSA made no official statement about the process of becoming a Slow City as a means of recovery from crisis, many within the organization perceive it as a coping strategy.

These narratives, as they were recounted to us during our fieldwork, situated recovery as embodied, sensory affective, and processual. That recovery also needed to have an economic element was also acknowledged, particularly in Goolwa. However, the approach to recovery manifested here is explicitly interwoven with a therapeutic narrative that goes beyond economic growth as recovery to focus on social, psychological, sensory, and embodied notions of wellbeing.

Researching Slow Cities in Australia

Australia is a predominantly urban country in terms of its population distribution (Australian Government 2015), most of which is concentrated along the east coast. Most urban research in Australia has been undertaken in and on its cities, leaving towns under-examined (Henry 2012). However, towns are increasingly popular with an influx of retirees and in some areas urban food and creative cultures have accompanied this, making towns increasingly interesting places to settle for people with families, including, according to our participants, returnees from larger metropolitan centers.

During our research, there were three accredited Slow Cities in Australia: Goolwa in South Australia, Katoomba in New South Wales, and Yea in Victoria. Goolwa is 1,300 km from Katoomba and 800 km from Yea. The network is geographically diffuse and the towns are at least two hours travel from metropolitan centers. Our research involved short-stay visits and drives out for meetings, events, and interviews in towns nearer to the major cities of Sydney and Melbourne. Our fieldwork methods were adapted to suit each local context and the time we could spend with participants, as well as the activities they were involved in and stages of their application and implementation processes. Earlier research included following a group preparing an application (Pink and Lewis 2014). We have also analyzed the Slow City documentation and process, including self-assessment documents and textual and video documentation of accreditation applications, and attended meetings and workshops organized by individual Slow City groups and CSA.

Slow City documents, documentation, accreditation, and translation sit precisely within, and are *part of* the encounter between the town leaders and the global movement. They are thus material and sensory actualizations of those moments where past-present-future temporalities are brought together as town leaders discussed, defined, remembered, imagined, and planned for their towns. It is to these processes that we turn in the next section.

Mundane future-making

Accreditation processes or applying for a future

The making of a Slow City, as was echoed in conversations with participants across Australia, UK, and Spain, cannot be manufactured for the application process. Town leaders consistently felt that their towns were already Slow Cities, and that the purpose of the accreditation process was to put this into a format that made it recognizable for the movement and, importantly, *acknowledged* this status and identity on a global stage. Pink and Lewis have suggested that in creating Slow City identities for their towns and areas, the Slow City leaders "delved into their biographical memories of a 'sense of place,' and imagined a future . . . It is by bringing these historical, environmental and cultural dimensions into a narrative about what they 'already are' that the present becomes invested in a future, framed by the movement" (Pink and Lewis 2014: 704). Indeed, the process of becoming a Slow City significantly balances between the local and the global and the past and the future. It makes possible a route into the future that is endorsed and facilitated through a globally acknowledged framework. Therefore, *possibilities* are imagined through the process of becoming a Slow City. The process does not make futures in any objective sense, but opens up ways of imagining futures and creating routes toward them.

Despite the lengthy and extensive collation of information and preparation of documentation involved in fulfilling the self-evaluation required for Slow City membership, many participants recalled this as a positive, useful, and collaborative process. Discussion at the CSA meeting in Goolwa on this topic, at which there were representatives from all Australian Slow Cities, centered on how to make the process relevant to the Australian context, and by extension, more accessible to prospective new member towns. For example, Adam from the Yea contingent observed that the accreditation process was a reminder of what they valued about their town, and of quantifying that in a productive, concrete way. Our interviews and conversations with participants showed how the accreditation process was not merely an intermediary step toward an imagined future. Slow City membership is rather an "enabling technology" (Pink and Lewis 2014) that is not activated merely at the point of achieving member status (or accreditation). Rather, the process of achieving membership itself is enabling. For our participants the inventory and evaluation mobilized during the accreditation application was critical in making the future of their towns; it enabled them to generate ways of knowing (about) and representing their towns and implicitly informed further action and thinking. The documents generated are not just bureaucratic "paperwork" but affective texts. Since 2005 we have been presented with or shown copies of application materials across several UK and Australian Slow Cities, and have been told the stories of application in most towns visited. The application process is thorough and can last one or two years. For example, for one UK town where the town leaders passionately felt their town fitted the movement but did not meet one of the criteria, this meant a long "battle" to become accredited.

The accreditation documents consisted of six areas and 60 or so criteria. They are often presented in tabular form, although one group of town leaders presented their application as a series of video-recorded discussions sitting around a table with a glass of wine and structured around the same themes and criteria. They felt this was in the spirit of the movement and of what they wanted to convey. These videos offered the group who accredited their membership of the movement, and us as researchers, ways to appreciate the feelings of belonging to the movement. The thematic frameworks that shape the applications ask the Slow City applicants to respond to a series of questions that are future oriented. Often these specifically ask the application committees to present their "plans for" securing particular objectives, thus requesting applicants to lay out their plans for making possible certain futures and seeking to avert others. For example, in Katoomba, Blue Mountains, which was one of the first towns to be accredited in Australia and had gone through the full international accreditation process which had included a visit from the movement's leaders based in Italy, Sue talked through the application process. When Sarah asked Sue how she thought Cittaslow would help she explained:

> because I wanted to reframe what we have here, that I saw as so valuable in terms of . . . landscape, heritage and built heritage, and I wanted to frame it in a way that . . . its value would be more easily recognized by others, because . . . some really quite highly educated people were fond of saying things like "oh you should just bulldoze it and start all over again," and it seemed to me that was really a tragedy.

For Sue these tragedies are part of a possible future, but by seeking ways to avert them, Cittaslow became a way to imagine another possible future. To put this into a more experiential context, when Sue and her partner Nigel walked Sarah and Tania around the town, as described elsewhere, Nigel accounted for its architecture not in its present manifestation but, for example, by taking us into a bargain store and showing us where the historical stage and gallery seating of a theatre was boarded over to make a commercial setting (Pink and Lewis 2014), invoking a hidden past and hope for its recovery in the future. Therefore, Cittaslow is not a predictive technology; it does not follow the logics of "prevention" of regulatory frameworks or forms of contingency management, and does not pretend to make the future knowable. Rather, it aligns with and supports ways to imagine the future as a series of possibilities in a context of uncertainties.

This non-linear temporality that characterizes how Cittaslow accreditation enables people to imagine futures in relation to past and present is manifested in multiple ways. For instance, in the Katoomba, Blue Mountains accreditation document, in a section about crime, past, present, and future are drawn together to represent a place in forward movement, and in a process where interventions are consistently being made toward a "better" future. For example:

> The Katoomba Chamber of Commerce and Community has organized for graffiti cleaning kits to be distributed to shopkeepers who require them and promote a zero tolerance of vandalism and graffiti in the area, encouraging prompt reporting and removal of graffiti. CCTV cameras will be put in place in Katoomba Street in 2007.

Such Slow City application materials cluster mundane local activities, policies, issues, and materialities into a single document. In calling these mundane, we do not suggest they are devoid of meaning; rather, we emphasize how they are the ongoing but hidden things and infrastructures that underpin it. In fact they are drenched with meaning, as they hold up what is seen, felt, and sensed. The accreditation documents thus relate to the present and to how the infrastructures they reveal will "hold up" the towns as they move into futures. They enable the applicants to engage with the future as something that is felt and imagined in a more corporeal or visceral way, as well as represented verbally. We might therefore see these apparently mundane accreditation documents as providing a scaffold for how people imagine their towns developing into the future.

Finally, accreditation is also a moment of trust; it is based on self-reporting, and usually on a guided visit from a more established set of Slow City leaders. Not all towns are accredited, or at least not immediately, and the movement has been particularly wary and vigilant of towns applying for Slow City status for tourism branding; it is precisely mass commercial tourism that the movement, and the leaders in its member towns, seek to discourage (Pink and Servon 2013). There is also an element of quantification, in that the towns are asked to score themselves against the criteria in a self-assessment against which they need to score 50 percent. Yet this is a subjective form of quantification, which is self-assessed and likewise is based on a form of morality and trust. Once accredited, towns are expected to improve on their scores, as part of a forward moving process, and they continue to be monitored through the submission of periodic self-assessment documents.

The temporalities of Slow City accreditation bring together the past with the present as it slips over into the immediate future, and the more distant aspirational, hoped for future. It is concerned with forms of safeguarding the positive elements of the past and present, and planning for a future that meets the movement's criteria for environmental sustainability, hospitality and sociality, heritage, and more. The futures mapped in such documents are rooted in the present-past; they are nostalgic, but at the same time practically oriented to documentable and experienced realities, yet they are also aspirational and anticipatory. Because they are often created to deal with perceived, actual, and experienced crises, they are additionally ways of creating forms of resilience against other possible anticipated or imagined futures. They offer frameworks for coping with uncertainty, which are embedded in what can be known about the present, and that call on the more-than-local context of the global Slow City movement for their endorsement. They form part of what can be experienced as a collectively imagined future. In the next section, we explore how the local-global elements of the movement are co-implicated in this process.

Translating and documenting or securing collective futures

The geographic and political anomalies and particularities of the Australian context, as well as Australia's distance from the governing body of the Slow City movement in Orvieto, Italy, has meant that Cittaslow International has devolved responsibility for local accreditation within Australia to Cittaslow Australasia (CSA). This follows their standard approach to giving national networks a certain degree of autonomy to adapt the movement's criteria to local circumstances. The creation of the CSA coheres with the Slow City movement's objectives in that "By reducing travel we reduce our ecological footprint and this is one of the aims of a Cittaslow" and also enables "the establishment of the Australian criteria based on the original Italian goals" (http://www.cittaslow.org.au/page.asp?id=39).

Efforts to translate criteria are future-oriented for the network itself as well as for the towns. At the 2013 meeting in Goolwa it was advanced that Australian Slow Cities should adopt regional identities by calling themselves Yea-Murrindindi, Katoomba-Blue Mountains, Goolwa-Alexandrina, therefore removing the focus from a single town. This is significant to the future sustainability of the network given that, unlike the Italian model, local government is not exclusive to a town. Because the survival of Slow Cities (whether or not they are actual towns or conglomerations of settlements) is dependent on their alignment with and the political turns of local and regional government, they need to engage existing local governance entities with them and their principles.

The complex and diverse responses to globalization amongst the movement's members often exhibited a pragmatic nostalgia. By this we mean a future-oriented acknowledgement of what one wants to "protect," or what one values, individually and/or collectively, about one's town that is informed equally by conservatism and an awareness of, and motivation to address the challenges of the present. An example of this can be seen in how the work of the Slow City movement is entangled with the flows of corporate and other national and global interests. Anne Elliott framed her introduction to Slow philosophy in terms of the fight against fast food chains in the Blue Mountains. She was comfortable with being called an activist. However, when Sarah and Tania were discussing Cittaslow with Sue and Nigel Bell in Katoomba, Blue Mountains, Sue emphasized how there is often no possibility of resisting certain developments that are not consistent with Cittaslow ideals. As she put it, "the development gets approved, it's past the point of no return, you know it's going to go ahead and the last thing you want to see is another empty shop site in your town so you know you've got to really make it work." Likewise, as Pink has shown elsewhere in the UK, town leaders found that given local planning approvals they were unable to prevent the building of large supermarkets in or just outside of their towns. Although they spoke quite bitterly about these developments, they also had to work with, rather than against, them (Pink 2009). As Sue said later in our discussion, Cittaslow is "a global movement . . . so hopefully it could . . . be a balance to the corporate global . . . [a] counterbalance, yes." In a sense, this notion of a counterbalance represents a realistic view of what Slow City leaders can hope for.

Indeed while, as we have shown, the movement offers ways for town leaders to imagine alternative futures to those they fear, there is a deal of ambivalence around the idea of activism amongst some local leaders of the movement. Although the Italian-based movement has emerged from left-wing politics in that national context, the local leaders of Slow Cities internationally are not necessarily committed to the same party politics and represent diverse groups in that sense. Likewise, they have a broad range of opinions about activism, and members of the network occupy different positions along the spectrum of activism. The subject of activism (or being "negative" as it was described by someone) in Australia was folded into a larger conversation about the identity of Slow Cities in the CSA network, and whether activism was something that was Slow City in and of itself. For instance, at a workshop at the 2013 meeting, it was suggested that CSA should not take an anti-, or negative stance in their advocacy such as being "anti-[fast food chain]," even though, as Lidia Moretti (Adelaide Slow Food) pointed out, the very origins of Slow Food (and consequently Slow City) were conceived through a protest against fast food. "We are not a transition town," another participant said. The group shared the view that if a fast food burger restaurant wanted to come to an Australian Slow City, they should not adopt a mandatory policy of opposition. Instead, they agreed that a Slow City should be able to dictate the terms on which they came to the town.

This conversation referred to Dandenong/Tecoma's fight against a fast food outlet (Pink and Lewis 2014), which some were concerned was not broad enough in its focus to really count as an activity of a Slow City. The discussion covered how, when a CSA contingent visited one town which had expressed interest in accreditation, it was clear that their objective in becoming so was solely to block a supermarket development. However, it was also suggested that groups who represented towns who were campaigning against development should not be discounted for this reason, but rather should be assisted in taking a more comprehensive view of why their town should become a Slow City. This was related to a more general motivation to "mentor" towns interested in joining the CSA network, and thus forming part of the processes and objectives of translation that were designed to encourage membership.

This national level debate is illustrative in that it situates the Australian Slow City network, not as a campaigning organization to directly resist capitalist growth, but rather as an organization that wishes to create environments in which the movement's criteria are represented and mobilized toward environmentally sustainable futures. This does not mean that the movement necessarily supports capitalist growth – internationally, nationally, or locally. Instead, it provides a realistic view of what the movement can actually achieve in terms of the political and economic power it wields and the objectives of its framework. Such an approach will not produce or support the degrowth agenda of political, social, and economic reform that is proposed in Kallis's chapter (this volume) in a substantial or dramatic way, but rather makes its impact on a local scale. However, its form of indirect activism can impact how businesses are able to trade in local environments. For instance, in the Katoomba, Blue Mountains area, certain large companies could not even set up due to local planning laws. In the UK examples, local Slow City leaders encouraged local people and organizations to use local services and businesses, which conformed to Slow City criteria, to shop at cooperatives and farmers' markets, *and* embedded these values and the activities and economies associated with them through local festive and ritual cycles. This produces forms of resilience; it is about coping *now*, in a way that is oriented toward a future which remains resilient because it can avert unwanted futures through the active practice and experience of the Slow City principles.

As such, the Slow City movement offers an alternative to models of capitalist growth, and embodies these by inviting people to actually live them out, thus keeping them alive, in the present and into the future. Yet it is also an alternative to direct resistance, which in the case of many of the things that the movements' members are opposing – such as the loss of local heritage architecture in high streets, the growth of supermarket chains, and the emergence of global fast food outlets – has often not been successful. Therefore, the Slow City movement, in its various manifestations around the world, can be seen as having a particular role, and one that indeed can encompass a range of diverse and potentially opposed party political agendas because it is about forming resilience rather than resistance.

Implications for making resilient futures

The future-oriented mode of resilience cannot resolve what movements like Slow Cities see as the ills of the world, stop the pursuit of capitalist models of growth, or replace the intensity of the pain and hope of direct resistance. Yet it offers a framework through which to achieve forms of everyday and anticipatory wellbeing that are of benefit in times of crisis, and to anticipate futures that will feel better than those which are feared or which are threatening the communities involved.

The Slow City approach to making alternative futures to those

202

that might be imagined through models of capitalist growth shows how an approach that engages with tangible possibilities, rather than more abstract and holistic solutions, can offer some respite – if not complete resolution in the face of threat or crisis. As argued elsewhere (Pink and Servon 2013; Pink and Lewis 2014), the Slow movement does not make alternative temporalities (e.g. as argued by Parkins and Craig 2006) and is not so much a corrective to "slowing" the fastness of modernity. Rather it seeks to make alternative ways of being and experiencing, which have an inevitably future orientation. These alternatives acknowledge the difficulty of achieving holistic solutions and instead create routes to futures that are inevitably partial and therefore can be understood only as relational to what "else" is there.

The future, like the present, will be mundane, messy and complicated. Any clear vision of it will be hijacked by the contingencies and the conditions created by "what else" is there. If we see the future as entangled, then approaches like that of the Slow City movement become threads, which through their relationships to other, perhaps as yet unknown threads, seek to constitute futures that are sustainable and fair.

Acknowledgments

The research discussed in this chapter was undertaken by Sarah Pink and Kirsten Seale and supported by the Design Research Institute and School of Media and Communication at RMIT University. We thank Tania Lewis at RMIT who contributed to an earlier stage of the research. Our biggest thanks go to the Slow City leaders who generously participated in the research.

References

Adam, B. and Groves, C. (2007) *Future Matters: Action, Knowledge, Ethics.* Brill, Leiden.

Anderson, B. (2010) Preemption, precaution, preparedness: Anticipatory action and future geographies. *Progress in Human Geography* 34, 6, 777–98.

Anderson, B. (2015) What kind of thing is resilience. *Politics* 35, 1, 60–6.

Australian Government (2015) State of Australian Cities: 2014–15. Available at: https://infrastructure.gov.au/infrastructure/pab/soac/files/2015_SoAC_full_report.pdf

Castells, M. (2012) *Networks of Outrage and Hope: Social Movements in the Internet Age.* Polity, Cambridge.

Cittaslow (2014) Cittaslow International Network. Available at: http://www.

cittaslow.org/download/DocumentiUfficiali/CITTASLOW_LIST_april_2014_
PDF.pdf

Henry, R. (2012) *Performing Place, Practising Memories: Aboriginal Australians, Hippies and the State*. Berghahn, Oxford.

Ingold, T. (2007) *Lines*. Routledge, London.

James, R. (2015) *Resilience & Melancholy: Pop Music, Feminism, Neoliberalism*. Zero Books, Alresford.

Parkins, W. and Craig, G. (2006) *Slow Living*. Berg, Oxford.

Pink, S. (2009) Urban social movements and small places: Slow cities as sites of activism. *City* 13, 4, 451–65.

Pink, S. (2012) *Situating Everyday Life: Practice and Places*. Sage, London.

Pink, S. and Lewis, T. (2014) Making resilience: Everyday affect and global affiliation in Australian Slow Cities. *Cultural Geographies* 21, 4, 695–710.

Pink, S. and Servon, L. (2013) Sensory Global Towns: An experiential approach to the growth of the Slow City movement. *Environment and Planning A* 45, 2, 451–66.

Sharma, S. (2014) *In the Meantime: Temporality and Cultural Politics*. Duke University Press, Durham, NC.

Simons, M. (2003) *The Meeting of the Waters: The Hindmarsh Island Affair*. Hodder Headline, London.

Tomlinson, J. (2007) *The Culture of Speed: The Coming of Immediacy*. Sage, London.

Conclusion
Manuel Castells

Economic crises reveal the cultural and political foundations of practices of production, consumption, and exchange of goods and services. I understand crisis as the condition in which the mechanisms that ensure the proper performance of these practices cease to function under the operating procedures embodied in markets and institutions. That is, financial institutions go bankrupt, investment dries up, mortgages are foreclosed, companies collapse, jobs are lost, salaries are cut, families are evicted from their homes, governments pile up debt, and social services and unemployment payments are cut at the very moment they are most needed. In such instances, institutions must implement emergency procedures, substituting public spending for markets and private investment as the engine of the economy. Meanwhile people, facing the need to survive outside of the ways of life they were promised if they worked diligently and complied dutifully, are forced to reinvent their practices and ultimately themselves. Some fight back against business practices and public policies deemed to be unfair and damaging for their lives. But how can they fight effectively against global financial flows, at the heart of the current crises, spiraling out of control from any given set of actors? How can they force governments to regulate capital and redistribute wealth, thus stimulating consumption, investment, and employment, when governments themselves are largely dependent on the financial whirlwind they contributed to create? And how can they activate the channels of political representation when they are clogged by the bureaucratization of politics and the control of political parties by financial interests and the ideology of market fundamentalism?

In some cases the dysfunction that provokes the crisis of the system results from contradictions internal to the programs of the system itself. In other instances, the obstacles to the performance of the system come from the feedback effect resulting from the unintended consequences of such performance on the system's environment. There are also limits that come from the inability of a given system to operate new technologies without altering its organizational logic. Furthermore, if the management of a crisis is hampered by a crisis of the managing institutions, the crisis may spiral out of control, inducing destructive effects on economy and society. Finally, since human action is not pre-determined, as soon as a system regulating life in all dimensions ceases to assure its expected goals, social actors challenge the rules and institutions of the system, deepening its crisis.

This volume has analyzed a series of social responses to the multiplicity of crises that in the last decade have shaken the global informational capitalist system, the dominant economic, social, and cultural form of our time. Crises are not exceptional for capitalism. In fact, capitalism, like all socio-economic systems, evolves and changes through crises. The characteristics of each crisis and the practices that attempted to restructure capitalism to restore its performance in the aftermath of each crisis determined new forms of capitalism. Thus, the crisis of laissez-faire capitalism in the 1930s was superseded, first, by the war economy during World War II. Then, the so-called Keynesian economic policies, characterized by the intervention of the state in the economy and the stimulus of consumption and employment via public spending and public policies, prompted a period of economic growth and productivity increase from the late 1940s to the mid-1970s. The economic crisis of the 1970s, marked by rampant inflation and declining profitability of capital, required a new set of economic and organizational strategies to assure the expanded reproduction of capitalism (Castells 1980). These strategies can be characterized as globalization (expanding markets, capital, labor, and inputs), organizational transformation (networking), and institutional reforms (liberalization, deregulation, and privatization of companies and markets, particularly of the financial markets). The new technological paradigm based on the revolution of information and communication technologies provided the necessary infrastructure for this profound transformation which induced a new form of capitalism: global informational capitalism, with finance capitalism at its heart, as I have analyzed in various works (Castells 2000a, 2000b, 2004). It must be said, though it is not feasible to elaborate in this text, that each one of these crises and transitions were not simply economic. They were social, institutional, cultural, political. Keynesianism was the result of the new politics in the 1930s and

1940s. The strategic creation of global capitalism by governments and companies in the 1980s was legitimized by the neoliberal ideology, the demise of trade unions and solidarity organizations inherited from the industrial age, and the crisis of social-democracy (Crouch 2004). A similar process of crisis and transition toward new forms of capitalism has been taking place in the last decade, with the new, emerging forms still in an embryonic state (Mason 2015).

The crisis that exploded in 2008 in the US first and then in Europe (but not in the rest of the world) is the most serious financial crisis since the Great Depression of the 1930s. In September–December 2008 financial capitalism collapsed, as the bankruptcy of key financial institutions propagated like a prairie fire. AIG, the mega-insurance company that ensures the majority of banks in the world, was unable to cover its liabilities, thus becoming in effect bankrupt. The decisive intervention of the US government, which *de facto* nationalized the company by purchasing 80 percent of its shares, avoided the collapse. Thus, the myth of financial markets' self-regulatory capacity was debunked. Ultimately, without going into the details of a well-known story that I have investigated elsewhere (Engelen et al. 2011; Castells et al. 2012), governments, both in the US and in Europe, saved the financial institutions using taxpayers' money on an unprecedented scale. Yet, while some shaky financial stability was achieved after several years, the social consequences of the crisis were devastating for millions, in terms of job loss, housing evictions, shrinking compensation, and deep cuts in health, education, and social benefits. Moreover, the massive indebtedness of governments to confront the costs of the crisis was used as a rationale to impose austerity policies, which increased their dependence on the financial markets, which in Europe aggravated the cost and the length of the crisis, leaving large segments of the population without a safety net. At the same time the upper classes increased their wealth both in absolute terms and in relation to 90 percent of the people, raising income and asset inequality to unprecedented levels (Piketty 2013). Thus, the crisis of financial markets in 2008 was triggered by the incapacity of households, companies, and governments to pay back the loans and interest due because of the irresponsible lending at the origin of economic growth, particularly in the real estate sector (Schiller 2008). This was not a mistake, but a systemic consequence of a financial sector that was expanding at an unprecedented rate by creating virtual capital through securitization and derivation of everything, using new financial and informational technologies. The dynamics of the system led to its demise.

At the same time, the global expansion of capitalism and the acceleration of industrial production and consumption everywhere in the world (with the incorporation of gigantic countries such as China, India, Indonesia, and Brazil into the global market) triggered potentially catastrophic environmental consequences, epitomized by the process of human-made global climate change. More generally, the ecological limits to this particular model of growth were fully revealed and added a major ecological crisis to the financial and economic crises (Castells and Himanen 2014). These intertwined crises induced challenges from different sectors of societies around the world.

The technological transformation of the financial system, at the source of a relentless trend toward the virtualization of capital, prompted daring experiments to counter the domination of high finance by innovating the means of payment, eliminating money and creating fully virtualized forms of currency, such as bitcoin and others, based on blockchain technologies. These virtual currencies challenged both financial institutions and the state by appropriating the use of advanced digital technologies to experiment with autonomous forms of payment and capital accumulation in the hands of a new generation of entrepreneurs. Underlying this technological wizardry there is a utopian culture that strives for freedom from the state and from corporate capitalism by using its knowledge and innovation capacity. As Lana Swartz writes in chapter 4 of this volume "Even if these projects turn out to be vapor, the blockchain is still meaningful as an inventory of desire. It is an engine of alterity: an opportunity to imagine a different world and imagine the mechanics of how that different world might be run."

Furthermore, governments, by quickly coming to the rescue of financial capitalism, deepened their crisis of legitimacy vis-à-vis their citizens. Indeed, the institutions of crisis management became in crisis themselves, as citizens/taxpayers opposed the one-sided policies under which they had to pay for the wrongdoing of the capitalist corporations and suffer the austerity imposed to restore the system. Social protests and social movements emerged as a result of this series of systemic failures, and destabilized the political systems in many societies, particularly calling into question the institutions of the European Union, and the legitimacy of traditional political parties in every country.

This is the context in which a number of alternative economic practices emerged in Europe, the United States, and elsewhere, as documented and analyzed in this volume. Some of them resulted from survival strategies, others from the search for new forms of economic life, and for a new way of life, less vulnerable to unpredictable, untamed global financial markets. Financial value, and value of life measured in financial/monetary terms was challenged by affirming the value of human life without financial intermediation. The satisfaction of needs and the desire of a meaningful existence came together in the quest for new economic practices beyond the constraints of for-profit markets.

Some of these practices aim at finding new forms of economic activity. Others include the search for ecological production and consumption that would be compatible with living together on the blue planet. Still others try to project a new monetary system out of technological utopias. And all converge toward an attempt to alter the power relations on which the flawed system of financial capitalism relies. From the diversity of these social and economic practices, a new understanding of the economy emerged, such as, for instance, a theory and policy of degrowth, projecting new forms of economic activity capable of producing, consuming, and creating jobs, and ensuring livelihood on new cultural foundations, ushering in an economy as if people mattered (see chapter 3 in this volume; Schumaker 1999). Another expression of the challenge to the presumed inevitability of the current economic system is the emergence of new local development strategies informing the "Slow City" movement, in which localities limit urban growth to aid the preservation of their residents' quality of life, thus inducing a transformative imaginary of a fulfilling existence (see chapter 8 in this volume).

It is hardly surprising that the most determined and more widespread of these practices took place in Southern Europe where the catastrophic crisis of a largely speculative financial and real estate system was deepened by stringent austerity policies imposed by Germany, the European Commission, and the International Monetary Fund to protect the interests of banks and governments in Northern Europe, particularly in Germany (Castells 2016). The Greek economy disintegrated, and the artificial boom of the Spanish economy went bust, with unemployment reaching over 25 percent and youth unemployment about 45 percent. As the empirical studies conducted in Greece and Catalonia show, multiple innovative economic practices blossomed during the years of the crisis, such as production and consumption cooperatives, barter networks, time banks, self-managed agro-ecological farms, urban orchards, solidarity networks, ethical banks, housing cooperatives, and self-sustaining urban and rural communities that bypassed the for-profit market. Moreover, in the case of Barcelona our study revealed that a substantial proportion of the population, beyond the relatively small experiments of alternative practices, engaged in non-capitalist practices that replaced typical economic practices in some of the dimensions of everyday life (see chapter 7 in this volume). Many of these practices in fact preceded the crisis as thousands of people were already exploring meaningful alternatives for their lives. The crisis expanded and deepened these practices, as many people felt betrayed by the promises of a market delivery of the goods and services on which their lives were dependent. While our direct observation was limited to Greece and Catalonia, anecdotal evidence from other countries, in Italy, Portugal, and Southern France, suggests there were (and continue to be) similar practices in many territories. Indeed, while a sharp separation with a dysfunctional market logic was largely a function of the severity of the economic crisis, the culture of a meaningful life that permeated these experiences connected with a much deeper trend that has always been present in capitalism, and has spurred new economic forms in recent times. Thus, the debate on reducing working time (with or without equivalent salary cuts depending on ideologies) has been at the forefront of the exploration for new employment policies that would use productivity growth to increase quality of life (measured in free time) rather than in economic growth per se. The notion of a sharing economy (exemplified by the shared use of cars, bicycles, facilities, etc.), while being part of the renewal of capitalism in the age of austerity, signals the rise of a utility function that privileges affordable consumption over the logic of capital accumulation. Self-management of production and consumption, according to various cooperative models, is back forcefully in the practice of collectives that learned the lessons from the crisis, and decided that their lives could not be trusted to capitalist corporations. Or, for that matter, to a welfare state that was under attack by governments and business at the very moment when it was truly needed.

An anecdote from our research in Catalonia may exemplify this significant social trend. In one of our focus groups there was a spirited debate between those engaged in a self-reliant form of communal livelihood, and those who, while being in agreement with the meaningfulness of this alternative way of life, were fearful of losing their pensions in their old age. The answer from the daring alternative subjects was as follows: "Well, if the evolution of capitalism continues as it goes, by the time you reach retirement age, the pension funds will be broke and they will not be able to cover your entitlement. While by investing in our solidarity networks, creating bonds among ourselves, we will always be able to count on friends and fellow members of our cooperatives." Between an exclusionary market and a bankrupt welfare state a new form of social solidarity was being projected in horizontal networks of reciprocity and support. It signaled a departure from the capitalist culture and the statist culture toward a culture of humanity, bonding people as human beings.

Yet, our observation and analysis has often been dismissed by the cynicism characteristic of media pundits and detached academics. However, it is from cultural change that major social reforms and the affirmation of human rights have emerged in history. The notion of paid vacations, unemployment insurance, or retirement pensions appeared to be utopian under capitalism before their implementation as workers' rights in the 1930s and 1940s. Their coming into existence was the outcome of social struggles, political change, and public policies that took place in that period. Ultimately, the strictly capitalist logic can only be enforced under power relations favorable to the culture and institutions of capitalism. When power relations change under the pressure of social movements and political actors, capitalism is reformed and new economic and social practices emerge, diffusing in society at large.

In the same vein, economic practices that appeared to be "alternative" and even utopian in the aftermath of the 2008 crisis were later proposed and implemented in those countries and institutions in which new social movements, triggered by the crisis, conquered social legitimacy and reached political power. Such has been the case in Greece, when the government led by SYRIZA created the Ministry of Solidarity to support and generalize many of the commoning practices that emerged at the grassroots level, as documented and analyzed in this volume by Kallis and Varvarousis. Similarly, on May 29, 2015, the municipal elections in Spain resulted in the largest cities – Madrid, Barcelona, and Valencia – electing a mayor from parties that had emerged from the Indignadas Movement of May 2011, particularly Podemos and its coalitions. This political change led to several policy changes that implemented some of the demands from the social movement, enacted in alternative economic practices during the crisis. For instance, an end to the evictions resulting from foreclosed mortgages, a tight control on the speculative practices of banks that were financing real estate, a moratorium in Barcelona on new tourist development (stopping hotel construction and the renting of private homes as B&Bs) to limit the commercialization of the city and to explore other models of economic development. Many of the cooperatives of housing and consumption that appeared spontaneously during the

crisis were supported by the municipality, and the semi-legal neighborhood social centers received legal protection and some funding.
Municipalities, at the time of this writing, were preparing legislation
to provide a livelihood subsidy payment to every person (including
immigrants) just for being a person, regardless of their entitlement.
And, with the support of the majority of citizens, the mayors of these
cities were offering protection to thousands of refugees from Middle
East wars, countering the policy of the Spanish government.

Thus, the rise of alternative economic practices, largely in connection with social movements that emerged during the crisis (Castells
2015) appeared to be the harbinger of significant changes in the lives
of people by transforming the culture, creating a new imaginary,
and implementing new policies on the basis of a change in power
relations. Although our evidence is limited, for the time being, to the
countries that we were able to investigate, our body of observation
relying on secondary sources is meaningful enough to suggest a tenta-
tive grounded theory on the interaction between cultural transformation, political change, and economic organization.

As has been established by a long scholarly tradition, economic
practices, like all social practices, embody culture and are rooted
in institutions. I understand culture as a set of values that guide
human action. However, cultures are diverse, in every society. Thus,
which culture permeates the entire society (local or global) depends
on the institutionalization of a given culture (or hybrid of various
cultures) that defines the rewards or sanctions for specific behaviors.
Institutions are based on power relationships, always in a state of
constant flux. When cultures change, for a variety of reasons, and
become contradictory to the institutionalized order, cultural domination may be challenged, and the modification of power relationships
(not just in the state but in society at large) may induce the prevalence
of a new culture. Cultural change precedes political change, although
there may be political change without cultural change, such as in
cases where a similar capitalist logic is enforced by different political actors. This is why deeper social transformations depend on the
emergence of new ways of perceiving, evaluating, and conceiving the
human experience. The institutionalization of a given culture, such
as the for-profit market as the organizer of economic activity, ensures
the smooth reproduction of a given economic system whose logic is
imposed on most social actors. To be sure, there are always dissenting
cultures and therefore the possibility exists of alternative economic
practices. However, as long as the orderly sequence of life can proceed
without major disruption, even with its inequities and inequalities,

economy as usual seems to be the only possible economy, to which everybody and everything must adapt.

Yet, the capitalist economy, like all economies, is subjected to periodic crises of variable intensity. When the crises are simply linked to the downturn phase of a business cycle, regulatory powers and market corrections restore the predominant logic without major changes, in spite of the human suffering linked to any recession, a suffering that is discounted in the capitalist logic or otherwise dispatched to charitable entities. But when the mechanisms of systemic reproduction are blocked, as in the 1930s or in the late 2000s, there is a disjunction between the dominant economic culture and the experience of the human subjects in their economic practices. And when the usual regulatory adjustments do not restore the usual economic activity for too many, or for too long, alternative forms of economic practices appear spontaneously, embodying different cultures. The scalability of these new economic cultures depends on specific circumstances in time and space. Yet, in all cases these are the cultural materials on which any major economic transformation could emerge. The new forms of understanding economic life, and life itself, can hardly be considered to be blueprints of economic policy. Instead, they are projects (or dreams) born from the autonomous capacity of humans to define, and redefine, the conditions of their existence. New cultures may eventually lead to new power relationships, as an outcome of social struggles, and eventually to new institutions enforcing a new kind of economy. Nevertheless, the critique of economic systems, specifically corporate capitalism, has traditionally been conceived as opposing to its logic the monolithic logic of a fully antagonistic economic system such as statism (ideologically labeled socialism or communism). In fact, human practices are more ambivalent in their nascent state. The passage to statism as a result of the challenge to capitalist exploitation in the twentieth century was determined by the capture of multiple economic alternatives that had emerged in the transition period by the logic of power relationships associated to a culture of state power rather than to a culture of humanity. Thus, the human experience was split between an economic culture subjected to the logic of the state, and various economic cultures unified by the overarching logic of capital accumulation for the sake of capital accumulation. This triumphant capitalist logic, embracing the entire planet in the age of capitalist globalization, has been called into question by a crisis that goes to the heart of the self-destructive capacity of the virtualization of capital in the global financial markets. It perseveres because any alternative is usually conceived in the same terms of an amendment to the totality that formed our political economic imaginary during the dramatic twentieth century.

And yet, the cultural materials emerging from the alternative economic practices nurtured in and by the crisis of the last decade embody a different culture: the culture of autonomy that characterizes the network society and that has been forcefully enacted by the networked social movements of our time (Castells 2015). These practices seem to be the harbingers of new forms of economic organization materializing the culture of autonomy. We do not know what these new forms will be. But we know – at least I know – that the current brand of unfettered global informational capitalism is unsustainable economically, socially, and ecologically. We also know that the substitution of a statist logic for a capitalist logic has been buried by history, and is despised by the large majority of humans, even under conditions of extreme distress, as liberty is their supreme value, considered to be compatible with equality. And while we do not know the precise contours of our future, if we are attentive to the creativity of alternative practices emerging from the crisis, we do know that another economy is possible.

References

Castells, M. (1980) *The Economic Crisis and American Society*. Princeton University Press, Princeton, NJ.

Castells, M. (2000a) *The Rise of the Network Society*, 2nd edn. Blackwell, Oxford.

Castells, M. (2000b) Information technology and financial capitalism. In: Hutton, W. and Giddens, A. (eds.) *On the Edge: Living in Global Capitalism*. Jonathan Cape, London.

Castells, M. (ed.) (2004) *The Network Society: A Cross-Cultural Perspective*. Edward Elgar, London.

Castells, M. (2015) *Networks of Outrage and Hope: Social Movements in the Internet Age*, 2nd edn. Polity, Cambridge.

Castells, M. (2016) *De la Crisis Economica a la Crisis Politica*. Libros de Vanguardia, Barcelona.

Castells, M. and Himanen, P. (eds.) (2014) *Global Development in the Information Age*. Oxford University Press, Oxford.

Castells, M., Caraça, J. and Cardoso, G. (2012) *Aftermath: The Cultures of the Economic Crisis*. Oxford University Press, Oxford.

Crouch, C. (2004) *Post-Democracy*. Polity, Cambridge.

Engelen, E., Ertürk, I., Froud, J., Johal, S., Leaver, A., Moran, M., Nilsson, A. and Williams, K. (2011) *After the Great Complacence*. Oxford University Press, Oxford.

Mason, P. (2015) *Postcapitalism: A Guided Tour to Our Future*. Allen Lane, London.

Piketty, T. (2013) *Le Capital au XXIème siècle*. Seuil, Paris.

Schiller, R. (2008) *The Subprime Solution.* Princeton University Press, Princeton, NJ.

Schumaker, E.F. (1999) *Small is Beautiful: Economics as if People Mattered*, 2nd edn. Hartley and Mark Publishers, London.

Index

Page references in *italics* denotes a table/figure

217